IVAN KOZLOV:

A STUDY AND A SETTING

IVAN KOZLOV:

A STUDY AND A SETTING

G.R.V. BARRATT

HAKKERT 1972 TORONTO

Set in Aldine Roman
by A. M. Hakkert Ltd.

Printed in Canada

International Standard Book Number
88866-516-4

Library of Congress Catalogue Card Number
72-78019

A. M. Hakkert Ltd.
554 Spadina Crescent
Toronto 179, Canada

For Georgette Donchin

PREFACE

Ivan Ivanovič Kozlov (1779 – 1840) occupies a unique place in the history of Russian poetry and a distinguished one in the records of literary translation. He was struck blind and paralyzed in early middle age. His verse – essentially a response to that blindness – both reflects and negates a personal misfortune. Unable to see, Kozlov composed verse that is full of colour; unable to move, he produced among the finest of all Russian versions of Byron's more violent and exotic tales. Translation could not, of course, make amends for a ruined career in the government service, lost freedom and a life wholly dislocated, but could and did make life tolerable.

There can be little doubt that Kozlov was the greatest of Russian translators of Byron. His celebrity in his own country, established by the rhymed tale *Černets* (*The Monk*, 1825), which briefly outshone even Puškin's *Evgenij Onegin*, came to rest firmly on his technically superb versions from Byron, Thomas Moore, Chénier, Ariosto, Schiller and Mickiewicz. But the original verse, too, inspired unfeigned respect among poets and critics of various persuasions; "A Venetian Night," "Kiev" and certain early elegies imbued with the very spirit of Christian resignation, moved Puškin "to tears of ecstasy."

It is appropriate that Kozlov's original and translated work alike be reconsidered now, and his still steady reputation reconfirmed. The past ten years have seen a remarkable growth of interest in the West both in the art and in the practice of translation, and it is certainly desirable that English-speaking readers know more than hitherto of one by whose efforts not only

Byron, but Moore, Burns, Wolfe and Wordsworth also have been made known to successive generations of educated Russians. Interest in the poetry of the Romantic era, moreover, continues to develop among those born since Hiroshima. Even Kozlov's conquest of personal disaster seems more likely to arouse interest and a reasoned respect now than ten or twenty years ago; now, such disasters are a pressing reality.

This is the first study of Kozlov's work in English. It was written with three kinds of readers in mind – the *comparatiste*, the student of nineteenth-century verse in general (and of Russian in particular), and those interested in the practice of translation. The problem, it followed, was to write a study neither too specialized for non-experts nor too simple for such specialists as may care to pick it up. I have tried to strike a mean, but in doing so have inclined slightly towards the latter group. Thus, while a brief section on the literary background *is* included, I have not hesitated to include a number of poems and letters by Kozlov never before published (pp. 31-32, 36-37, 40-41, 115, 118 etc.). I wish to thank Professor Marfa Malova, Director of the Manuscript Division of the Institute of Russian Literature (*Puškinskij Dom*), Soviet Academy of Sciences in Leningrad, for free access to these materials. Thanks are also due to Professor G. Makogonenko, of Leningrad State University (Philological Faculty), for advice and encouragement.

TABLE OF CONTENTS

ABBREVIATIONS

A. S. Puškin	A. S. Puškin, *Sobranie sočinenij v IO tomax*, Moscow, 1959-62.
Poln. sob.	*Polnoe sobranie* (Full Collection)
PD	*Puškinskij Dom*

IVAN KOZLOV:

A STUDY AND A SETTING

CHAPTER ONE
A GENERAL SETTING

Like Vasilij Žukovskij, his immediate contemporary and mentor, Ivan Ivanovič Kozlov was born in a country more backward culturally than any state of western Europe – and into a class highly conscious of the fact. Russia was backward in 1800 for essentially the same reasons that she was backward in 1600 or, indeed, at any time in the previous five centuries. Cut off from the West by physical barriers, Muscovy scarcely emerged from its middle ages until the eighteenth century. Neither the Renaissance nor the Reformation, certainly not that flowering that marked the literatures of France and England in the late sixteenth and early seventeenth centuries, were felt or seen beyond the high "dumb wall" (*gluxaja stena*) of central European Russia. Such light as glimmered in the north had penetrated through the chinks of Kiev and of Poland.[1] Encouraged and coerced by Peter the Great, Russians or, rather, a minute percentage of the Russian population, absorbed from the West not only the techniques that he so valued and considered necessary to the future of the state but also, though Peter neither planned nor even wished it, ideas concerning all the arts. Racine accompanied French cannon, Petrarch Italian architects and engineers; no less than astrolabes, Leibnitz and

1. On Polish influences of various kinds (literary, architectural, musical), see A. S. Orlov, *Perevodnyje povesti feodal'noj Rusi i moskovskogo gosudarstva XII-XVII vv.* (Leningrad, 1934); A. I. Sobolevskij, *Perevodnaja literatura moskovskoj Rusi XIV-XVII v* (St. Petersburg, 1903), pp. 37-51; on Ukrainian influences, V. O. Ključevskij, "Zapadnoe vlijanie i tserkovnyj raskol," *Očerki i reči* (St. Petersburg, 1897), pp. 373-454, and any large Soviet history of Russian, that is, pre-Revolutionary, literature.

Corneille came to impinge increasingly on the awareness of a new aristocracy and gentry – men whose advancement depended on service, not on birth, and whose minds were receptive, in varying degrees, to Western concepts and values. With unprecedented energy, Russian writers and propagandists for the *status quo*, the state or both experimented between 1720 and 1820 with all literary genres favoured and practiced in the West and invented some of their own. The triumphal ode (*toržestvennaja oda*) and *poema* were both verse forms of native, but not folk, Russian origin.

Being backward in their literary development (and so men of Kozlov's birth regarded themselves as a nation, ignoring for the most part folk tales and songs that reached a high pitch of technique several centuries before), Russians found themselves well placed to imitate both what and whom they chose. For, as Čaadaev wrote in his celebrated "Lettre Philosophique" (1836), "We are constituted into a veritable jury by the very nature of things . . ."[2] There was no need blindly to follow any one model or school. To be sure, France was accepted even in Kozlov's youth and early manhood as the source of examples, the fount of models in all Russian literary circles save those in which an archaic reverence for the earlier, syllabic prosody was curiously preserved. Through French literature, as through an imperfect prism, the classics reached St. Petersburg. Still in 1820 those ancient poets best known to Russians – Horace and Anacreon chief among them[3] – were those whom the French had taken as their own exemplars in the various genres. But the France of Sumarokov's time, the 1750s and 1760s, looked back to its Golden Age; it was

2. Published in *Teleskop* without Čaadaev's knowledge, the letter resulted in the journal's closure by the censors. Among the ideas propounded in it were i) that Russia was neither of the East nor of the West, ii) that Russia's strength had always lain in the despotism of her princes and the vastness of her territories – not in the education or welfare of the populace, iii) that new ideas from the West yearly swept away older ones because they did not spring from the older ones – that is, Russia lacked intellectual tradition of an organic kind, and iv) that Russia, being backward, could choose which path to follow. Čaadaev was subsequently declared insane and subjected to humiliating "medical examinations."

3. See M. Ehrhard, *V. A. Joukovskij et le préromantisme russe* (Paris, 1938), pp. 28-32.

a faded, silver classicism that Russians imitated with such care and conscientiousness. Worse, the rules for poetry and drama that the French had accepted unquestioningly – rules divorced from the purposes of which Greek authors had approved, that is, from the attainment of decorum and the quest for humane happiness[4] – were also accepted blindly by the Russians.

Even before Sumarokov was laid to rest, however, some felt unwilling docilely to "follow the Roman Catholic highway," as Čaadaev put it; nor did they see adequate reasons why French neo-Classical norms should be binding on them, the new Russians. That movement called Romantic by its practitioners and enemies alike was embodied, so far as Kozlov's generation was concerned, in the figures of Rousseau and Byron. Not that this Romantic current was the only current flowing counter to the failing neo-Classical tradition – a tradition, as educated Russians understood perfectly, essentially alien to Russia's own literary past; during the reign of Catherine (1763 – 96), Russian *littérateurs* of noble birth discovered their native folk literature. None other than the Empress herself saw fit to develop traditional songs,[5] while her *Novgorodskij bogatyr' Boeslaevič*(1786), no less than Xeraskov's amazing *Baxarijana* (1796 – 1801),[6] still stands as a memorial to false epic and pseudo-mediaevalism. The wizard Čornomor, released from the confines of a strictly oral tradition, openly stalked Petersburg literary almanacs. How could the spirits of Otahiti fail to entrance Russians so suitably prepared, and with imaginations so receptive?

4. See Aristotle's *Poetics* and *Ethics*; essential to the Aristotelian concept of decorum is the conviction of achieving greater happiness and humaneness by limiting one's modes of thought and conduct, and adhering to a predetermined and accepted norm. Often in neo-Classical art, restrictions were applied with no adequate or justifying end; thus art became a complex game played to elaborate rules for its own sake, for the author's own pleasure or because such rules were acceptable to the public – certainly not with a view to making that public more humane. Decorum was, of course, no more a natural quality in ancient Greeks than it is in their modern descendents; see Bertrand Russell, *History of Western Philosophy* (London, 1961), p. 36.

5. "Perekatno, krasno solnyško," "Po seničkam, seničkam" and "Ty rasti, rasti, čado miloe," for example, appear in her *Načal'noe upravlenie Olega*.

6. Russians and Greeks rub shoulders unconcernedly in this "*poema*-epic," in which the Tsar-Devitsa, Ilja Muromets and Knjaz' Ivan keep company with Scylla and Charybdis and a group of nameless nymphs.

Wearied by imitations of the verse of Millevoye and de Parny, Legouvier and La Fare, tired of the constraints imposed by grand tradition (constraints which, because they were seen as somehow embodying reason, would bring reason itself into disrepute before Kozlov's first piece appeared in 1821), Russians sought out the delights of Swiss mountains, Pacific exotica,[7] and the delicious fears found in "black forests and precipices at one's side that scare one wonderfully."[8] Few authors were translated into Russian more often in the course of two decades (1790–1810) than Ossian-Macpherson; following Kostrov's fine version of the great Gaelic hoax came versions by Karamzin, Gnedič and half a dozen no less hopeful, but less happily inspired paraphrasts.[9] In a thousand poems by Russians anxious to follow fashion, moons broke through misty clouds over jagged and moss-grown cliffs.[10] In a thousand odes and elegies as, *par excellence,* in Venevitinov's fragment from "Kolna Domna," winds whistled wildly as the pines groaned long.[11] Nor was Scandinavian mythology – Nordic and Finnish elements mixed with cheerful unconcern – an original strain in Kostrov's work. Assembled around the throne of the Slavic god Perun in Catherine's dramatically unfactual representation of life in the time of Rurik (*Istoričeskoe predstavlenie iz žizni Rjurika*), were not only Odin's regular assistants, Truda, Milla and Golla (now attired in the Russian fashion, but still quite recognizable), but such distant cousins as Ron'griza and Rotlaza! In his dying moments, Gostomyl' addresses, not his Slavic courtiers, but – the Valkyries![12]

7. See M. Ehrhard, *op.cit.*, pp. 95-101.

8. "Il me faut des torrents, des rochers, des bois noirs, des précipices à mes côtes qui me fassent bien peur"; Rousseau, *Les Confessions*, Pt. 11.

9. *Ossian, syn Fingalov, bard tret'jego veka: gall'skie stixotvorenija, izdannyje na anglijskom jazyke g. Makfersonom* (St. Petersburg, 1792) created a sensation. It is improbable that Ermil' Kostrov himself believed that Ossian wrote in the 3rd century A.D., but the presentation is masterly. Karamzin's Ossianic essay is usually headed "*Pesni Sel'mi*."

10. For a fine ironical description of the Ossianic *paysage*, see B. V. Tomaševskij, *Puškin: kniga pervaja* (Moscow, 1956), p. 88.

11. "The night is fearful, and I am alone/ Here on this solitary peak./ Around me is a war of elements./ In the ravines of the high mountain/ I hear the dull whine of the winds./ A roaring stream rushes below . . . " (My translation). No holds are barred.

12. Scandinavian mythology also plays a prominent part in Deržavin's "The Waterfall" ("Vodopad," 1791) and, still more obviously, in Batjuškov's "The Dream" ("Mečta," 1802-03); see N. Zamotin, *Romantizm dvadtsatyx godov XIX-ogo stoletija v*

Byron was not the only English poet to produce a greater impact on the literature of Russia than of his own country; indeed, he may be said to have continued a tradition begun, under the aegis of N. M. Karamzin, by Sentimental poets such as Cowper and Young and Thomson. The extraordinary popularity of these, as well as of Sterne, among the Russian reading public as the century of reason ended, is almost a commonplace of Russian literary history[13]; yet the English Sentimental experience, it will be stressed in this study, did not inspire in Russians of Kozlov's generation an equally ardent devotion to English Romantic verse. Only after 1820 was Byron able to eclipse the lasting glory of Rousseau, and no other English Romantic enjoyed comparable popularity in Russian literary circles.

Born in 1779, Kozlov could hardly have escaped the shadow of Sentimentalism – he was, after all, a well-read adolescent in the time of Karamzin's *Poor Liza*, and his emotional fate was sealed. There was, perhaps, a new piquancy in the notion of premature death as presented by Young and adapted by Karamzin: death by a mossy tombstone, death by a besilvered stream or lake, the moon shining palely down. It was in *attitude*, however, rather than subject matter that change came about in Russian poetry in the time of Kozlov's youth. Of course subject matter could not remain constant; yet it is true that Žukovskij expressed, in terms of deepening aesthetic mysticism, ideas expressed by Sumarokov forty years before – the joys of solitude, for example, and the necessity of meditation. But whereas meditation had been necessary for the princely heroes of Sumarokov's drama chiefly to help them gather strength for future (moral) conflict, for the Žukovskij of 1820 only what was subjective, or perceived in meditation had reality.[14] Batjuškov and Baratynskij might reproach Žukovskij for his "weary psalm-chanting" and imitation of

russkoj literature, 2 vols. (St. Petersburg, 1911), vol. 1, chaps. 2-5. Batjuškov served in Finland during the war of 1808-09, and turned it to good account (see also "Na razvalinax zamki v Švetsii").

13. Sterne's impact on Radiščev has been well covered by Soviet scholars. Even in 1830, Russians continued to take their Sentimental Journey in French paraphrase; see V. Nabokov's erratic glosses to *Eugene Onegin*, 4 vols., (New York, 1964), vol. 2 and 3, p. 158 and p. 143 respectively.

14. See M. Ehrhard, *op.cit.*, chap. 5.

"weeping half-Russians" and German Jeremiads[15] – a bitter reference to the latter's predilection for minor German elegiacs of the eighteenth century's close – yet still it remained true that for most poets of Puškin's generation, certainly including Puškin himself, Žukovskij was a teacher.[16] And Žukovskij, "wet-nurse" to Del'vig and Kjuxel'beker, Baratynskij and Odoevskij, did what he could to introduce the English pre-Romantics and early Western Romantics to his countrymen.

By 1818 Kozlov might read the works of Young, Sterne and Cowper either in Russian or in French translation;[17] he knew *La Nouvelle Heloise* and Sterne's *Sentimental Journey* from cover to cover and had suffered with the young Werther. In Deržavin's verse as in Xeraskov's enormous *Rossiad* and the outpourings of L'vov, Dmitriev and Šalikov, he might pore over Sentimental literature of purely Russian origin. He was alive, in other words, both to Western influences on Russian literature of his own day and to indigenous developments; and Western influence was enormous.

Some indication of its strength during the first three decades of the nineteenth century on Russian literature of all kinds is a list of the works by French, German and English writers that appeared in Russian literary journals of the time. In his invaluable *Essay In Russian Bibliography* (*Opyt rossijskoj bibliografii*), compiled in St. Petersburg in 1813, V. Sopikov provided the numbers of poems, articles, prose pieces or works in translation by Western authors that appeared in the city's journals in that single year. Here is a brief extract from Sopikov's findings:[18] Rousseau, 30; Florian, 26; Young, 19; Gellert, 19; Shakespeare, 8; Schiller, 5; Chateaubriand, 4.

15. See Baratynskij's "Bogdanoviču" (1824), ll. 25-33; also, on A. A. Bestužev's and Ryleev's anti-Žukovskij sentiments, *Mnemozina* (1824), Pt. 2, pp. 3-4 and A. G. Tsejtlin, *Tvorčestvo Ryleeva* (Moscow, 1955), pp. 235-49.

16. See M. Ehrhard, *op.cit.*, chaps. 2-3.

17. Among Letourneur's translations that sold in quantity in M. D. Ol'xin's and A. Plavil'ščikov's establishments by the Moika were *Les Nuits d'Young, traduites de l'Anglois par M. le Tourneur* (Marseilles, Jean Mossy, 1770), and *Ossian, Poesier Galliques, traduites sur l'Anglois de M. Macpherson* (Paris, 1777); for details of Plavil'ščikov's holdings and prices, see André Meynieux's excellent study, *Pouchkine, homme de lettres* (Paris, 1960), p. 545 ff.

18. This reference is from pp. 34-35.

It was entirely natural that an interval of years should elapse before a book or lengthy poem was translated into Russian. First, its fortunes and success had to be tested. Moreover translators were few in the first years of the nineteenth century.[19] Inspired, in part, by Žukovskij's indefatigable example – the master devoted himself entirely to translation work in 1800 – 1801 – Kozlov, too, would translate what he felt to be most needed by Russia's still backward literature and readers, and so expose himself to criticism by those of a younger generation who thought his choice unfortunate.[20] Even massive efforts at translation by more than the dedicated few, however, could not have brought the simple fact that there existed a French or German Romantic literature to the attention of more than a tiny minority of Russians; the vast majority of Kozlov's fellow countrymen were quite illiterate. Still in the last months of the third decade, an interval of years commonly passed before the *grand succès* of Weimar, Edinburgh or Paris finally reached the shelves of St. Petersburg and Moscow booksellers. Aleksandr Smirdin, a prosperous and liberal St. Petersburg bookseller and publisher, produced regular lists of books in stock and expected. Here, on the same basis as those of Sopikov, are certain most illuminating figures from his *Rospis' rossijskim . . . knigam dlja čtenija* of 1828:[21] Florian, 21; Young, 14; Gessner, 9; Byron, 5; Goethe, 2; Tieck, 1; Walter Scott, 23. So popular in St. Petersburg, the bulk of Sir Walter Scott's work was not fresh in 1828, or even in 1818. By 1828, when Goethe's work first appeared with some regularity in several Russian literary journals and almanacs, and so became known to more than the handful of Germanophile connoisseurs headed by Andrej Turgenev,[22] Goethe was fast approaching death.

19. The work of the Friendly Literary Society (*Družeskoe literaturnoe obščestvo*), 1800-03, founded by Žukovskij, A. F. Merzljakov and the brothers A. I. and N. I. Turgenev provided a strong, albeit short-lived example of selective translation from Western verse and drama; see O. Muratova (ed.), *Istorija russkoj literatury XIX-ogo veka: bibliograficeskij ukazatel'* (Moscow, 1962), p. 67.

20. An attack typical of the period – not directed against Kozlov, however – is Puškin's epigram "Kukuška i solovej" (1825).

21. Smirdin, like Plavil'ščikov, printed annual and tolerably detailed lists, of which that given here is typical in format. Smirdin published *Evgenij Onegin* in the first complete edition of 1833. Delivery was punctual; see Nabokov, *op.cit.*, vol. 1, pp. 80-81.

22. See M. Ehrhard, *op.cit.*, p. 54. It was "the *fuoco* of Werther," Turgenev

The Classics, too, seemed to be heading for their demise and swift oblivion. Though failing, however, they did not vanish in the first or even the third decade, as had seemed probable in 1790 when, under the influence of Freemasons, institutes in both capitals had taught modern languages at the expense of Greek and Latin, even gently mocking the latter. Still in 1810, Žukovskij found that some knowledge of the ancient languages was not only to be gained in the *Pension Noble* of Moscow University but, somewhat to his surprise, was even thought important.[23] Submerged by modern languages at the turn of the century, largely, it may be stressed, as a result of Masonic influence in printing and education,[24] the Classics had regained some of their earlier positions by the time Kozlov reached early manhood. But it is of obvious significance that throughout the 1780s and early 1790s, the time, that is, of his education and of Novikov's and Schwartz's greatest influence in the two capitals, a thorough knowledge of Italian, French and Russian was considered more useful and necessary for him than a command of Latin and Greek. No less than Onegin, it would seem, Kozlov was able to recite his two lines from *The Aeneid* and scatter *vales* at his letters' ends – a weakness of Puškin's also.[25] Kozlov, too, knew only enough of Latin literature "to expatiate on Juvenal's morals."[26] He was an accomplished modern linguist, on the other hand, and fluent in five languages.

English literature, it bears repeating here, made a less forceful impression on the Russian reading public, until the rise of Byron's star, than either French or German literature. It was, therefore, between supporters of these two literatures that clashes occurred, with increasing frequency and sharpness, in pre-Decembrist literary circles; few Russians, now that Young was *démodé*, troubled

explained, that "so drew him."

23. *Ibid.*, p. 75.

24. See A. N. Pypin, *Russkoe masonstvo XVIII-ogo veka i pervoj četverti XIX-ogo veka* (Petrograd, 1916), *passim*.

25. See A. S. Puškin, *Sobranie sočinenij v desjati tomax*, vol. 9 (Moscow, 1959-62), pp. 30, 33, 39.

26. *Evgenij Onegin*, chap. I, VI, 1-8; see also D. P. Costello, "Pushkin and Roman Literature," *Oxford Slavonic Papers*, 1964, no. 2, pp. 46-55.

themselves with English verse.

It need hardly be emphasized that French influence on literature, on fashion and artistic values remained immense in Russia and wherever Russian officers assembled throughout the 1830s, as fifty years before. Strolling the boulevards of Paris after reviewing his victorious armies, Alexander I entered the conquered capital in 1814 as though returning to a second homeland, and hundreds of *dvorjane* followed him in the succeeding years. Some stayed, others returned often. In Russia, those unable to visit the blessed city might feast their eyes on full-page illustrations of the latest wigs and carriages in Paris. Also in Nikolaj Polevoj's francophile *Moskovskij telegraf* were long and frequent extracts from *Revue des deux mondes*, the latest literary news – from Paris, French verse sometimes translated, sometimes left in the original. (Why, after all, should one translate when all one's readers perfectly understood *la langue de la politesse*?) Kozlov, like Puškin and each member of the so-called Pléiade excepting only Kjuxel'beker, was educated in a literary tradition of French, not German, origin. Like them, he wrote and commonly conversed in French.

Those of the German party were slow in grouping their forces. Once organized, however, and provided with an organ – Kjuxel' beker's and Odoevskij's *Mnemozina* (1823 – 25) – they presented a systematic challenge to the old French domination of Russian literature. Even before the nineteenth century had begun, Andrej Turgenev was enthusing over Goethe in his correspondence with Žukovskij.[27] Shortly afterwards, Vjazemskij felt the charm of an undisciplined, misty, ill-defined tendency to revolt, but tried to dismiss it. At first among a few, later among ever expanding circles, interest in German literature, aesthetics, and even, after 1820, ethics continued to develop in Russia until Kozlov was dead and his earliest verse a memory. And from the first, Russians saw German philosophy and literature as linked. Here, at least, Madame de Staël showed prescience, forestalling the Muscovite

27. See V. Žirmunskij, *Gete v russkoj literature* (Leningrad, 1937), pp. 20-60; also V. I. Kulešov, *Zapadnyje vlijanija na russkuju literaturu v XIX-om veke* (Moscow, 1964), pp. 26-9.

Ljubomudry or Lovers of (German) Wisdom by a good twenty years. "Il est impossible," declared the baronness, "de faire connaitre l'Allemagne sans indiquer la marche de la philosophie qui, depuis Leibnitz jusqu'à nos jours, n'a cessé d'exercer un si grand empire sur la république des lettres."[28]

As among individuals, whose feelings on the subject led to epigrams and verbal vendettas, so also in journalistic circles two distinct camps began to form between 1810 and 1815 – the French and the German. If, as Baratynskij later wrote to I. V. Kireevskij, "each man . . . extracted his opinions from his age," and if "organs were formed in accordance with the concepts with which minds were fed,"[29] then many had their views formed by such journals as *Moskovskij vestnik* and *Mnemozina*. Chief literary organ of the Lovers of Wisdom, that is, of Kjuxel'beker, V. F. Odoevskij, Venevitinov, S. P. Ševyrjov and their lesser followers, *Mnemozina*, so its editors announced in the opening issue, was "to propagate certain new ideas . . . even a little understanding of the reflections of the great philosophers of our time, especially of German philosophers."[30] And what kept these grown men up in the early hours? "Discussion of . . . the most fashionable authors of that time – Kant, Schelling and Fichte."[31]

Seldom did French and German authors meet in one issue, or English writers appear in any, unless it were Scott or Byron. The subject is a wide and complex one. Here, it must suffice to note that between 1825 and 1835, *Moskovskuj vestnik*, *Biblioteka dlja čtenija* and *Atenej* proved, in the main, hostile towards Romantic writings of French origin or inspiration, while *Moskovskij telegraf, Severnyje tsvety* and *Sovremennik* took the opposite, pro-French position more frequently than not. To detractors of Hugo's and Barbier's work, "French" was synonymous with "violent," "recherché" and "over-colourful" – precisely the epithets, in fact, which Polevoj, as editor of *Moskovskij telegraf* and a leading

28. *De l'Allemagne* (written 1808, pub. 1810), chap. 1.

29. E. A. Baratynskij, *Stixotvorenija, poemy, proza, pis'ma* (Moscow, 1951), Letter 53 (4.12.33).

30. "Neskol'ko slov o Mnemozine samix izdatelej," *Mnemozina* (1824), Pt. 4.

31. *Zapiski A. I. Koševjova* (Berlin, 1884), p. 12; all translations mine – GB.

advocate of "the new direction"[32] so deliberately applied to verse which he approved![33] By "German", on the other hand, supporters of German and German-inspired Romanticism as well as the movement's critics meant "possessed of idealist traits," "stressing the need and value of harmony (or, rather, Harmony)," "tending to reconcile opposite forces."

For Russians, it is true, German literature also brought fantasy. E. T. A. Hoffmann's influence is plain enough in Kjuxel'beker's "Ižorskij," Gogol's "Portret" or Puškin's tale of a coffin-maker. It also brought open revolt against the rational, or supposedly rational, order of neo-Classicism, and if Hegel, in his belief that all society is the product of reason, was no less "rational" than those who held that reason is moulded by society, still it is plain what the *philosophes* were held to have stood for, and on what grounds the Germans of *Sturm und Drang* – Herder, for example – were held by Russians to have attacked them. As Sir Isaiah Berlin succinctly puts it, "Whereas they believed that reality was ordered in terms of universal, timeless, unalterable laws which rational investigation could discover, Herder maintained that every activity, situation, historical period or civilization possessed a unique character. He was held to stimulate the growth of particularism, literary, religious and political irrationalism." And so, broadly speaking, he did.[34] It was a fresh and elevated respect for abstract thought, however, that German literature brought most emphatically to Russia. That abstract thought, idealist and Utopian, was the most valuable German contribution to the rapid development of Russian literature, and of poetry in particular. Later, when Nicolaevan oppression weighed heavily on those who reached maturity only to see Liberal hopes thrown down in the fateful December rising of 1825, its charm and

32. Polevoj's idea of a "new direction" in Western literature, itself, of course, no novelty in 1831, is first expounded in his "Vzgljad na nekotoryje žurnaly i gazety russkie," published in his own *Moskovskij telegraf* (1831), Pt. 37.

33. *Hernani, Lucrecia Borgia* and *Cinq Mars*, for example, and all Balzac's work; see N. Polevoj, "O romanax V. Gjugo i voobšče o novejšix romanax," *ibid.* (1832), Pt. 43, and "Inostrannaja literatura," *ibid.* (1833), Pt. 49.

34. Isaiah Berlin, "Men and Ideas: J. G. Herder," *Encounter* (London), July, 1965, p. 29.

peculiar appropriateness to Russian needs would merely grow more obvious. To many whose lives were dislocated by the Decembrist aftermath, German thought and literature offered prospects of escape and harmony; many young Russians, both before and after Rudin and Turgenev, went like them to Berlin, "the new Athens," and returned with similar beliefs in Thought and the Word, its winged steed.[35]

In Kozlov's youth and adolescence, then, "à une époque où la France classique semblait épuisée, L'Angleterre trop limitée au sentimentalisme, l'Allemagne en pleine jeunesse littéraire ... faisait craquer les vieux moules et promettait à l'Europe la rajeunissement qu'on appelait romantisme."[36] But was England "too limited"? It seems curious to suggest so, when one remembers Byron, or, if Sentimentalism was truly to be preserved, Young, Cowper and Gray. Yet Kireevskij, Odoevskij and Ševyrjov, men most aware among their countrymen of German Romantic literature and thought, could recognize only one "opposition party" – the French. As Kireevskij puts it simply: "In the composition of our literature there entered two elements, that is, the French and German ways of thought. Our literature presented two warring bases."[37] Two elements, not three; English verse and criticism were of little or no concern to Kireevskij. It was one of Kozlov's more obvious achievements to bring English poetry before wide Russian audiences, and so do much to rectify that grave imbalance.

Kozlov could not quickly reverse so well-entrenched an attitude. Still in 1841 Ševyrjov could declare (with more justice than wilful blindness, since he spoke of education as much as of literature), "One may divide all educated Russians into two camps, the French and German, according to the influence of one or other form of education."[38] But every year since 1820, Kozlov

35. See G. Jaëger, *Schellings politische Anshauungen* (Berlin, 1939), esp. chaps. 2-4; also P. N. Sakulin, *Iz istorii russkogo idealizma: knjaz' V. F. Odoevskij* (Moscow, 1913), p. 210 ff.

36. M. Ehrhard, *op.cit.*, p. 279.

37. I. V. Kireevskij, "Obozrenie russkoj slovesnosti na 1829 god," *Sob. soč.* (Moscow, 1911), vol. 1.

38. S. P. Ševyrjov, "Vzgljad russkogo na sovremennoe obrazovanie Evropy," *Moskvitjanin* (1841), Pt. 1, p. 246.

had been presenting the English case; it was all but inevitable that something of its essence penetrate the educated Russian consciousness. Castles, fox-hunting in scarlet coats, the rich eccentric lord – those English motifs or symbols took root in Russian prose only after Byron's celebrity had reached its zenith in the late twenties, thanks in large measure to Kozlov's efforts. Translated by Kozlov, Charles Wolfe and Thomas Moore ceased to be merely names vaguely remembered, and became, for the first time in Russia, individualistic poets.

Of course the central notion of Idealism as presented by Schelling and Schiller (and it was as a Romantic theorist, as much as a playwright, that Schiller came to the notice of others than the "Archive Youths" in Russia),[39] was perfectly in keeping with the needs of countless Russians after the débâcle of 1825. Hundreds of individual careers and Liberalism itself were disrupted by the Decembrist tragedy.[40] But Byron, too, had a powerful appeal. It was to the towering figure of Belinskij's imagination, the creator of *Childe Harold* and *The Corsair*, the immense, storm-scarred personification of proud, injured and misunderstood Individualism, that a whole generation turned. Byron and, in and through him, English Romantic poetry, was Liberty's arm and agent, and a bastion against soulless, corrupt society. To Russians, Byron was and always remained the Lover of Liberty; interpreting "liberty" as they saw fit and wise, admirers of conflicting political persuasions could extol him with unwonted unanimity.

"Only Byron is on our tongues now," complained Jazykov in the spring of 1825; "He is the *nec plus ultra* in literary judgements ... everyone is thought his imitator."[41] Valid in 1820, the

39. See V. I. Kulešov, *op.cit.*, pp. 26-9. Coined by Sergej Sobolevskij, the phrase was applied to Venevitinov, Odoevskij and Ševyrjov – a none too happy youthful group of employees of the Ministry of Foreign Affairs (Office of Records) – and was taken by Puškin; see *Evgenij Onegin*, chap. 7, 49, 1. The Office was the only Government department in Moscow in which *dvorjane* felt themselves permitted to serve with proper dignity.

40. For an admirable general account of the Decembrist rising and Liberal movement in Russia, 1812-1825, see A. G. Mazour, *The First Russian Revolution, 1825* (Stanford, 1963). The bibliography provided is more than adequate for most needs.

41. Letter of 3.5.25; *Jazykovskij arxiv: Pis'ma N. M. Jazykova rodnym za derptskij period jego žizni* (St. Petersburg, 1913), p. 182.

"two-base theory" of Russian literature was no longer so in the Decembrist year; further contemporary evidence simply stresses the point: English verse was published in Russian journals and almanacs with increasing frequency after 1823; A. Bestužev-Marlinskij exiled in the Siberian township of Yakutsk, "took nothing into his hands besides Byron" (save the tools with which he built his log cabin);[42] Kjuxel'beker's private diary bears eloquent testimony to his lively interest in "the bard of Albion."[43] It is Belinskij's rush of rapturous comments that finally underlines what is already clear enough – that for Russians, English poetry, having lain dormant twenty years, had awoken. In Byron's gaunt and splendid figure (for the limp they had no eye), men of Puškin's generation saw the embodiment and triumph of English Romanticism. In Byron's wake came all other British Romantics, while beside him even Shakespeare paled into relative insignificance. To be sure, certain plays by Shakespeare continued to appear in theatres and literary journals throughout the third and fourth decades, but these were plays with suitably arresting and "Byronic" plots and heroes.[44] How typical of Shakespeare's greatness that it seemed to echo the better parts of Byron's "Eastern Tales"! The irony escaped the ardent Vissarion. "Byron," the critic assured his readers in 1842, "was a Prometheus of our age, chained to a cliff, tormented by the vulture: a mighty genius . . . Bearing in his breast the sufferings of millions, he loved humanity."[45] One wishes that Byron might have lived to read and ridicule such phrases.

As it was, a Russian named Kozlov had to remove him from the pedestal on which he had been placed – a pedestal so high that almost nothing could be seen of him. Bringing life to, and humanizing, the grandiose monument, Kozlov also, inevitably, threw the finer aspects of Byron's verse into refreshing, sharp relief. Kozlov was not the first to introduce that verse to a Russian

42. A. N. Veselovskij, *Etjudy i xarakteristiki*, 2 vols. (Moscow, 1912), vol. 1, p. 519.

43. Interesting extracts may be found in *Russkaja starina* (1875), vol. 1, pp. 83-4.

44. Translations from *Hamlet, Macbeth* and *King Lear*, by Vrončenko and A. Rotčev for example, appeared in the pro-French (and therefore, by a strange quirk of loyalties, pro-English) *Moskovskij telegraf* seven times, in 1827-29 and 1832.

45. "Russkaja literatura v 1842 godu."

audience. Translations had appeared by Orest Somov and other students of "the mighty genius" some years before the ill-fated rising.[46] Even in 1818 M. T. Kačenovskij had published versions of, and favourable comments on, poems by Byron,[47] while early in 1819 P. A. Vjazemskij was writing enthusiastically of *The Corsair* to Andrej Turgenev and to others.[48] Yet it was Kozlov who first translated Byron frequently and in a systematic manner. He, more than any other, offered his countrymen acceptable versions of the English poet's work of all periods – and first introduced to Russians, not Byron the martyr or the champion of abstract freedom, but Byron the poet; he, finally, more than any other Russian, opened the way to an appreciation of other English Romantics. As a translator alone, his contribution to Russian literature was great.

46. Somov's translations appeared in *Blagonamerennyj* (*The Well-Meaner*) for 1821, Pt. 15, pp. 211-12, Pt. 17, pp. 122-26, and were well received by the public.

47. A slim booklet edited by Kačenovskij, and entitled *Vybor iz sočinenij Lorda Bejrona*, appeared for sale in Moscow only in late March, 1821.

48. See *Ostaf'jevskij arxiv knjazej Vjazemskix*, 6 vols. (St. Petersburg, 1896-1913), vol. 1, pp. 326-7 and p. 334.

CHAPTER TWO
THE LIFE

Ivan Ivanovič Kozlov was born into a family of old Muscovite gentry on April 11, 1779. It was not a family of ancient Russian aristocracy. Before 1720, indeed, since when it had advanced in wealth and influence by service in all three Petrine ladders – the civil, naval and military – it was of small account outside its own rural domain. Yet even in service, the members of the family whose portraits Kozlov found in his cousins' drawing-room in prominent positions – Commodore Ivan Ivanovič, his paternal grandfather, Ivan Pavlovič his great-grandfather – had kept a sense of measure. Had they been courtiers they would have lived in St. Petersburg, but they preferred Moscow. This very fact suggests that considerations of social prestige and advancement weighed with them less decisively than with either the Puškins or the Baratynskijs.

Kozlov's paternal grandfather and namesake reached the rank of a Captain of Navy, and was entrusted, at one stage in his career, with the general administration of naval construction in the shipyards of Kazan.[1] It was a responsible post, and brought him into contact with those who could further his son's career far better than he. The son, the poet's father, became an officer of artillery, *General-Reketmejster* in the capital and a familiar figure in the Senate in Catherine's reign.

On Kozlov's mother's side, too, there were military traditions. Anna Apollonovna Xomutova was a daughter and grand-daughter

1. "K Kozlovu" (1825), l. 7.

of soldiers. Little wonder, then, that with his parents' strong approval, he married into another military clan – his wife, Tat'jana Semjonovna, was the daughter of Brigadier Sergej Davydov and a member of the family of soldiers whence came the poet and hero of the wars against Napoleon, Denis Davydov.[2]

As was usual among the wealthier gentry and nobility his name was "written into the lists" of a socially exclusive and prestigious regiment of Guards. The choice fell on the Izmajlovskij. So it was that, by the age of four, he was a sergeant and eligible for regular, unearned promotion. Better than any memoirs, the dramas of Fonvizin and of Griboedov reflect something of the society in which Kozlov grew up during the 1780s; through the parody and extremes of characterization one glimpses the reality.

There is no reason to think that the Kozlovs were more uncivilized than the run of gentle Muscovite families. To the contrary, the facts of Kozlov's later careers as poet and translator plainly suggest that certain of them were far better read than was common among their contemporaries and peers. There was a fortepiano and an extensive library in the house of the richer cousins with whose children, according to Kozlov's daughter, Aleksandra Ivanovna,[3] her father was educated from an early age. According to that short biographical fragment (which, though less factual than one might wish, provides almost the only details known of Kozlov's first years), he was taught "by several foreign governors and tutors," "read various foreign literatures" but "always . . . loved what was simple and Russian." Perhaps Aleksandra Ivanovna added the last detail wishing to show her father in a favourable patriotic light, but in any event, it is clear that he received an education typical for his class and generation. Heavy emphasis was placed on the acquiring of a first-rate knowledge of French, and an acquaintance with ancient literature and history, was held desirable. But it was an ability to converse

2. For a short biographical sketch (there is no reliable study) of Kozlov's mature years, see V. Jakovlev, "I. I. Kozlov," in *Russkij biografičeskij slovar'*, 25 vols., (St. Petersburg, 1903), vol. 9, pp. 49-52.

3. A biographical fragment by Kozlov's daughter is included by K. Ja. Grot in his article "K biografii, tvorenijam i perepiske I. Kozlova," *Izvestija Otdelenija Russkogo Jazyka i Slovesnosti* (St. Petersburg, 1904), bk. 2, pp. 77-78.

on equal terms with Western Europeans, to be receptive to ideas brought from the West both in print and orally, on which Kozlov's tutors most insisted. Like all educated Russians of the time of Catherine, General Kozlov's heir was expected to evince those qualities also expected of ambassadors: to be lucid in several languages; to be extremely well-informed of recent happenings, political, social and literary; to be a citizen of Europe. Not until the 1820s would the emphasis be moved from the Russians' obligation to join the world of greater Europe to their duty to be citizens of Russia.[4]

Kozlov was an apt pupil. From the few early letters and notes that have survived, it is plain that he learned French and some Italian as a boy. Later, in early manhood, he perfected his command of Italian and learned Polish well. Still later, between 1818 and 1825, he added German and English. Untroubled by the need to pass examinations, he was able to devote his energies to those studies which interested him – modern languages and literatures; in privileged conditions, a penchant became a rare skill.

But the study of literature was hardly a career, and French was acquired to be spoken with *le beau monde*, not with tutors and friends. Pressed to enter his regiment and active service, Kozlov acceded to his father's wishes and in February 1795 joined the Izmajlovskij, then stationed in St. Petersburg. He served in it forty months.

From the first, he disliked the military life, with its endless parades and its tiresome restrictions on his own comings and goings. Nonetheless he scored a series of marked social successes. Only his skill with the épée and sabre equalled his talents as a dancer.[5] Having achieved such triumphs in his first months as a subaltern, and, without the smallest effort, having attained the rank of *podporučik* (second lieutenant), he could most probably have pursued a distinguished career as an administrative officer. The future promised well. Yet one has only to read the memoirs

4. On this question, see A. G. Tsejtlin's lucid work, *Tvorčestvo Ryleeva* (Moscow, 1955), esp. chaps. 5-7.

5. Vjazemskij, in a letter to N. I. Turgenev of 1819 speaks gaily of "the retired dancing-master . . . who has taken to scribbling verse."

of men who witnessed the unbalanced Prussomania of the Tsarevich Pavel Petrovič – and were disgusted by it[6] – to understand why Kozlov should have preferred civilian life. The time was yet to come when Arakčeev, Aleksandr's organizing martinet, would do his best to turn the whole state into a prison or parade-ground,[7] but there was discipline enough, and regimentation to spare, in 1797. Pavel's deepening neuroses were reflected not only in Gatčina and Kameno-Ostrov, where he maintained his private, Prussian-helmeted troops and personal spies, but also, and with unpleasant faithfulness, in the standing army. Kozlov hesitated, then requested a transfer to the Civil Service.

The request was granted, and ex-Lieutenant Kozlov entered the Chancery of the Procuror-General with equivalent civilian rank and status – Provincial Secretary (*Gubernskij Sekretar'*). The procedure, which was allowed for by Peter the Great's parallel tables of rank, was simple. The transfer in no way affected Kozlov's career prospects, and within three months, in October, 1798, he was again promoted, this time to Collegiate Assessor.

It was apparent from the first that his career would be a distinguished one; by 1812 it seemed most probable that it would be brilliant. From the dark, fortress-like building of the Procuror-General's chancery off the Fontanka he moved to the Chancery of Heraldry, and from there, in 1807, to the still more inviting Chancery of the Commandant of Moscow. Each move was calculated; each year brought him advancement, or its promise. The Commandant of Moscow, Count Tutol'min, liked Kozlov. And in November, 1807, at the age of twenty-eight, he was appointed Court Councillor (*Nadvornyj Sovetnik*), a position which took him to St. Petersburg.

Later he wrote about the "Moscow period" of his life, which this appointment interrupted, in the introduction to his third narrative tale, *The Mad Girl* (1830). His affection for his

6. See P. Moranne, *Paul I-er de Russie avant l'avènement, 1754-1796* (Paris, 1907); also C. de Grunwald, *L'Assassinat de Paul I-er, Tsar de Russie* (Paris, 1960). Both works have useful bibliographies.

7. For a sketch of Arakčeev's career, see A. G. Mazour's excellent study of the Decembrist movement, revolt and aftermath, *The First Russian Revolution, 1825* (Stanford, 1963), pp. 41-5, pp. 51-63.

birthplace never lessened; "Moscow, Moscow!" he could write in his fiftieth year, "where joys and grief/ Embraced my youthful spirit, burning –/ Where the alarm of passions, like a sea in storm/ So often agitated my life!/ Thou art the cradle of my memories,/ Of my heart-felt thoughts and daring hopes. . . . " If one believes certain Soviet commentators,[8] the passions' alarm certainly rang like a clarion for the young officer and mandarin. The life he led was worldly. He became well-known as a dancer, celebrated as a wit, and was a welcome figure in many a noble salon. If he did not lead the debauched life that the young Tolstoy would lead as an army officer some thirty-five years later, then at least he enjoyed himself in every possible way. And it is pleasant to learn that he did, since his illness was imminent.

Still his interest in literature seems to have been a passive one, for it is most improbable that every single piece that he composed before 1818 – granted that he wrote any – should have been lost. Since the smallest album-pieces by his contemporaries, lost in obscure corners of fashionable scrapbooks, could not elude the watchful eye of literary scholars and historians such as P. A. Pletnjov and Baron N. Drizden, it seems most likely that he wrote little or nothing, or destroyed all that he wrote. Yet, as Nikolaj Polevoj observed in 1833, talent in poetry does not appear and vanish "like the morning mists,"[9] and it is hardly reasonable to think that Kozlov was so lost in the joys of the social life as to have neither time nor leisure for literature. The ease with which he formed a friendship with V. A. Žukovskij, "teacher of harmony" to Puškin and his generation, in itself discredits the view. If Kozlov was a dandy, as even his daughter does not fully deny, he was a cultured one and alive to literary developments in Russia, as in England and France.

The meeting with Žukovskij, which took place in the autuman of 1808, was a formative one for Kozlov. Recently arrived in Moscow to assume the editorship of the literary journal *Moscow Messenger*, the celebrated poet at once formed an

8. E. Kuprejanova, for example, in the 1948 edition of the verse; see chapter 9.

9. N. Polevoj, "Sočinenija I. I. Kozlova," *Moskovskij telegraf*, 1833, no. 10, pp. 317-8.

attachment for Kozlov, and quickly introduced him to the members of literary circles where he was himself the leading figure. Of those whom he met at this time, A. F. Merzljakov, classicist, author of briefly popular songs and future Professor of Russian Literature at Moscow University, I. A. Krylov, the so-called Russian Aesop, became life-long friends; others became respected acquaintances. (It was within six months of his meeting Kozlov that Krylov earned his first overwhelming success, with twenty-three fables published in book form; he read them aloud to Kozlov.)

Secure in his career by 1809, and confident of lasting financial stability (the family estates were small and poor, scarcely sufficient to maintain his parents, still less himself and a future wife), Kozlov resolved to marry. The wedding took place in Moscow, in the summer of that year. Tat'jana Semjonovna bore him a daughter, Aleksandra Ivanovna, later his personal helper and faithful secretary, and one son, also christened Ivan.[10] The marriage seems to have been successful and to have brought both partners happiness.

Meanwhile his civil career continued to progress well. On the outbreak of war in 1812 he found himself appointed to the committee formed to organize a citizens' home guard, or militia, in Moscow. Both his administrative and his military experience served the city well; he left three days before the entry of Napoleon's vanguard, retiring with his family to the small town of Rybinsk. There he remined until the French retreated.

For the fourth and last time he changed ministries, joining the Department of State Properties early in 1813. On July 24, he was appointed assistant to its head (*Pomoščnik Stolonačal'nika*), and in September, 1814 to the rank of Collegiate Councillor. For a man of thirty-five, it was a position of no small importance, and bode well for the future.

The future, however, had a harsh surprise in store, and

10. The poet's son left a small collection of papers to the Imperial Petersburg Public Library (now the Saltykov-Ščedrin Public Library, Leningrad), on his death in January, 1883. "Iz bumag poeta," based on those papers, appeared anonymously in *Russkij arxiv*, 1886, bk. 2, pp. 177-94.

Kozlov's administrative career had, without his knowing it, entered its final phase in 1814. Almost certainly the disease that led to his paralysis and blindness was not contracted in 1816, when it first showed itself, but had been in his body for some years, gradually worsening. The symptoms suggest sclerosis, but it is dangerous even to speculate at such a hazy distance from the years concerned. Nor can one say with certainty when signs of partial paralysis in one leg became obvious; the diary is silent on the question, while contemporaries, perhaps from various and confused motives, do not allude to it. It was no later than 1818, and probably in 1816 – 17. At first the muscular seizure caused him merely grave inconvenience and discomfort; later it gave him lasting pain. But more troublesome by far was his constantly weakening sight. By 1821 he was completely blind, and his career ended.

"Misfortune," wrote Žukovskij tersely, "made Kozlov a poet."[11] The fact cannot be denied. Even in 1818 – 19 the ailing civil servant had found solace in paraphrasing Byron's "The Bride of Abydos." What had been earlier an interest and pastime became, under the impact of an unforeseen and horrible disaster, a stay and support. The version of Byron's tale, which was in French, not Russian, spoke eloquently of Kozlov's distinction as a linguist.[12] More than this, it stood as a monument to a phenomenal energy and persistence. There is no record of his having known English before blindness threatened him seriously in 1817. Yet within three years, perhaps less, he was able to translate English verse into both French and Russian! Little wonder that A. I. Turgenev, slightly exaggerating the reality, perhaps, but understandably impressed, claimed bluntly that Kozlov "learned English in six months"![13] It was a feat of memory and will.

But will-power was not Kozlov's only asset; indeed, although afflicted, he was also curiously favoured in some ways, for he had strength and temperament to bear misfortune. Others might have

11. Žukovskij's obituary for Kozlov appeared in *Sovremennik*, 1840.

12. On this whole subject, see chapter 7.

13. Letter to Vjazemskij of 22.10.19; *Ostaf'evskij arxiv Knjazej Vjazemskix* (St. Petersburg, 1896-1913), vol. 1, p. 335.

reacted violently, imprecating God, where Kozlov faced facts objectively, first recognizing his dependence on others for help, then granting that he needed a supplementary income. Puškin, A. A. Del'vig, P. A. Vjazemskij and Nikolaj Turgenev are merely four of the many friends and acquaintances who carefully record the blind man's customary cheerfulness. Perhaps their insistence on the matter is itself enough to cause one to view their statements with caution; yet the kernel of truth, even if they, like A. I. Turgenev, exaggerate a trifle, need not be questioned. P. A. Pletnjov, too, states that to visit Kozlov was a pleasure, not a task, and one that he never dreaded.

In one other way Kozlov had good fortune: he met and came to know Puškin in 1819, before his sight had completely failed. The friendship between the two was not, and never became, intimate. Shortly after their first meetings Puškin was exiled to the south, a number of his "revolutionary epigrams" having come to Alexander's notice. But it was as to "an old friend" that Puškin alluded to "the dear blind poet" in 1825,[14] and Kozlov continued to write to him throughout the thirties.

Poets' works, as Belinskij remarked, are the records of their lives, and certainly Kozlov's personal and literary concerns grew ever more closely enmeshed after his blindness. Friendship with Puškin heralded a new phase in his life, and from 1820 until his death twenty years later, his private existence was scarcely separable from his literary career; for that career, too, was private, drawing its inspiration chiefly from personal misfortune and changing responses to it. It would be true to say, at all events, that his private life became so private, after 1825, that we can know little of it. Nothing is known of his adjustments to the cripple's life but what is reflected in his verse – a fact which handsomely substantiates Belinskij's comment.[15]

When he went blind, Kozlov was forty, by which age the character is formed. If character cannot be changed, however, it can most certainly be coloured, and illness coloured Kozlov's very

14. Letter of 31.5.25; *A. S. Puškin*, vol. 9, p. 126, p. 155.

15. V. G. Belinskij, "Literaturnyje mečtanija," vol. X (1834), *Poln. sob. soč.* (Moscow, 1954-9), vol. 1, pp. 91-4.

outlook. It would have been strange indeed, Kozlov being an educated and reflective man and his disease incurable, if he had not given much thought to such questions as Providence, salvation and the prospects of another life after death. His verse is the result of that reflection. For as his outlook grew increasingly religious, so it found ever clearer reflection in his verse, which is in essence elegiac (see Chapter 3). In vain early Soviet commentators attempted to under-emphasize the element of pure religion in Kozlov's original verse (a tendency happily rectified in recent years).[16] There is no shadow of doubt that Kozlov firmly believed in God and in personal salvation.

"Pardon my transgressions, O God,/ And revive my wearied spirit,/ And grant that I may suffer my torments/ In hope, in faith and love": so begins the poem written barely eight weeks before Kozlov's death in January, 1840, which is, as the title makes plain, "A Prayer." And Kozlov did evince Christian virtues during his lifetime. Not least among these, though not mentioned by the most recent of his Soviet commentators, was simple patience. "There are," he informs us in "The First Meeting" (1837), "two secrets/ By the power of which suffering on earth blooms/ . . ./ Patience is a blessing in misfortunes;/ In a new life, it changes a crown of thorns/ Into a crown of roses."[17] He was charitable and, as numbers of epistles demonstrate, loving towards all he knew. Total dependence on others, one might suppose, would hurt the pride of one so recently and wholly independent, yet there is no indication that Kozlov suffered from bruised vanity – or even tried to conceal such a feeling from himself. More, he does not appear to have been overly sensitive about his handicap, a fact the more remarkable when one remembers that now his financial position was far from being sound. It was natural that contemporaries should pity him, remarkable that pity neither distressed nor aggravated him. Perhaps he was able to conceal frustration and annoyance; certainly no visitor came face to face with it. Yet he must surely have approved Nikolaj Polevoj's judicious irony at the expense of those "whose articles begin: 'Kozlov's fate must evoke

16. See chapter 9.
17. ll. 33-7.

sympathy in every tender heart . . . ' "[18] Either he displayed an almost superhuman self-control for twenty years or – far more probable – he was by nature benign and tolerant.

The roll-call of those who visited him on Petrovskaja Storona, across the Neva from the Winter Palace, is an impressive one: Vjazemskij and Krylov, Griboedov and Ryleev, Gnedič and Kjuxel'beker, Glinka, Tjutčev and Baratynskij. These visitors came from no one social or political grouping – what had Gnedič, the distinguished translator of *The Iliad*, in common with Ryleev, so soon to be hanged for his part in the Decembrist rising, if not a shared interest in, and concern for, literature and its potential benefits to Russia? They came because they chose to; because Kozlov, as the author of *The Monk*, a rhymed tale which so briefly rivalled Puškin's *Evgenij Onegin* in popularity among the St. Petersburg littérateurs, was a distinguished poet; because, finally, his company and conversation were far from being onerous, especially to those who, like the Countesses Aleksandra Laval' and Dar'ja Fiquelmont, wife of the Austrian Ambassador, imagined themselves, like him, destined to suffering on this earth. (Like Mar'ja Pototskaja, Aleksandra Voekova and several other women from fashionable Russian society, these two cast themselves in curiously ambivalent roles, now seeking to comfort Kozlov in his affliction, now seeking solace from him, as from a supposed connoisseur of pain. There can be little doubt that his illness and firm response to it exercised a certain fascination over high-born women, notably those with literary penchants and little to occupy them.)[19]

Visited by some writers occasionally, by others frequently and by Del'vig and Pletnjov often,[20] it was easy for Kozlov to remain *au courant* of literary news and happenings in Russia, as in Western Europe. It was through Del'vig that he had come to know Puškin; and, as Del'vig's friend, it was natural that he collaborate

18. See note 9.

19. This emerges from A. A. Voekova's many letters to Kozlov, 39 of which, dating from 1823-27, may be found in N. V. Solov'jov's *Istorija odnoj žizni*, 2 vols. (Petrograd, 1916), vol. 2, pp. 24-55.

20. See K. Ja. Grot, *op. cit.*, note 3.

on the Petersburg almanac, *Northern Flowers* (1825 – 32).[21] Through Del'vig, too, lay the path to close friendship with Orest Somov, author of "The Dream" and an ecstatic student and translator of Lord Byron. Somov was critic of poetry for Del'vig's almanac, and reviewed Kozlov's translated and original work alike with consistent warmth and approval (see Chapter 5). Nor was Del'vig without influence on Kozlov's style as an author, that is, on his way of viewing his own verse, others' literary work and, for that matter, Russian literature in general. Encouraged by Del'vig, Kozlov became an active member of a progressive literary society, the Free Society of Lovers of Russian Letters.[22] By direct implication, he became the enemy of such writers (or hacks) as A. E. Izmajlov (editor of the rival journal *The Well-Meaner* and pillar of the opposition party, the Petersburg Society of Lovers of Letters, Sciences and Arts), V. Panaev, and A. Lobojko. Thus even his friendships and literary enmities were, to a point, determined by contact with Del'vig. But it was a natural decision to assist Del'vig, Puškin, Pletnjov and Vjazemskij in their new almanac which would oppose A. F. Voekov's *Russian Invalid* and, still more energetically, *Son of the Fatherland*, controlled by the detested Faddej Bulgarin, secret agent of the Government and enemy of all progressive thought. His literary mentors, too, were Karamzin and Žukovskij (see Chapter 3); he, too, "from the first assumed an attitude of mirthful disdain towards militant neo-Classicism and enthusiastic support of Romanticism"[23] – or, rather, of those facets of Romanticism that he cared for: the colour, *brio* and drama of Byron, Schiller, and Mickiewicz. Since "one of the common denominators of *Northern Flowers* throughout its eight years of existence, expressed not only directly in its literary criticism but indirectly by the orientation of its contributors, was . . . a positive interest in and admiration for Western European Romantics,"[24] it was entirely logical that Kozlov – through whose translations Russians first encountered the true

21. A recent study of that almanac in English, J. Mersereau's *Baron Del'vig's Northern Flowers* (Carbondale, 1967), alludes briefly to Kozlov's participation in it.
22. V. Bazanov, *Učonaja respublika* (Moscow, 1964) pp. 335-6, pp. 434-44.
23. J. Mersereau, *op.cit.*, p. 45.
24. *Ibid.*, p. 43.

Byron and Thomas Moore, and not the fictions of Letourneur's grand imagination – should contribute enthusiastically towards it. And he did so.

Still more reliable as a contact with literary circles in St. Petersburg and Moscow (for the indolent Del'vig rarely left the newer capital), was the gentle and diligent Pjotr Pletnjov (1792 – 1862). The son of a provincial priest, Pletnjov's career in St. Petersburg, as a teacher, editor and, finally, academic, was one of unforeseen brilliance. He was an indifferent pupil, abandoning mathematics for physics, physics for history and everything for pleasant soirées with his friends. "Discovered" by A. Borx, an intimate of the Empress, he gave lessons in Russian history and literature to the Imperial children; in 1832, thanks to the influence of S. Uvarov, Minister for Education, he found himself appointed Professor of Russian Literature in St. Petersburg University. Eight years later, in the year of Kozlov's death, he became its President (*Rektor*).[25]

"You once published my uncle," Puškin wrote to him in October, 1824; "The author of *Dangerous Neighbour*/ Was most worthy of it/ . . ./ Now, old pal, publish me./ But who in the name of Phoebus, my Pletnjov,/ Will be *your* publisher?"[26] The uncle in question was Vasilij Puškin (1767 – 1830), Aleksandr's paternal uncle and the author the lengthy satirical poem mentioned here; Pletnjov did agree to publish Chapters One and Two of *Evgenij Onegin*; and he published his own, weak verse.

Pletnjov was a reliable literary agent, and seems to have acted on Kozlov's behalf, as well as Puškin's, though he was not mentioned on the fly-leaf of Kozlov's first verse collection, of 1828. I cannot discover what financial arrangements Pletnjov had with Kozlov, but there is a casual, almost unmercenary, air about those notes which the poet scrawled to him in the years of his blindness. Here is one such note, published for the first time here and taken from the Pletnjov archive in *Puškinskij Dom* (*Institut*

25. Pletnjov, Kozlov's close neighbour on Petrovskaja Storona, proved a good and efficient friend in times of trouble; see my article "P. A. Pletnjov and A. L. Baratynskaja: Unpublished Correspondence," *Scando-Slavica*, vol. 15 (1969).

26. For details, see V. Nabokov, *Eugene Onegin*, 4 vols. (New York, 1964), vol. 2, pp. 20-24.

Russkoj Literatury Akademii Nauk), in Leningrad. Unable to control the flow of ink from a quill-pen, Kozlov chose to write in soft pencil; but still he had no more control of his script than has the average ten-year-old and was often obliged to break simple words in two at the ends of lines:

(Side 1)	(2)	(3)
Thank you	I'm alone	I shall
sincerely	now and	reply
dear Pjo-	there is	tomorrow
tr Alek-	nobody to	I embrace you
sandrovič	read	dear
for the five	your lett-	friend with
hundred roubles.	er, to which	all my heart.
		Ivan Kozlov[27]

Why Pletnjov should have sent Kozlov 500 roubles in 1825 – 28 one can only guess; Pletnjov's preceding letter has not survived. Perhaps it was an advance payment from A. Smirdin, publisher of *Verses of Ivan Kozlov* (St. Petersburg, 1828), or payment for one of the narrative tales printed in book form, *The Monk* (1825) or *Princess Natal'ja Dolgorukaja* (1828); possibly Pletnjov visited a St. Petersburg banker on Kozlov's behalf. To speculate further is pointless. Two things are amply clear: Kozlov and Pletnjov were on the closest terms; and Kozlov was receiving considerable sums of money for his work, assuming, as seems reasonable, that the transaction mentioned here *was* connected with his poetry or translations, and not an entirely separate matter. Five hundred roubles, incidentally, was exactly the sum that Pletnjov received, via Vjazemskij, for arranging the publication of Puškin's uncle's poems, in April 1822. It was sufficient to rent spacious rooms off Nevskij Prospect for three months.

Other notes, scrawled almost illegibly or, more often, dictated to Aleksandra Ivanovna, cast interesting light on Kozlov's changing

27. Preserved in *Puškinskij Dom* (*Rukopisnyj otdel'*), under reference: *Fond* 237, Op. 3, N. 312. The note is on coarse paper, 7 inches by 6 inches, folded once at centre vertically; on side 4 is "Petru a loksandrovu pletnyo vu." I thank Professor Marfa Malova, of PD, for permission to publish this and other notes and materials concerning I. I. Kozlov.

work habits. Particularly curious in this respect is a note to Mixail Lobanov (1787 – 1846), translator, critic and "Classicist" of August, 1827:

> I would have sent you my Princess, respected Mixail Evstaf'evič, but she is not yet written out – as is customary with me, certain extracts have been thrown down on flying bits of paper; the last hundred lines or so are not yet done, but are ripe, and everything will be finished this week. I ask you, dear friend, to call on me, now, or tomorrow, or when it is convenient – and I shall read it to you and make use of your observations. I embrace you. I.K.[28]

There are three points of interest in the letter. First, it is noteworthy that Kozlov had little method in the actual writing of his works. Some of the "flying bits of paper" have happily survived, and one marvels that all were not lost within hours of being torn from the exercise-book. Even the note to Pletnjov was jotted down on a piece of coarse grey paper, torn from a larger sheet, that measures scarcely seven inches by five. The fragments measure anything between nine inches by eight inches and the area covered by six postage stamps! Although disorganized in this respect, however, Kozlov was very highly organized in the matter of creating verse; and, one realizes on reading this note to Lobanov, creation for Kozlov was not at all the same thing as composition. Writing and dictation were time-consuming and laborious processes. Not unnaturally, he preferred to avoid them as much as possible, working out long passages in his head, amending and even re-forming sections without recourse to pen or paper, and calling his faithful daughter only when dictation could be given fluently. It was a process combining common-sense with a phenomenal retentive power – a power already well developed when, in 1828, Polevoj published a review of *Princess Natal'ja Dolgorukaja* ("my Princess" of the note to Lobanov) that was also, in parts, a paeon. Contemporaries marveled at the blind poet's ability to recite long passages from the Old Testament, from Shakespeare, Milton, Dante and Racine. "Speaking to him,"

28. *Fond* 93, op. 4, N. 46 (*Sobranie P. Ja. Daškova*).

Polevoj writes simply, "I forgot that he was blind and that a burden of suffering weighed him down onto his couch. We talked of many things, and his remarkable memory and wide-ranging knowledge amazed me. I listened with wonder as he recited to me by heart the verse of Puškin, Moore and Byron – quantities of verse by Byron . . ."[29]

It is interesting, lastly, that Kozlov should have been on close terms with Lobanov. Eight years the poet's junior but still, in comparison with such young men as Puškin, Yazykov or Baratynskij, one of his own generation, Lobanov served under Krylov in the Imperial Public Library of St. Petersburg, where he met Del'vig and Kozlov. He was a writer, critic and translator, but distinguished himself in none of those fields. Among his works which Kozlov cared for were an exceedingly patriotic "Song on the Capture of Paris" (1816) and ponderous translations of "Phèdre" (1823) and "Iphigenia in Avlida" (1816); but it was his play "Boris Godunov" that brought him notoriety in his own time. The drama, "classical" in style and without Puškin's intervals of humour, appeared within a year of the latter's *Boris Godunov*, and was an instant failure. Lobanov is remembered now, if at all, for a famous reactionary speech read to the Academy of Sciences (to which he was elected in 1845), on "the spirit of Russian literature." It appeared in *The Contemporary*, I (1836), where it was deftly and ironically refuted by that journal's founder – Puškin.[30]

Plainly Kozlov thought highly of Lobanov's criticism, or wished him to think so. The fact reveals others – that Lobanov was a scholar, albeit a pedant also. His contribution to the compilation of the Academy of Sciences' Russian Dictionary (1845) was a major one. More than this, his circle of acquaintance was, broadly speaking, Kozlov's too. As time passed, Kozlov came into ever closer contact with his contemporaries, men and women

29. N. Polevoj, "O sočinenijax I Kozlova," *Moskovskij telegraf*, 1828, no. 4, pp. 549-50.

30. The speech was entitled "O duxe slovesnosti, kak inostrannoj, tak i otečestvennoj"; for Puškin's refutation, see *A. S. Puškin*, vol. 6, pp. 134-42; see also my article "Eight Unpublished Letters of E. A. Baratynsky," *Canadian Slavonic Papers*, vol. XI (1969), no. 1, pp. 115-6.

in their late twenties during "the golden start of Alexander's reign." One perceives a double, or parallel process of rapprochement – on one level, with literary, scholarly, above all, *serious* circles; on another, with those able to recall the time of Catherine, Dmitriev, Deržavin. It is a far cry from the post-Decembrist years to Kozlov the dandy and brilliant army officer!

Kozlov was of an older and more conservative generation than Puškin and his circle. Those closest to him – Countess Laval', Žukovskij, Pletnjov, Pavel Gagarin and P. M. Volkonskij – were close to him in age also. A Muscovite, he was never a member of the St. Petersburg critical and literary circles as younger poets were, and by 1821, when his first piece was published, there was a mighty psychological ravine between the two cities. Moscow threatened to become a back-water; that it did not was almost entirely the result of the Karamzinians' decision, in 1810 – 12, to make it their rallying point (see Chapter 3). Not even Lermontov could escape the stigma – to Baratynskij he seemed "somehow stuffy, Muscovite . . . ,"[31] and this in 1839!

In other ways, too, Kozlov stood apart from those with whom he consorted and who were his regular correspondents. The influence of Karamzin on his verse, and on his first rhymed tale *The Monk* in particular, was so strong as to be obvious to all but the prejudiced; on Puškin, and other poets of his generation, it was less lasting and less deep. Vissarion Belinskij was not, properly speaking, prejudiced against *The Monk*; he merely wrote with *partis pris* – and, such were his ready-made demands of literature even in 1834 that he could never do more than commend Kozlov's poetry in measured terms. Like a solitary signal his comment that *The Monk* was a *Poor Liza* for the 1820s heralded the forthcoming attack and caused the tide of criticism to turn against Kozlov;[32] yet, as even Pletnjov acknowledged, it contained a grain of truth.

But for two women, Kozlov always remained without re-

31. Letter to A. L. Baratynskaja of late 1839, cited by M. L. Gofman in *Poln sob. soč. E. A. Boratynskago* (St. Petersburg, 1914-15), vol. 1, p. 303.

32. Pletnjov was echoed by Del'vig, writing in *Literaturnaja gazeta* (1830), no. 68, p. 261, and by N. I. Nadeždin in *Teleskop* (1831), no. 1, p. 177; even the principal points are basically identical – that Kozlov, having once given of his best in 1825, had yet to repeat that performance.

proach. (Unfortunately, Tat'jana Semjonovna left no record of her feelings for her husband.) Both Žukovskij's niece, Aleksandra Voekova (1795 – 1829), and Aleksandra Laval' (1772 – 1850) maintained close friendships and a warm correspondence with him throughout their adult lives. Though both attractive bluestockings, fashionable hostesses and accomplished pianists, the two were separated by a quarter of a century; the fact is reflected in the very nature of Kozlov's different, though equally intense, relationships with each.

Aleksandra Voekova was sixteen years younger than Kozlov, and he was approaching forty when they first met. Both were married, and there are no grounds for thinking that the relationship was ever other than platonic. Within those bounds, however, it was ardent; for Kozlov, as slightly earlier for Žukovskij who had dedicated to her his marvellous ballad "Svetlana" (1812), she became as it were a private Muse – a spirit of inspiration (as he put it in a letter to her).[33] "So much do you bring gladness with you," he began his epistle "To Svetlana" (1821), "That the heart seems to burst out laughing;/ Something in it responds, part of itself,/ To your welcoming voice./ . . . / Always, Svetlana, you/ Shall be my heart's friend!"[34] Between 1823 and 1827 alone, Voekova wrote more than eighty letters to him. Naturally, being "an epistolatory hero" (as Žukovskij said),[35] he responded in kind.

Countess Laval', on the other hand, was older than "the dear friend" of her later years. A daughter of Catherine's State Secretary, Ivan Kozitskij, she married Nicholas's Master of Court Ceremony, Ivan Stepanovič Laval' (1761 – 1846), a man, in his turn, far older than she. Together with the Fiquelmonts, husband and wife,[36] she represented Kozlov's main link with Court circles. To her he dedicated two considerable poems, "The Promised

33. See note 19.

34. ll. 1-5.

35. Letter to Kozlov from Venice of 4.11.38, reproduced in my paper "Žukovskij and Manzoni," *Forum Italicum*, vol. 8 (1971).

36. Kozlov introduced Puškin to the Count, and Puškin, too, became a family friend, as is clear from a note to Natal'ja Puškina of 8.12.31 (*A. S. Puškin*, vol. 10, p. 83): "Has Xitrovo or Fiquelmont been to see you?" etc; Puškin was expected at the Countess's next ball (*ibid.*, p. 94), and, unlike Kozlov, dutifully attended.

Land" (1832) and "To Countess Laval'" (1839). Here, to give some flavour of the friendship that existed between the two, is an extract from the second of these poems:

Your birth was a feast for all
Who live and love in the soul,
Joys and griefs are the feast of all
Who have met you in this life.

How faithful is the cloudless purity
Of your ardent friendship!
With you, sadness is lighter, joy
More tender in the hearts of friends.

And, believe, heatedly I pray
To Him whose kingdom is over the stars
That He in everything
May strew your life with flowers. . . .
(ll. 5 – 16)

Aleksandra Laval' visited Kozlov often, more, it seems, to discuss the nature of human destiny than to listen to his work, although she would do that too, when in suitably exalted mood. Certainly she read everything that he wrote, as is plain from her many letters, each replete with references to ballads, songs, and idylls. Certain letters, indeed, seem to reflect the mood of his fantasy "A Venetian Night," with their languid cadences and balmy air, and of these none more so than one written from St. Petersburg on April 14, 1832. In its transparent desire both to give and to receive comfort, as in its allusion to the Countess's own "peines" (her eldest son, Viktor, shot himself on the family estate in Penza shortly after his twenty-first birthday),[37] it may be said to typify those of the years 1832 – 39;

A Monsieur Kozloff ce 14 d'avril

Je suis toute honteuse, Monsieur, de n'avoir pas repondu

37. On this tragedy, see Vjazemskij, *Staraja zapisnaja knižka* (Moscow, 1963), p. 179 (under July 5, 1830).

jusqu'à présent à votre I-er billet – je m'empresse de repondre à celui du 14, que je viens de recevoir dans ce moment. La journée se passe comme la vie, elle finit: voilà tout ce qu'on sait positivement. Souvent elle ne laisse aucun souvenir, ou bien en donne si peu qu'ils ne valent pas la peine d'être rappellés! Je vis du monde, par entraînement plus que par choix; je me promène en chalupe, j'écoute les sérénades qui se donnent sur la Néva. Le beautemps, les 20d. de chaleur à l'ombre me font vivre et me rendent paresseuse en même temps. Je jouis du 'dolce far niente' – cette vie indolente est cependant la vie. L'absence des agitations, des inquiétudes, du mal est déjà un bien-être. Je crois que le repos du corps amène un peu la paix de l'âme. On rêve; on voit le monde avec le prisme de l'imagination; on voit les hommes tels qu'on voudrait qu'ils fussent. Après ce beau rêve, on se rencontre en Société, et tout le monde joue fort bien le rôle du salon; on se sépare autant les uns des autres, en faisant semblant.

Et l'âme reste en paix. Pourquoi n'avons-nous pas toujours 20d. de chaleur en été? Je n'aurais pas eu des causes de troubler (?) la paix de l'âme avec Balk, et il ne m'aurait pas retiré son amitié comme il l'a fait. Cela me fait de la peine lorsque j'y pense.

Je suis de votre avis, Monsieur, vivre et souffrir vaut encore la peine de vivre. *Souffrir* n'est qu'une condition de la vie. Quand le corps suffre, l'âme se trouve plus désaisie des biens terrestres; quand l'âme souffre, la vie et l'espérance sont devant elle – l'âme s'y transporte. Cette ennuyante présente (?) l'épure et la prépare pour la gloire. Pourquoi donc la plaindre? Vous dites très-bien: "Il y a plénitude d'idées, de sentiments et sensations dans la souffrance." Mais quand vous aurez besoin de soulager votre coeur, parlez-moi, Monsieur. Vous savez que je ne sous pas étrangère aux peines de la vie.

Venez je vous prie Monsieur passer la journée avec nous vendredi à b.h. Recevez l'assurance de toute l'amitié que je vous ai,

de Laval

Acting sometimes on impulse, Countess Laval' was capable of

great generosity to those in need or pain. One such "movement of the soul" is recorded by the all-embracing Vjazemskij. Aleksandra Grigorevna, it seems, was in some circles "reputed a miser, and unsympathetic . . . Having learned from Žukovskij that a certain clerk, who had lost government funds, needed more than 10,000 roubles to save himself from misfortune, she . . . gave him a banknote for that sum."[38] Like so many of the anecdotes and comments in Vjazemskij's invaluable *Old Notebooks* (*Staryje Zapisnyje Knižki*), containing an incomparably rich survey of literary developments and personal affairs in the years 1812 – 1848, it has a pleasing, almost aphoristic pithiness.

The Countess, it may be emphasized, succeeded in her aim of comforting Kozlov, though less through her sensibility (which, other letters indicate, she thought of an unparalleled acuteness and fine delicacy),[39] than by her willingness simply to keep him company if and when he required it. She saw him often; little by little, she came to identify with him, sharing his attitudes, his apprehensions, even his successes. Not that she lacked an independent mind and spirit – proof enough of that is the real interest with which, at the age of sixty, she embarked on a study of early Spanish and Catalan poetry; but why did she study poetry, and not, like numbers of her contemporaries in London, Paris, Trieste and St. Petersburg, herbals or the occult? She studied it (not merely read it) because this was the interest of Kozlov. Why Spanish and Italian verse? Because he had a friend in Paez de la Cadena, Spanish Ambassador to St. Petersburg, and had translated Dante, Grossi, Ariosto, and Manzoni. It was not for herself alone that she would copy out extracts from the Spanish verse that she best liked: "Quant à moi, je me propose de transcrire tout ce qui fera impression sur moi afin de retrouver ensuite quelques impressions sympathiques avec vous."[40] The sentence conveys more than its component parts, taken separately, seem to allow. Here, to emphasize the curiously blended personal

38. *Ibid.*, p. 108.

39. "Dva pis'ma grafini Aleksandry G. Lavalja," *Russkij arxiv*, 1886, no. 3, pp. 316-18; author not certain.

40. Letter of 20.7.31.

and literary flavour of that friendship (which lasted as long as Kozlov lived), is an extract from another letter to him, also of 1831. It is taken from *Russkij Arxiv* for 1886 (no. 3, 316 – 18), where it appeared for the first time in print, together with a second letter of February 10, 1831 containing the Countess's views of Titian, of Dante's earlier work and of Princess Zinaida Volkonskaja, already settled in Rome, who had recently read Kozlov's tale *The Mad Girl*:

> Je vous remercie beaucoup, Monsieur, de la charmante traduction du Tasse que vous m'avez envoyé. Ces deux strophes portent la fraîcheur de la rose, on la voit s'épanouir et se flétrir – et quelles tristes réflexions cela amène. Je ne puis m'empêcher de vous transcrire ces 4 vers, sur la rose, tirés des poésies Cattalanes, que je vous enverrai dans deux jours avec la dette pour les deux vol. de vues de l'Ecosse et d'Angleterre. Je suis sûre du plaisir que vous feront les poètes espagnoles du 16-ième siècle: je serais heureuse de pouvoir en causer avec vous. En attendant, voici les derniers vers adressés à la rose.
>
> "A peine tu viens de paraître
> Que déjà envolent tes débris
> Et les pleurs de l'Aurore ont plus coulé, peut-être,
> Pour ta prochaine Mort que pour te faire naître."
>
> Rioza
>
> Quelle pensée gracieuse et touchante, tout-à-fait nouvelle!
>
> M. Paez m'a chargé de vous dire qu'il sera charmé de vous faire passer quelques heures en vous faisant connaître les poésies de son pays . . . Milles tendresses pour Mme Kosloff et mille compliments pour Vous.
>
> *A., Ce de Laval*

The quatrain, it must be said in Rioza's defence, is less appalling in the original; nor, it is good to know, is there the least indication that Kozlov also believed the thought expressed was "gracious, touching" or even "completely new." But it is of patent significance that Aleksandra Grigorevna should *feel* that such verse would appeal to him; hackneyed imagery apart, it was to do with swift decay and death. Always, in contemporaries' eyes, Kozlov was and remained "the suffering poet" (*poet-stradalets*), one expert in pain spiritual and physical. It was to be expected, perhaps, that such a reputation should provoke pity; coupled with a knowledge of the man's uncomplaining cheerfulness and obvious strength of spirit, it also evoked deep respect.

Karl-Ludwig Fiquelmont (1777 – 1857), from 1829 to 1839 Austro-Hungarian Ambassador in St. Petersburg and another of the poet's numerous friends in the diplomatic corps, felt that respect particularly deeply. Kozlov was on intimate terms with the whole Fiquelmont family, but to none was he more attached than to Dar'ja Fjodorovna, *née* Tizengauzen (1804 – 63). To her Kozlov dedicated his "Dream" (1831) and two excursions into foreign poetry: "Alla Contessa Fiquelmont (Graziosa quanto bella . . .)" and "To Countess Fiquelmont," a piece no less charming for its slight gaucheness;[41] to her, he addressed a poem on the birth of a son; and it was to him, in return, that the blue-stocking grand-daughter of Kutuzov, the celebrated beauty and mistress of a large *salon* in St. Petersburg turned in moments of trouble. Fiquelmont was aware of this and, to his credit, seems to have felt no resentment or jealousy. Nor is there more than the subtlest of suggestions that he and his wife were not close, by 1839, in the noble but sad letter that now follows. Fiquelmont wrote to Kozlov, and not to any other, because he felt that he, if anyone, could offer solace in a time of great trouble. We do not know what this trouble was, but one thing is clear enough: "une femme," as Fiquelmont puts it delicately, was in reality "sa femme":[42]

> J'ai l'honneur de vous faire savoir, Monsieur, que c'est hier ou aujourd'hui ou demain, ou enfin dans ces jours, à ce qu'une femme doit recevoir la nouvelle qui lui brisera le coeur; sa pieuse resignation soumettra pour elle à cette épreuve, mais les nerfs, déjà si malades, n'auront pas (- -) de piété pour les soutenir; ils obéissent à d'autres lois. Ecrivez-lui Monsieur, vous lui ferez du bien. Vous savez qu'elle vous aime, qu'elle porte respect à votre courage; vos paroles iront donc à son

41. Letter preserved in *Puškinskij Dom, Fond* 88, Op. 3, N. 33.
42. *Fond* 88, Op. -, N. 37, dated 24.5.39.

coeur, non pas comme une consolation qu'elle ne peut pas trouver, mais comme un adoucissement. Les paroles de ceux qui sont heureux ne pourront jamais produire sur elle l'effet qu'auraient les vôtres. Je vous remercie déjà de votre intention.

Je lui ecrirai samedi; s'il pouvait vous convenir de m'envoyer votre lettre, je la joindrais à la mienne. Veuillez agréer, Monsieur, l'assurance de ma considération distinguée.

Fiquelmont
ce 24 mai 1839

Much is obscure, at a distance of a hundred and thirty years; Kozlov's letter, which was almost certainly written, has not survived. One cannot know if or how he alleviated the pain spoken of here. His being asked to write at all, however, tells us a great deal.

So far various Kozlovs have emerged and blended in this brief narrative, and none has been seen in close detail – the highly successful young army officer, the later society figure, Kozlov the sufferer and consoler of others. It is trying that one cannot present a single facet of the poet in minute detail (though the temptation to stress one aspect of his career or character at the expense of others is thus neatly removed), but such is the fact – one cannot. Specific, factual details are extraordinarily few. Kozlov played no part in the campaigns of the Napoleonic War or its long aftermath, and so is not mentioned in the memoirs of military heroes and contemporaries. Nor do those details of his earlier life that are known – dates of promotion, records of transfers and awards – cast light on the man himself. When he is mentioned by contemporaries it is in terms that one can almost predict, such is their uniformity – "the dear blind poet," the *good* Kozlov, "the Russian Byron" and so forth. As elusive game through snares, so the author of *The Monk*, a work that briefly rivalled *Evgenij Onegin* in popularity at home, slips through memoirs and court records, civil lists, correspondence and biographies. Thus it seems only natural that a single portrait of the poet should be known (that given in the frontispiece of the 1960 Soviet edition of his verse), and that there is no sketch, no profile, no cartoon even from which one might form an impression of the artist as a young man.

The biography, as Belinskij said, lies in the work; and, it must be conceded, only letters provide one with an alternative source of pertinent information. For this reason alone, numerous letters are cited here; for this reason too Chapter Four, on the original verse itself, may be seen to complement and add depth to this section.

But there are two aspects of Kozlov's life as a poet that do not emerge from poetry, and these may well be touched on here. First, his ability to empathize with foreign poets – and to quote from their works at tremendous length – may be mentioned. Second, it is of interest to consider the growth of his popularity against the ever-changing background of a growing reading public in Russia, and, in connection with this, his attitude towards that public and towards all literary journalism. The questions are best treated separately.

Nikolaj Turgenev and N. A. Polevoj were merely two of many who, during or shortly after Kozlov's life, recorded his phenomenally retentive memory. It was a skill in which the poet consciously trained himself after the loss of his sight. Able to count on it with confidence, he had no need of copies of his letters or, for that matter, of verse which he had heard read twice with care. "With amazement," Polevoj declares ingenuously, "I listened as he read to me (that is, declaimed – GB) by heart verses by Puškin and Byron, quantities of verse by Byron and Moore."[43]

Many years later, in 1855, another piece on Kozlov by "N. A. P." appeared, this time in *Library for Reading* (*Biblioteka dlja čtenija*).[44] In it, Polivoj reminisced on evenings spent with Kozlov, and on Kozlov's verse in general. An extract from that second article bears quoting here:

> Any lover of fantasy might say, not without reason, that the souls of Walter Scott, Burns and Byron, flying across mountains and seas, came at certain hours to that poor labourer (*k bednomu truženiku*) and held converse by his bed. There is, among his verses, an epistle to Walter Scott in

43. See note 29.
44. *Biblioteka dlja čtenija*, 1855, vol. XXXIV, sect. 5, pp. 10-11.

> which the blind man thanks the Scottish bard for the pleasures granted by him and, finally, imagines himself at Abbotsford, at the tea table, among Scott's children and grandchildren. A whole evening in the life of the author of *Ivanhoe* is described as, one would think, only an old family friend could describe it. Scott's married daughter (Sophie Lockhart – GB) pours tea. Around the hostess sit guests – foreigners come from distant regions to meet the laird of Abbotsford. . . . For Kozlov, both Walter Scott and Burns were not merely poets, but *men*.

Opinions may differ as to the merits of Kozlov's epistle, but there is no denying the essential point of Polevoj's somewhat baroque paper: Kozlov did, indeed, imagine himself in Abbotsford, and, when the fancy took him, at home with the Moores, Byrons and Wordsworths. Only in body did he pass the last twenty years of his life by the banks of the Neva.

Throughout those years, he contributed to a small number of literary journals – no more than seven in all.[45] It is of note that one so prolific should be so scrupulous in choice of vehicle. Baratynskij, Puškin, Jazykov, all contributed to at least eighteen or twenty journals or almanacs, many destined to bloom but briefly. In one other respect, too, Kozlov stood apart from these three poets and from others of the period – he wrote and published in a measured, regular fashion. Not for him the stops and starts of a Jazykov, the periods of silence and moments of inspiration of Puškin or Baratynskij (who, in 1833 – 34, produced barely ten lines!) The graph of Kozlov's activity is constant; in vain one seeks sudden declines and rises. 1828 was an exceptional year, it is true, producing eighteen poems for the waiting public, as well as the "Crimean Sonnets of Adam Mickiewicz"; but 1832 produced twenty-four. Both in 1825 and in 1835 he published eleven pieces, six in 1822, 1824, 1827, 1829, 1830, five in 1823 and 1837, three in not only 1821, 1826 and 1833, but also in 1839, the last full year of his activity! It is a steady record, and reminds one not only of the poet's lifelong habit of reworking

45. For details, see the most recent (1960) Soviet edition of Kozlov's verse, *Stixotvorenija I. I. Kozlova*, I. Glikman, ed., p. 443.

poems many times, until quite satisfied with them, but also that he was obliged to write. Perhaps Kozlov spurned deadlines; Del'vig's urgent letters pressing him to send a promised piece for *Northern Flowers* seem proof enough that he did; but he could not, as both Del'vig and Baratynskij might have, had they chosen, abandon literature. Payments from almanacs, journals, song-books, all formed a necessary income.

And that income rose each year from 1828 until 1840. It would be foolish to pretend that Kozlov had not merited financial security – his translations from the English, Italian and German alone opened extensive new horizons before the Russian public. Of course it would be bad for Byron, as Bestužev-Marlinskij remarked acidly, were his work judged only by Kozlov's versions in Russian;[46] but the suggestion is ridiculous, and does not change the fact that, more than any other single man, Kozlov introduced the Byron of *Lara* and *Childe Harold* – the true, enigmatic Byron and not the grandiose visions of earlier paraphrasts – before the Russian reading public.

Success was merited – and the reading public alone could grant it. (Kozlov enjoyed no Imperial or other patronage.) Here is the point: the reading public *did* grant it, but only when it was of a size, of a power to grant success. Lomonosov, Deržavin, Bogdanovič had enjoyed success, of course, and even Imperial favour and acclaim; but it had been in narrow, albeit exalted, circles. Theirs had not been popular successes. Kozlov enjoyed a national, popular celebrity. His songs were adapted by artists of every class. They were adapted because they were known. They were known because they were published in great numbers. And so, once again, one returns to the major, the central point of reference in all bearings of triumph or disaster during the 1830s and 1840s, as in all subsequent decades in the West and until 1918 in Russia. Kozlov reached maturity as a writer at a time when his reading public was expanding enormously, and by 1835 it, too, had reached maturity. Its uncertain agents, literary publishers, could and did bring him success and fame which, if it did not quite reach the glorious heights of 1825 and *The Monk* at least outlasted

46. See A. S. Puškin, *Poln. sob. soč.* (Moscow, 1937), vol. 13, p. 149.

him and maintained his reputation.

In 1821, when Kozlov's first poem appeared in print, far fewer books, journals and almanacs were published in the entire Russian Empire than in the Low Countries. Four years later, 600 titles were published in that Empire of some fifty million persons. Whereas in England, France and Germany a run of 20,000 copies was common enough to warrant no special comment, in Russia one of more than 1,200 was exceptional.[47]

But things changed greatly between 1824 and 1834. In that ten-year period, according to A. Smirdin, co-editor of *Library for Reading*, the number of readers of journals and almanacs in Russia quadrupled.[48] Kozlov was fortunate to have been born when it was becoming possible, for the first time in that country, to make a livelihood as a regular contributor to literary publications. Twenty years earlier, in 1800, it had not been possible; fifteen years later it would be difficult. But in the years 1815 – 30, poetry reigned. Baratynskij, Vjazemskij and Ivan Kireevskij might object to the malodorous new commercially-based literature, and others deplore the advent of "the iron age" of railways and counting-houses in the once sacred groves. But new times brought fresh advantages to writers, as well as to entrepreneurs. By 1830 *The Northern Bee*, a reactionary journal viewed with favour by the government and with scorn by radicals, boasted a circulation of more than 3,000. Where it led, others could follow. Twelve months later, *Roslavlev*, a wordy "historical novel" by Zagoskin, a leading Russian Scottophile, sold 4,800 copies in eleven weeks.[49] This was

47. The figures, given in *Moskovskij telegraf*, 1828, no. 1, pp. 519-21, are among those cited by A. Meynieux in *Pouchkine, homme de lettres* (Paris, 1966), p. 475 ff., where other statistical data is admirably presented.

48. According to "Russkaja literatura," *Biblioteka dlja čtenija*, vol. 19 (1836), pp. 49-50; see A. Meynieux, *op.cit.*, p. 471.

49. Moreover, according to *Severnaja pčela*, 1829, no. 40, that writer's *Ivan Vyžigin* sold 2,000 copies in five days (March 26-31, 1829). The steady fall in book prices from 1825 to 1835 was a further factor in Kozlov's favour. The holding lists (*rospisi knigam*) of several booksellers of the period have survived, among them those of Smirdin and Plavil'ščikov, who dealt with poetry. Prices of small verse collections dropped dramatically between 1800 and 1830, and continued to fall; Chapters Seven and Eight of *Evgenij Onegin* cost R10 in 1832, but only R2 in 1837 (from Ol'xin's catalogue, no. 5364). In 1828, Kozlov's, Del'vig's and Baratynskij's verse all cost R10 a copy. In its third edition, of 1831, Puškin's *Baxčiserajskij fontan* cost a modest R5, while

something different from Karamzin's devoted following of a few hundred to perhaps two thousand at most. Suddenly, there was a sizable reading public in Russia, a swift and unprecedented expansion. It was, of course, a direct result of increased literacy, not among the gentry who were, broadly speaking, literate by 1775, but among the *raznočintsy* – "the men of various classes"; and Kozlov was one of the immediate beneficiaries. Supported by merchants' clerks and priests' sons, who cared for his elegies and songs, almost as ardently as by the gentlefolk who wept at the adventures of Princess Natal'ja Dolgorukaja, heroine of his second tale, how could he fail in the new age of busy printing-presses?

The first separate edition of his verse appeared, in a single slim volume, in 1828. It was a success. A second edition, this time in two plumper volumes, appeared in 1832 – 33. It, too, sold well. For those without the means to purchase hard-bound editions of anybody's verse, his poems appeared year by year, sometimes month by month, in literary journals. His songs and ballads might be found in any one of ten song-collections, or *pesenniki*, published in St. Petersburg and Moscow. In 1835, for example, the musically inclined reader might find them both in *A Full and Most New Song-Book* (!), handsomely bound and with fine engravings by an unknown gentleman, and in *Spring Flowers, or a Collection of Romances, Ballads and Songs*, a volume as substantial as the title promises, in 13 parts.[50] Kozlov's name, in other words, was well-established with his readers. Publishers ensured that it remained so – to the point, indeed, that by 1838 Belinskij was driven to remark that "usually one may be sure, on settling down to read a new journal or almanac, that one will find something in prose by Prince Odoevskij and at least one poem by I. I. Kozlov"![51] In this instance, however, the critic was wide of target, for Kozlov contributed to few "new journals or almanacs" after Del'vig's death in 1831.

Bogdanovič's *Dušen'ka*, in its tenth printing by that year, was R4. This was within the means of hundreds of government clerks, merchants and traders, as well as of the traditional book buyers, the gentry.

50. *Polnyj i novejsij pesennik*, and *Vesennie tsvety, ili sobranie romansov, ballad i pesen*.

51. V. G. Belinskij, *Poln. sob. soč.*, 13 vols. (Moscow, 1957), vol. 2, p. 387.

Respected as a poet by foreigners and Russians, Kozlov was loved by most of those who knew him.[52] In his last years, he moved little, finding that pain outweighed the pleasure. Žukovskij, who was close to him throughout his adult life, described his death in an obituary that is, to say the least, coloured. It is a Christian who, sustained in life "by faith . . . and the sacred fire of poetry," died the death of a believer, that is presented for inspection. (Žukovskij's theology was never over-precise.) A brief extract from that obituary notice will serve to illustrate both its message and its tenor: "Blind, motionless and constantly suffering, but deeply penetrated by Christian humility, he bore his grievous destiny with a wonderful patience, and Divine Providence, which sent him that wearisome test also gave him a great joy: Providence revealed to his dimmed sight the varied but unchanging world of poetry, lit up by faith . . ."[53]

When Kozlov died, after weeks of sharp pain, on the morning of January 30, 1840, it was natural that his contemporaries should think of him as "one who bore his cross with patience" and "found solace in religion, his family, his songs." No doubt he did suffer his misfortune in a Christian manner, showing faith, hope and charity; but it is unfortunate that this should have been the image of him to be handed down to younger generations – an image that is current still. It is more suitable, and in better accordance with the known facts of his life, that Kozlov be presented as a strong-willed, cheerful man, a poet of some stature and highly distinguished literary translator and intermediary.

52. Such, with some foundation, is K. Grot's conclusion (see note 3).
53. See note 11.

CHAPTER THREE
KOZLOV AND THE PRE-ROMANTIC MOVEMENT

Kozlov was a grown man of thirty when Žukovskij introduced him into his own Moscow literary circle. Of those whose acquaintance he made in 1809 – 11, some, like I. I. Dmitriev (1760 – 1837), Ju. A. Neledinskij-Meletskij (1752 – 1828) and Prince I. M. Dolgorukij (1764 – 1823), were established sentimentalists, authors of songs, short odes and elegies already antiquated in tenor and style by the time of Alexander, while others like V. A. Ozerov (1769 – 1816), author of *Fingal*, a sentimental tragedy with choruses in an Ossianic setting, were close to death. As if to emphasize that the opposition party to Nikolaj Karamzin's new style and sensibility – "the cult of feeling, the obedient submission to emotional impulses, the conception of virtue as the outcome of man's natural goodness, all prepared by the slow infiltration of sentimental novels and the emotional pietism of the Freemasons"[1] – was a party of ageing men, Semjon Bobrov, friend of the arch-conservative A. S. Šiškov (1753 – 1841) and author of *Tauris or My Summer Day in the Tauric Chersonese*, promptly died on Žukovskij's arrival in Moscow.

But Kozlov witnessed a new spirit and time of experiment in verse and drama, and his meeting with Žukovskij in 1809, as he quickly discovered, coincided with the start of a new era in Russian poetry – that of the universal and informed interest in verse that led to the so-called "Golden Age." Never was poetry more an avowed passion in St. Petersburg and Moscow, at least

1. D. S. Mirskij, *History of Russian Literature* (New York, 1955), p. 60.

among the liberal gentry, than in the months preceding the French invasion of the Western provinces. "De quoi nous occupions-nous dans nos réunions?" demanded Dmitriev rhetorically, twenty years later; "La Poésie, elle, elle seule nous était donnée comme objet . . . l'harmonie des sons de la lyre et le vrai code de la langue."[2] The fever was not confined to Russia, as any French schoolboy knows. "It was," wrote Wordsworth in 1815, "a passion yet to cool. For poetry is, like love, a passion. And for much the greater part of those who have been proud of its power over their minds, a necessity soon arises of breaking the pleasing bondage . . . thoughts being occupied in domestic cares."[3]

In Russia, "domestic cares" assumed a political colouring; and already in 1815 the process had begun that would destroy – for a while – poetry with no obvious political or social relevance. But the process had yet to begin when, encouraged by Žukovskij, Kozlov first took a steady interest in literature. In taking that interest, one must stress, he merely began to share a general preoccupation of his class and generation.

It would, of course, be foolish to suggest that Kozlov lived in ignorance of literature until one fateful week in 1809; as N. A. Polevoj remarked, an interest or skill in poetry does not come or vanish "like the morning mist."[4] Under the eye of his tutors, he had studied Western literatures ("always," however, "loving what was simple and *Russian*"). Scansion of Classical lines was still, as Žukovskij discovered at the *Pension Noble* of Moscow University in 1797, considered an integral part of the liberal education.[5] Later, frequenting Moscow *salons* as the youthful mandarin first of the Chancery of Heralds, then of the Moscow Commandant's Department, it was entirely necessary that he at least pretend familiarity with the latest play and epic. And so he went to see Katerina Semjonova, one of the most distinguished of Russian tragediennes, in Ozerov's culminating triumph, *Dmitrij of the Don*.

2. Cited by V. Gofman in *Ryleev-poet* (Leningrad, 1929), p. 2.

3. Wordsworth, "Essay of 1815," *Coleridge Biographia Literaria and Wordsworth, Preface and Essays on Poetry, 1800-1815* (Cambridge, 1920), p. 217.

4. N. A. Polevoj, "'Knjaginja Natal'ja Borisovna Dolgorukaja'; sočinenie I. Kozlova," *Moskovskij telegraf* (1828), no. 9, p. 539.

5. See M. Ehrhard, *op. cit.*, pp. 15-31.

(The play was acted within days of the battle of Eylau (1807), and its patriotic tirades received with huge enthusiasm.) Nor, judging by his private correspondence of the period, was he less careful to remain *au fait* with developments in poetry and prose.

It is unfortunate that we have only a private diary and occasional hints in letters from which to form an impression of Kozlov's earlier reading; how easy that task would be, had his library, like Puškin's, been preserved and catalogued. Such brief and casual references as one finds in the letters (the diary hardly touches on childhood or adolescence), tell a conventional tale: Montaigne, the Encyclopaedists, Voltaire, Karamzin, Petrarch and – more surprisingly – the Bible. The memoirs of friends and contemporaries, even the paper of Kozlov's son who died in 1883,[6] throw scant light on the subject. One thing is clear, however: if Kozlov's consciousness of literature may be said to have awoken in any given period of its development in Russia, it was in the time of Karamzin.

Through the verse and prose of Karamzin and the verse of Žukovskij, Kozlov inherited the weight of sentimentalist tradition in Europe, as in Russia. Only of their work, among Russian sentimentalists, would there be reverberations in his own. In the linguistic controversies of Bludov and Šaxovskoj, Vasilij Puškin and Šiškov he took no interest, judging them superfluous. Of the polemic, too, centred on Karamzin's innovative journal, *The Messenger of Europe* (from the pages of which Russians first sampled the delights of *Atala* in 1803 – 4),[7] there are no traces in his correspondence. And, indeed, why should Kozlov, writing in 1820, concern himself with the struggle, so recent although forgotten, between the protagonists of Karamzin's new, Gallicized language and fervid adherents to Šiškov's "purified" "Slavic" tongue? He wrote in the time of Puškin; and who, as Puškin said, would choose to read or publish "poems in the Nikonic style" when Žukovskij's ballads were available?[8] Though he wrote in the

6. The papers left by Ivan Ivanovič Kozlov the younger (d.6.1.83.) appeared in *Russkij arxiv* (1886), bk. 1, pp. 177-204, as "Iz bumag poeta."

7. See my article "Chateaubriand in Russia, 1800-1830," *Comparative Literature Studies* (1972), vol. 9, no. 2.

8. "Žukovskomu" (1817).

age of Puškin, however, Kozlov belonged to a much earlier generation. It was without disrespect to Šiškov that he admired Karamzin; indeed, one inclines to think that Šiškov's *Dissertation on the Old and New Styles in the Russian Language* (1803) struck chords of sympathy in him, at least in its *political* orientation. "Our letters," he might read, "by following the model set by the new French and Frenchified-German literatures, have begun to lose all resemblance to Russian";[9] but he, no less than Puškin, well understood that it was Liberal thought rather than Gallicisms (which are rare in his verse) and neologisms (which are wholly absent) that the Admiral attacked. To be sure, Kozlov spared little thought for the noxious effect of Chateaubriand on the pristine language of Fénelon; but he, too, regarded the French Revolution as "having trampled upon all that was based on the principles of Faith, Honour and Reason. . . . "[10] The question of Kozlov's political beliefs, and their connections with his literary work, will be returned to.

It was all but impossible that one born of a cultured Muscovite family, in 1779, should not deeply feel the impact of the Karamzinian poets – those who, abandoning the "high style," the ode and epistle of the age of Deržavin, had devoted themselves to the cultivation of the *poésie légère* of Chénier, Delille, Millevoye. In the event, two poets of the Karamzin côterie, Vasilij Puškin, author of the best-received burlesque of Kozlov's childhood, *A Dangerous Neighbour*, and A. F. Merzljakov (1778 – 1830), his immediate contemporary, later Professor of Russian Literature at Moscow University, became his personal friends.

In one sense, their work was far from being revolutionary. There were no startling new themes or metres, to be sure, in Karamzin's *Poor Liza*, in the prolix and didactic "adventure romances" of Fjodr Emin' (1735 – 70), Neledinskij-Meletskij's and N. A. L'vov's tales of unhappy love and "popular" comic operas. There was, perhaps it now seems, little to celebrate in

9. A. Šiškov, commenting on his own translation of two French essays by La Harpe, 1808; taken from *Pis'ma N. Karamzina k Dmitrievu*, P. P. Pekarskij, ed. (St. Petersburg, 1866), p. 263.

10. See M. Ehrhard, *op.cit.*, pp. 200-01.

finding, dressed in the new Karamzinian Russian of "tenderness" and "délicatesse" (*nežnost' i delikatnost'*), tales written forty years before, dealing with poor maidens in distress – maidens rescued, of course, by a tall hero and happy chance. Yet such tales, published with great commitment in Karamzin's *Messenger of Europe* from 1802 – 08, did represent progress; for they were written in a smooth if, to our eye, rather prettified style. The treatment of theme, too, was fresh; and compared with the aesthetic of Šiškov and Kačenovskij,[11] Karamzin's was both vigorous and modernist. In *The Messenger of Europe*, moreover, Kozlov read German ballads that inclined him to learn for himself the language of Burger.

Nikolaj Mixailovič Karamzin (1766 – 1826), best known in the West as a historian (his *History of the Russian State* was an unprecedented triumph, the total printing of 3000 copies of the first eight volumes selling out within a month in February, 1818), was the first great Russian sentimentalist. In danger of becoming a dissipated young squire, he met I. P. Turgenev, a prominent Freemason, who introduced him to Novikov. Masonic influences, it may be said, played a principal part in the formation of Karamzin's mature outlook. Their opaquely religious, sentimental, cosmopolitan ideas paved the way to an appreciation of Rousseau and Herder. Through Žukovskij, those same Masonic ideas would reach Kozlov, who was thirteen in 1792 when both *The Letters of a Russian Traveler* and *Poor Liza* appeared.

If descriptions of merchants, students and noblemen in Germany, England, France and Switzerland spoke to Kozlov's imagination (though he did not care to travel greatly), the sad fate of poor Liza appealed to him more immediately. Seduced from her aged mother and a peaceful country cottage by Erast, a frivolous noble, Liza is brought to unspeakable ruin near a moonlit pond in the grounds of the Simonov Monastery, on the outskirts of Moscow; she promptly drowns herself therein. It was possible to walk from the house of the Kozlovs to the sentimental shrine.

11. Further on this question, see A. Martel, *Michel Lomonosov et la langue littéraire russe* (Paris, 1933), pp. 101-05.

Karamzin's impact on Kozlov was deep and lasting. As Kozlov came, in middle life, to reflect attitudes towards literature adopted thirty years before by "the Russian Sterne,"[12] so in expression of those views also he came unconsciously to echo him. The very terms in which their mutual admirations were couched were not dissimilar; it might have been Kozlov, and not Karamzin, who praised Shakespeare thus: "All his splendid canvases imitate Nature directly; every degree of man, every age, every passion speaks with its own, proper voice."[13] It was precisely the "naturalness' (*estestvennost'*) of Shakespeare's characters that drew Kozlov's admiration also.

Karamzin's first work to appear in book form was a translation of *Julius Caesar* (1787). Kozlov's earliest extant work is a translation of Byron's *The Bride of Abydos* (1819). Few Russians of either generation had sufficient command of English to read these works in the original;[14] and the mere fact of Kozlov's ability to do so – and to comment intelligently on Karamzin's remarks on eighteenth-century English literature – indicates that a knowledge of English created a bond between the two. Both were international in their literary outlook; both held English literature in special esteem. True, Karamzin was a citizen of Europe in a way that Kozlov, for all his education, could not imitate. Yet his preoccupation with the inner country of "the good and tender heart"[15] was one with which Kozlov could deeply sympathize.

Subject-matter in eighteenth-century Russian poetry, as G. A. Gukovskij has shown so lucidly, did not change greatly from one decade to another, and it is in attitude, not theme, that one best

12. V. V. Sipovskij, *N. M. Karamzin* (St. Petersburg, 1899), p. 70.

13. N. M. Karamzin, *Izbrannyje socinenija*, 2 vols. (Moscow, 1964), vol. 2, p. 80.

14. Attempting in 1822 to translate the first fourteen lines of *The Giaour* into French, without a crib, Puškin rendered "the Athenian's grave" as "la grève d'Athènes." Again, attempting a literal version of the beginning of Wordsworth's *The Excursion* in 1833, this time with a dictionary, he failed to understand such phrases as "brooding clouds," "side-long eye," "twilight of its own"; small wonder that only a few pages, in several places at random, are cut in his lycée copy of P. J. Pollock's *Cours de langue anglaise* (St. Petersburg, 1817); see B. Modzalevskij, "Biblioteka A. S. Puškina," *Puškin i jego sovremenniki*, vol. III (1909), pp. 9-10, p. 312.

15. See P. Berkov, "Žizn' i tvorčestvo N. M. Karamzina," *Izbrannyje sočinenija* (Moscow, 1964), vol. 1, pp. 22-36.

seeks originality.[16] It is hardly surprising that Kozlov stands in the debt of Karamzin for his themes; he wrote of matters that have always been the common property of verse: the joy and transience of love, the warmth of friendship, the fleetingness of life and the inevitability of death.

Like Karamzin, Kozlov regarded poetry as something at once more personal and exalted than had G. R. Deržavin, "whose idol," Puškin declared, "is one quarter gold, three quarters lead";[17] like Karamzin again, Kozlov came to believe that, as the elder man put it simply, "the evil person cannot be a good author."[18] Four years in the company of Muscovite Masons produced in Karamzin a moralizing, didactic trait stronger and more obtrusive than that later instilled into Kozlov by his foreign governors. (It may be noted in passing, however, that not even Karamzin's passing interest in Utopianism – "More's work," he found, "describes an ideal republic just like Plato's" (!) – failed to produce distinct echoes in Kozlov's correspondence.)[19] No less than Karamzin, Kozlov tended to universalize his personal experience; like the older poet, he declined to treat political or, indeed, any controversial topic in his poetry; like Karamzin, finally, he too expressed the essence of sentimentalism, that love and the emotional life is all. These couplets, one from a piece by Karamzin, the other from a later poem by Kozlov, might have come from the same elegy:

Love is delight, the life of feeling souls:
In poetry, it is the end and the beginning.[20]

16. G. A. Gukovskij, *Russkaja literatura XVIII-ogo veka* (Moscow, 1927), pp. 48-66.
17. Letter to A. A. Bestužev of May-June, 1825; *A. S. Puškin*, vol. 9, p. 158.
18. See Karamzin's "Protej, ili nesoglasija stixotvortsa" (1798). Karamzin imbibed from Fénelon a peculiarly moral literary outlook which found a highly emotional expression in his prose. He contributed generously to M. Xeraskov's *Pleasant and Useful Pastime*, the opening issue of which, in 1794, began: "O Coeur sensible! Je bénis ta force magique qui console, je te bénis . . . Coeur tendre! Coeur bon!" Žukovskij echoed that same note. "Je peux dire," he informed Dmitriev (letter of 18.2.16), "qu'il y a dans mon âme une faculté particulièrement bonne qui s'appelle Karamzin . . ."; *Soč. V. A. Žukovskogo* ed. A. Alferov (Moscow, 1902), vol. 1, p. 496; also A. N. Pypin, *Russkoe masonstvo XVIII-ogo veka i pervoj četverti XIX-ogo veka* (Petrograd, 1916), index under Karamzin.
19. *Moskovskij žurnal* (1791), Pt. 1, p. 359.
20. "Protej, ili nesoglasija stixotvortsa."

Thou dost not dwell on earth,
Love, unseen seraphim . . . (1828)

But what is "love?" Here, suddenly, similarities between Kozlov's and Karamzin's aesthetic outlooks end. For the latter, it is plain from "Il'ja Muromets," love is, like poetry itself, escape; it is concerned with the pleasant aspects of life – with lies:

Falsehood, Untruth, Apparition of truth,
Be my goddess now!
Ah! We are not all to pour rivers
Of tears over existence's misfortunes!
Let us forget ourselves for a moment
In the sorcery of wondrous fancies!
(ll. 93 – 8)

For Kozlov, on the other hand:

There is a delight in the sad shadows,
And there are two secrets, by whose power
Suffering on earth flowers . . .
One of these is in sacred love.
("The First Meeting," 1837)

It is true that Kozlov viewed his tales and verse and, indeed, all poetry as an escape from his predicament; he translated those pieces by Byron best suited, in his view, to serve that function. But poetry was also, he assured Žukovskij (to whom the fact was indisputable), an expression of Christian tenets – that faith and courage, charity and love, delightful in themselves, surely bring their ultimate reward. For Kozlov as, in a more mysterious fashion, for Žukovskij, poetry sprang from and expressed a temperamental piety. The same is not wholly true of Karamzin.

Kozlov was a Muscovite. It was, therefore, after a brief stay in Rybinsk while French troops ransacked his house, to Moscow that he returned in 1813. And there he found members of the triumphant Karamzinian party, A. F. Voekov, Dmitriev and Merzljakov. Moscow, not St. Petersburg, was the stronghold of the

Karamzinians, though the master, deep in his historical research, lived on the Fontanka. Occupied by his career and young family, however, Kozlov did not choose to involve himself in literary polemics. It was from a respectful, even amused distance, that he observed the verbal and epigrammatic combat between, on the one hand, the massively formal *Forum of Lovers of the Russian Word* and, on the other, the Society of Unknown Writers of Arzamas. Founded by Šiškov in March, 1811, the Forum included – nominally, at least – both Deržavin and Krylov, but was essentially a group of elderly grandees. Hierarchical and pompous, it drew its members from among high dignitaries willing to support "Classical" (that is, neo-Classical) forms of Russian against Gallicisms and other Western infections. Inevitably, a younger group of men picked up the gauntlet. By its very *raison d'être*, Arzamas was politically committed.

Two hundred members of the Forum settled in Deržavin's drawing-room for the opening meeting. Hoping for the Imperial visit which did not materialize, Deržavin had composed an ode.

> Soigneusement préparées par des réunions privées, les séances publiques avaient lieu dans le grand salon; les places, autour de la table au tapis vert ou sur les fauteuils et les chaises du public, étaient fixées selon les règles de la hiérarchie russe; les uniformes brillants des hauts fonctionnaires, les costumes ecclésiastiques, les robes de bal donnaient à ces réunions littéraires un caractère à la fois solennel et mondain, très académique.[21]

To Russians, Arzamas, a market town in the province of Nižnij, was the Slavic equivalent of Motiers-Travers. The meetings of Arzamas consisted of roast-goose dinners followed by the reading of facetious minutes and trivial verse. The carousers donned red calpacks, and referred to one another by their nicknames, taken from Žukovskij's ballads: Vjazemskij was Asmodeus; A. I. Turgenev, Eol's Harp; Puškin, The Cricket.

Hostile by temperament to both pomposity and sheer facetiousness, Kozlov joined neither group. To remain wholly unaf-

21. M. Ehrhard, *op.cit.*, p. 87.

fected, however, was beyond his power. As it bears on his political and literary outlook alike, so the decline and fall of the Society of Arzamas bears also on the study of his work.

Marcel Ehrhard captures the flavour of Arzamas so well that one can only cite him:

> On voit dans quel esprit se fonde la nouvelle société: il s'agit avant tout de s'amuser, et la parodie de la solennelle société rivale sera la base des plaisanteries. Dès le premier soir, Joukovski, mis en verve par la perspective de joyeuses réunions, improvise des statuts comiques. Les members, qui sont liés entre eux par 'un effroyable serment,' prononcent comme discours de réception l'éloge funèbre d'un membre bien vivant de la *Béséda* (Forum – GB).[22]

Parodying Masonic rites, gaily mocking one another, the members of Arzamas consolidated the success of Karamzin's reforms of language; practice, not theory, won the day.

The spirit of irreverence, however, quickly began to flag. By March, 1817, even Vasilij Puškin, the least serious-minded of men, was urging his colleagues to find "some serious aim" – a journal, perhaps. In retrospect, one sees that the election of Mixail Orlov and Nikolaj Turgenev to the Society (1817) was a clear premonition of coming schism. Turgenev, a future Decembrist, could not long sit easily beside Bludov who was later to sentence Decembrists to exile and death.[23] Nor was the very informality of Arzamas without political significance; in 1818 the Society foundered on the rocks of practical politics.[24]

Kozlov's first known translation dates from 1819 – one year after the geese of Arzamas had flown in disarray; but he was not in tune with the new age, in which Žukovskij's ballad *Svetlana* was outmoded, Karamzin's prose gently mocked. To the extent, indeed, that he was weakly Liberal, rather than reactionary; conscious of isolation and in need of friendly encouragement;

22. *Ibid.*, pp. 94-5.

23. See M. V. Nečkina, *Russia in the Nineteenth Century* (Ann Arbor, 1952), under Turgenev, N. I.

24. See M. Fonvizin, *Obščestvennyje dviženija v Rossii v pervoj polovine XIX-ogo veka* (St. Petersburg, 1905), p. 35 ff.

unwilling to deal in verse with Russian political problems of immediate import, yet patriotic, Kozlov was heir to the Arzamas tradition. He, like the Arzamasists, regretted that happiness is not for "the sons of Prometheus,"[25] but made no move to make that happiness possible for a majority of his countrymen. Like those who so exasperated Nikolaj Turgenev, with whom he was on close terms until 1820, he willed the end but not the means. His aim was to describe the realities of life, his own and all men's; but Russian life, with its deplorable realities, he did not see even before his sight failed. In these respects particularly, Kozlov had affinities with those who wrote verse in Russia before Napoleon came to Moscow; who lived when literary questions ruled the intellectual scene, and merely to write well, regardless of political import or its complete absence, ensured success.

In the abrupt decline of the Society of Arzamas one sees, clearly reflected, a stage in the development of Russian intellectual life. It is, of course, a great step from Mixail Orlov's speeches of 1817 to Ryleev's anti-autocratic position, from Turgenev's anglophile address[26] to the programme of Nikita Murav'jov. But still, even in 1818 – 19, the Muse found herself a handmaiden to a national, political cause with increasing frequency; to read the verse of V. F. Raevskij, "The Voice of Truth," for example, or "The Road to Happiness" (1819), is to acknowledge the fact.

As Žukovskij's and the Turgenevs' Friendly Literary Society in 1801 cast Novikov's grand philosophical and altruistic plans into the shade, so now, sixteen years later, political realities advanced on literary ground. Kozlov did not choose to dwell on those realities; for him, indeed, politics did not impinge on literature or, if it did, it was in an acceptably modified guise. (Thus Alexander Ypsilanty is transformed to "The Captive Greek.") Like both Žukovskij and Karamzin, Kozlov was highly conscious of the gulf between political and literary convictions among his contemporaries – and thought it a most proper one.

The Karamzinians' triumph was a comprehensive one, affect-

25. E. A. Baratynskij, "Del'vigu" (1821), ll. 1-4.

26. On this, and Turgenev's *Opyt teorii nalogov* (1818), see E. I. Tarasov, *Dekabrist*

ing not only style but also choice of genre and metre. It wrought a profound change in Russian poetry, and went far to determine the general form of Russian pre-Romantic verse, that of Kozlov included. Yet, such was its sweepingness, that it could not precisely chart the course of pre-Romantic poets; for in Russia, pre-Romanticism took no less than three distinct, though interconnected guises. First, there was the scenario of Ossian and Burger – a wild seascape, with pounding waves, skalds, flaming oaks; then there was the gentle paysage of Thomson and Lamartine, a land of calm lakes and villages, country churchyards and spires; finally, Russians might choose a stylized Central Asia, an exotic, distant land replete with khans, harems and dark-eyed odalisques. "The poet of mysterious visions, of love and dreams and devils,"[27] Žukovskij led his fellow-countrymen through the second of these landscapes (the green and misty meadows of his version of Gray's *Elegy* were rapturously received in 1802 by readers of *The Messenger of Europe*), and, more diffidently, through the third. It was Kozlov and Puškin, however, who would provide the finer details for the southern Moslem palace: its seraglio and plashing fountain, high, rose-grown walls, eunuchs and nightingales.[28]

Žukovskij-Gray was a commanding presence in the Moscow of 1805 – 12. Long before appealing to him for assistance from semi-exile in Finland, Baratynskij had "wept over his verses";[29] Del'vig "knew collections of verse published by Žukovskij almost by heart";[30] Puškin considered him "our wet-nurse." ("Why bite her breasts," he reproached Ryleev in 1825, "because we have cut our baby teeth?")[31] Through Žukovskij, Russians found other sentimental pleasures, as they would shortly know English and German Romantics in Kozlov's numerous translations.

No Western pre-Romantic authors enjoyed a more brilliant

N. I. Turgenev v aleksandrovskuju epoxu (Samara, 1922).

27. A. S. Puškin, *Ruslan i Ljudmila*, Song 4.

28. See Chap. 7, on Kozlov's versions of Thomas Moore's orientalia.

29. Letter from Ročensal'm, Finland, late 1823; E. A. Baratynskij, *Stixotvorenija, poemy, proza, pis'ma* (Moscow, 1951), pp. 463-9.

30. *A. S. Puškin*, vol. 7, p. 293.

31. Letter of 25.1.25; *ibid.*, vol. 9, p. 130.

vogue in St. Petersburg and Moscow, in the time of Kozlov's adolescence, than Macpherson (Ossian) and Young. For the latter, Kozlov entertained a considerable respect, having first read him at an early and impressionable age.[32]

Young's popularity in Russia, as in Germany and France, was still greater than in England. From the *Night Thoughts*, first translated into Russian in book form in 1778 and, in a burst of enthusiasm, rendered separately in 1785, 1799, 1803 and again in 1812,[33] Russians discovered a new way of viewing natural scenes. More than any other eighteenth-century poet, Young inspired in educated Russians the mode for death and moonlight. If Robespierre kept a copy of *Night Thoughts* under his pillow during the Revolution, Kozlov kept it within hand's reach. Russians of his generation were much taken up, under the influence of the Masons, with the old opposition of social and natural man, and it was therefore perhaps natural that Merzljakov and Karamzin should much admire the work. There were other aspects of the poem to which Kozlov, too, could respond warmly – Young's concept of man's fellowship with nature, for example, his belief in the might of conscience and his conviction that man's lot on earth is a basically wretched one.

Alas! Not only my small bark
Of hope was smashed by waves,
Not only I was drawn by the stars
Into an uncertain distance!
And who has not been troubled by anxiety,
Who reached his cherished aim,
Who has not parted with a favourite dream
But passed the vale of tears?
Could you, O sea, cast up
From your angry waves
All that of elevated thought
And feeling lay in wrecked vessels:

32. His attitude towards Young precisely echoed that of Karamzin; see V. Sipovskij, *op.cit.*, p. 43.

33. For an excellent survey of English sentimentalism in Russia, see E. J. Simmons, *English Literature and Culture in Russia* (Cambridge Mass., 1935), pp. 161-203.

Were someone to appear from out the abyss,
To tell the tale of those perished,
Then, perhaps, the world would wonder
At what no one know.
"The Swimmer" (1835)[34]

The tolling bells, ivy-grown tombs and dirges, all seemed to Kozlov's contemporaries the proper setting for that most *engaging* sadness that pervaded the poem, and it was this melancholy, not the underlying structure of ideas – in truth, an extremely rickety one – that captivated Russian readers. Young is praised in many periodicals during the years 1772 – 1802,[35] but it is "That poet sad, both of lyre and of soul,"[36] not the real writer, who is sung. Would one find Genius? (cried a nameless poet of 1797):

Hearken to the spirit of the storm
In Ossian's mournful verses, or with Young
Pour tears.[37]

Invariably, Young is praised as the singer of sadness. On his "Morning Stroll," another Russian admirer of the poet usually bends his steps (so we are told), towards "a nearby graveyard." There he sits pondering, and Young and Gray are his companions, and "sacred melancholy" comforts him.[38]

Such, then, was the extraordinary influence of Young in Russia. The youthful experience of S. N. Glinka (1776 – 1847), a minor writer of the period, is not an exaggerated example of the effect produced on "feeling souls" by *Night Thoughts*: "In my youth, dreaming of Young, I would wander in remote places, into deep woods. Once, dreaming under the pouring rain, and composing in the vein of the *Nights*, I was aroused by a clap of thunder; returning home, I transferred my sombre reflections to paper."[39] Like Thomson's *The Seasons*, which Karamzin trans-

34. ll. 9-24.
35. E. J. Simmons, *op.cit.*, p. 131.
36. "Envoy to Young's Nights," *Aglaja* (1808), vol. 1, pp. 78-9.
37. "Sila Genija," *Aonidy* (1797), vol. 2, p. 125.
38. *Ippokrena* (1799), vol. 2, p. 322.
39. *Zapiski Sergeja Nikovaeviča Glinki* (St. Petersburg, 1895), p. 363.

lated as "Hymn on The Seasons" (1789), Young's poems were regarded by young Russians as an unfailing source of solace from which they took deep draughts when the sentimental or melancholy thirst came upon them. There is no reason to suppose that Kozlov was averse to such draughts.[40]

But it is Ossian, among Western pre-Romantics, whose impress is clearest on Kozlov's original verse. To Ossian, "the great, the inimitable,"[41] as Karamzin hails him in "Poezija" (1787), Kozlov and his contemporaries turned for the strain of bitter-sweet memories of glories that once were. It was Macpherson's Caledonia and its poet, not Young, who seldom wanders in imagination over the vanished glory of ancient civilizations, that filled the hearts of Russians with that melancholy well reflected in Kozlov's epistle "To Walter Scott" (1832), "Brenda" (1834) and "Byron in the Coliseum" (1834). As Batjuškov had treated Sweden and its crumbling fortresses in an Ossianic manner (in "A Castle In Sweden," 1814), so Koslov, like Baratynskij (in his ode entitled simply "Rome," 1824), viewed Italy and its past through the eyes of a Russian Fingal.

Few authors were translated more often into Russian, in the course of twenty years, than was Macpherson, the history of whose splendid hoax is well-known in the West. Ossian's first appearance in Russia was as a fragment in *Werther*, translated in 1781, but it was not until 1788 that a substantial rendering of "the songs of the third-century Gaelic bard" was published.[42] Thereafter, versions followed thick and fast, from Ermil' Kostrov's monumental attempt (based, unfortunately, on the French of Letourneur)[43] to the essays, more or less appalling in point of literal accuracy, of Karamzin (*Songs of Sel'ma*), Gnedič, Ivan Zaxarov, N. F. Grammatin, V. N. Olin, and a dozen other

40. See Ja. K. Grot, "K biografii, tvorenijam i perepiske I. Kozlova," *Izvestija Otdelenija Russkogo Jazyka i Slovesnosti*, 1904, bk. 2.

41. *"Just as the ocean's roaring waves, that sound*
Through forests far from shore, bearing sadness
To hopeful hearts: so are Ossian's songs,
Pouring sweet anguish into languid minds . . ."

42. A. I. Dmitriev's *Poems of the Ancient Bards* (*Poemy drevnix bardov*).

43. Cf. V. Sopikov's *Ukazatel' k opytu rossijskoj bibliografii* (St. Petersburg, 1908), nos. 8742, 11544, 11545. Letourneur's first edition of *Ossian, fils de Fingal; barde du troisième siècle, poésies galliques*, etc., appeared in Paris in 1777.

paraphrasts. It would, as Professor E. J. Simmons so reasonably says, "be wearing a commonplace threadbare to point out the similarity between the indigenous sadness of these so-called Gaelic songs and the sad temperament characteristically associated with Russians. Native critics, however, have laboured the point."[44] How Kozlov could be other than sad contemporaries failed to see.

Russians' *penchant* for Northern mythologies, Finnish and Nordic mixed in a carefree way, preceded the advent of Macpherson. It was Kostrov's translation, however, together with the discovery of Russian oral or folk-literature during the 1790s, that brought a fashionable interest in Scandinavia's past to its highest pitch. (In Russian eyes, the Western Isles lay within sight of Uppsala.)[45] Already in the years of Kozlov's adolescence, Northern myth was finding an increasingly prominent place in Russian verse and drama. We have mentioned Catherine the Great's bizarre *Historical Presentation from the Life of Rurik*.[46] As they are prominent in Xeraskov's vast narrative poem on the introduction of Christianity into Russia, *Vladimir* (1785), so mountain mists, sighing winds and dismal Northern regions loom large in works as disparate as Deržavin's "The Waterfall" (1791), Batjuškov's "Dream" (1802 – 3) and Kozlov's own epistle "To A. I. Turgenev" (1832).

Kozlov had a high opinion of Xeraskov's *Vladimir*. In his library, to judge by his correspondence of post-Decembrist years, was at least one edition of Letourneur's *Ossian, fils de Fingal* – perhaps the second edition of 1805.[47] Žukovskij's early elegiac verse, which he openly admired, is thickly populated by the tribes of "Rino, the highland chief," Malvina, "Ullin's daughter" and Finn mac Cumhail, alias Fingal. Small wonder that Kozlov's ode "To the Sea" (1828, from *Childe Harold*, Canto 4), "Jealousy" (1832) and "The Poet and The Storm" (1836, from Lamartine's *Jocelyn*), to mention three pieces at random, echo the clash of swords and howling storms that he met in Macpherson's realm.

44. E. J. Simmons., *op.cit.*, p. 182.
45. See. I. Zamotin, *op.cit.*, chaps. 4, 5.
46. See chap. 1, p. 3.
47. See V. Nabokov, *op.cit.*, vol. 2, pp. 254-5.

"The kings of Morven, their blue shields beneath the mountain mist upon a haunted heath, the hypnotic repetitions of vaguely meaningful epithets, the resounding, crag-echoed names, the blurred outlines of fabulous events, all this permeated romantic minds with its nebulous magic so unlike the flat classical backdrop colonnades of the Age of Taste and Reason."[48]

Macpherson, of course, wrote in several veins, and a storm is not always raging through his more or less rhythmic, rough-hewn English prose. Here, in a brilliant quasi-parody, is the Soviet scholar Tomaševskij's presentation of Macpherson in tranquil mood: "The time is either night or late evening. Necessarily, the moon would figure, peeping through the mists; around would be seen a forest, mossy for the most part. Cliffs, too, are necessary, also overgrown with mosses. And here there must flow a stream or rivulet. . . . "[49] But Russians were more familiar with the darker, wilder aspect of Macpherson's work – the savage, unwelcoming landscapes of Dmitrij Venevitinov's fragment of "Kolna Domna," of Baratynskij's "Waterfall" (1824) and Kozlov's "To the Sea." Kozlov could sympathize with those who, like Jazykov, loved the wildness and the gloom more reminiscent of the paintings of Jacob van Ruisdael than of his own earliest work, "To V. A. Zukovskij," for example, or "To Svetlana" (1821). More than this, he chose to translate works by Byron and Lamartine that are essentially evocations of that darker, wilder country. One comes to a central point in the study of Kozlov's life and verse: Kozlov's verse is, with few exceptions, an expression of an unrebellious outlook. Of course there are complaints – about his personal misfortunes, the transience of life, friends' absences or deaths; but these are not protests, and particularly not protests against political, Russian realities. Sighs do not gather into a storm, but are controlled. And even where they are not well controlled, as in "An Elegy. (Yesterday in the Woods, Distracted by Grief)" or "The Song of Marco Visconti" (1836) – the former giving vent to religious doubts and worries, the latter to a vision of helmets and blood – they do not prompt reflections of an immediate, political nature.

48. *Ibid.*, vol. 2, p. 255.

49. B. V. Tomaševskij, *Puškin; kniga pervaja* (Moscow, 1956), p. 88.

But the anger and frustration, hatred and jealousy of most mens' lives is not a mystery to Kozlov. He was not the saint of Žukovskij's conceit, and could respond with pure pleasure to the image of war and rebellion. The war, to be sure, is fictional, and neither bloodshed nor pain obtrude on a consciously developed pageantry in "Jaroslavna's Lament," for example, or "The Warrior's Dream" (1828). In the latter, the poet-warrior, gazing at the camp-fires after a gruesome battle, and hearing the "heavy moaning" of those wounded, falls into a reverie; and he sees – a rustic church, and hears the song of reapers and – dogs barking! Again, in "The Secret" (1836), it is the "sword of steel, witness of awesome battles," not those battles or their causes or results, that concerns the poet; "On the shield can be seen a star and cross,/ And near the shield shines a sharp sword./ And a shady oak overshadows a fresh grave,/ And the darkness of the fateful secret/ Is terrible . . ." (stanza 2). Can one believe for an instant that a fresh human corpse, its arms or head mangled, lies beneath that magic oak? It comes as no surprise when, in the sixth stanza, "a most aged hermit" approaches the mound of earth, a torch in his "trembling hand," and proceeds to pray. The poem is, after all, a ballad.

Kozlov, then, could respond to the anger of others; *other* mens' fury, indignation, passions struck ringing chords, and his sympathy with them (but not, by any means, with their concrete aspirations – it is as though Byron's political convictions pass through an objectifying filter before emerging in the Russian) is plain from numerous pieces, both translated and original. "What a holiday for the imagination!" he might have cried with Karamzin,[50] who translated Ossian's *Carthon* on board a ship during a raging storm.[51] Not only did Kozlov show a fondness for the wilder aspects of nature – a fondness that both complements and stands in stark contrast with his liking for idyllic rural scenes (in "The Country Life," 1837, "Blessed is he who quietly lives/ In his forefathers' unknown hamlet/ And knows of white-walled Moscow/ Only from passers-by") – he attempted deliberately to harmo-

50. *Pis'ma russkogo putešestvennika* (St. Petersburg, A. Smirdin, 1848), vol. 11, p. 786.

51. Later published in *Moskovskij žurnal*, 1791, no. 2, pp. 115-47.

nize natural descriptions, in Ossianic fashion, with the actions of his *Icherzaehlern*, especially in the more tragic or melancholy scenes. In Lara's castle, all is tranquil; the night is therefore moonlit and calm. But Lara's vision having disturbed that peace, and the peace of all his household, the servants go in fear of "the squeak of doors,/ The sound of wall hangings, the doleful howl/ Of the wind in the darkness of night. . . . " Again, in *The Monk*, the hero would ride in the woods and hunt – and the sun shone gaily and the leaves sparkled around him. It is as though his coming to the monastery somehow provoked a clap of thunder and a downpour.

Ossian's influence, as Tomaševskij observes, is more readily perceived in sense or mood than in specific passages. Nonetheless, its presence in "Jealousy" is hardly open to question. Here are the first fifteen and last four lines:

The midnight hour struck in the cemetery.
Darting from behind clouds,
A trembling ray wandered
Onto the dead's silent resting place.
Hiding her sweet countenance beneath a shroud,
Casting off a secret horror,
A certain beauty stands in tears
Over a fresh grave.
Confused involuntarily
By dark reflections' troubling alarm,
Over the turf inclining, she said
With hopeless grief:
"Unhappy friend! Forgive me, O young shade,
For the destruction of your life, . . .
For avoiding you.

And vengeance eclipsed a burning love,
In his hands there gleamed a dagger –
And her blood watered the grave,
But he vanished in darkness.

Kozlov's admiration for the sound and fury of Macpherson's

masterpiece did not disappear as he grew older. (Though Karamzin's respect for the *effects* of Ossian scarcely diminished, he did begin to complain of "too much sameness.")[52] But, of course, Kozlov took up the Gaelic bard only occasionally and in proportion to changing emotional needs; thus his appetite never became surfeited. Here, now, is the opening section of "The Poet and The Storm," based on Lamartine's *Jocelyn* and written when Kozlov was fifty-seven and no longer of an age for transitory enthusiasms:

O wondrous Ossian! Dreaming of the mists,
Of Innistor's mysterious barrows,
Your song in my soul, and harp in hand
When I roamed the slumbering forests in winter,
Where storm and snowstorm, raging, would alarm
The hearing and, like corpses, howl in the dark glade;
Where, raising my hair, a blizzard whistled,
And a waterfall roars from horror over an abyss
And, flung down from the skies above long cliffs,
Would strike my brow with foam and spread its cry
In streams; where pines, scattering snow,
Trembled like reeds, a raven raising its cry above
Their tops, and where a frozen mist breathed
Darkness from the crag and, like the son of Morven,
I was clothed in a storm;
Then, should lightning suddenly rend the mist,
Or the sun gleam stealthily . . .
Then, animated by a steppe-like wildness,
And by the fresh air and the holiness of night,
The organ of sound was sweeter;
There would be ecstasy, delight in its soul

Byron and Ossian answered one part of Kozlov's emotional need, Lamartine, Young and Moore another. The point need not be laboured further. Macpherson's Caledonia, Dante's Hell (in "A

52. See Karamzin's "Ossian," in *Panteon inostrannoj slovesnosti* (Moscow, 1798), vol. 1, p. 201.

Dream," 1832), Scott's border country all offered a certain refuge from a potentially tedious present. It was to another, calmer version of pre-Romanticism that Kozlov most often turned for relief from the all-pervading darkness. Not Schiller or Ariosto, but Burns; not Ossian but Moore offered *tableaux* in which he could feel most at ease. But from that world of piety and country churches, it must be emphasized, it was a short and easy step for the author of *The Monk* to the land of Manfred and the Giaour. Sometimes, as in "Irish Melody" (1824), Kozlov seems uncertain which of the two adjoining lands to sojourn in; at other times, the *loci* of Gray's *Elegy* and Byron's Eastern Tales seem strangely to blend, elements of each emerging in the other. "Not While Awake, Not in a Dream" (1832) is merely one of many pieces by Kozlov pitched, so it seems, at precisely the key in which grief becomes indistinguishable from measured optimism:

In fancy having left the earthly life,
I look timidly into the dark distance;
I know not myself for what I grieve,
I know not myself what I regret.

By a wave, broken among rocks,
Made silver by a moonbeam,
By the daybreak, by a favourite song
My senses are at once confused.

Hope, terror, recollections
Quietly press around me;
My heart's involuntary dreaming
I cannot express in words.

And it seems to me that I hear singing
From beyond misty clouds . . .
And I am ready in my heart
To foster my secret agitation.

Does the piece, well called "a fantasy" by Kozlov, end on a buoyant note? Certainly it is not depressed; and yet one cannot say that it is optimistic – agitation, after all, may not lead to happiness. All is obscure, nothing is settled or precise. Disparate elements meet in the poem: the *dark* distance and *silver* wave, terror and hope, recollections and anticipation. The poem reflects in microcosm qualities of Kozlov's verse of every period.

It was, all critics agree, Kozlov's unique distinction to have formed a clear connection between Thomson and Byron. In his person, devotees of *The Seasons* and *The Giaour*, of pre-Romantic and Romantic Western verse, found a common exemplar and protector; in his verse, aspects of poetry admired by two generations separated by twenty years found a meeting place, and fused. And, of course, it says much of his character, as of his verse, that he could so deftly combine elements of Karamzin and Byron, Young and Ossian in his work, now translating Lamartine's idylls, now *Manfred*. The Monk, it has been stressed, is certainly cousin to the Giaour, sharing his outward characteristics, his disastrous love affair, his departure, confession, confessor, cloak; yet, apostate from Byron but not from God, he meekly repents of his past and submits to the will of God, hoping for absolution of his sins.[53]

Bound by sickness to a chair or, in later years, his bed, Kozlov could only respond to the colour and restless movement of Schiller's, Byron's, and Dante's verse. Would it not have been strange, granted his love of poetry, had he refused to do so, closing his eyes on the inner world, as they had been closed on the outer? Of course exotic, distant lands and peoples spoke to him:

And when I plunge into myself,
As in a dark abyss,
With what a magical shield
Do I defend myself from black reflections!
I hear the wondrous sound of the harp,
I hearken to the singing of the favourites
Of the Muses, enlivened by celestial fire;
And inspiration floods into my soul,
And the heart beats, the spirit seethes,
And a new world stands before me;
I live in it, I dream in it,

53. *Černets*, stanzas 10, 12.

I find almost bliss in it.[54]

No less than the élan and *brio* of distant, bloodless battles (even the sanguine beginning of "The Song of Marco Visconti," from Tomaso Grossi's "In morte di Marco Visconti" – "Blood! Blood! Whose castle do I see/ With crenellated tower? The sombre entrance/ Steams yet in streams of blood"; – seems strangely disconnected from the fact of human pain), it was the splendour and romance of a stylized mediaeval world, now Russian (in "Kiev," "Jaroslavna's Lament"), now Italian, now German or English that plainly charmed Kozlov. In this respect, it may be added, he stood apart from those who, in the late twenties and early thirties, acquired an interest in historical realities, whose interest in Russia's past was not merely that of poets. Puškin visited Orenburg, scene of the great peasant rising of Emil'jan Pugačov (1773 – 74), before writing a study of that rising and, for good measure, *The Captain's Daughter*; he also searched the Imperial archives for materials relating to a matter "of which little was known." Despite the crude nationalism and cardboard psychology, Mixail Zagoskin's novel *à la Walter Scott, Jurij Miloslavskij* (1829) is an acceptable romance of its kind. Zagoskin, too, took, some trouble over his subject matter, carefully introducing the proper terminology for seventeenth-century clothing, armour and tactics. The novel enjoyed an enormous success, and set the fashion for the "Waverley" novels and I. I. Lažečnikov (1792 – 1869), the finest of the Russian Scottophiles. It is true that Kozlov adheres to the broad outlines of Natal'ja Dolgorukaja's personal history, but it is the *broad* outlines that he follows, and there is the point. Kozlov read the princess's posthumous memoirs as they appeared in St. Petersburg periodicals, from 1810 to 1816. We, too, may do so, and read that she "had not the custom to love someone today, another tomorrow . . . and so proved to the world" that she was "faithful in love."[55]! In the intrigues around Prince Ivan Dolgorukij, in the cause of his exile and death Kozlov had no obvious interest. Had

54. "K drugu V. A. Žukovskomu" (1822), ll. 367-73.

55. "Zapiski Knjagini N. B. Dolgorukoj," *Russkij arxiv*, 1867, bk. I, p. 16.

they been colourful, dramatic, foreshadowed by strange auguries or followed by grim battle, he would, one may be sure, have found these things no less arresting than the princess's conversion, pilgrimage and visions.

Kozlov was not born in the age of Byron. He belonged, by disposition, to another generation, and grew in the time of Catherine and Deržavin. His contemplative melancholy was not that of a man who reached maturity to find the dead weight of oppression under Nicholas; rather was it literary Russia's chosen mood when he had been an adolescent and most vulnerable to all influences, literary or not. For his contemporaries, one recalls on reading his "To Svetlana" or any one of seven elegies set in bucolic frames, "the joy of sadness was to be found while sitting at night in the cell of some ruined monastery with moonlight streaming through the window."[56] And, to be sure, the moon shines in a good third of his poems, translated or original.

Early impressions were not easily erased even by such as Lara or the Giaour, and those impressions were preponderantly sentimental. Here lastly, to underline that indelible mark left on him by the age of Karamzin, are two passages from *The Monk*, Part One, 8 – 9. The hero tells his tale to the abbot, and a Karamzinian spirit, so it seems, restrains the shade of Byron:

I left our deserted region;
Alone, in despair, in tears,
I wandered, my heart orphaned,
In dense and distant forests.
My cries, my moaning, my reproaches
The dark ravines and mountains
Heard seven years in horror.
Sombre, grieving, wild,
I tormented myself with the former dream;
I sobbed for what was no longer.
Night's shade, a mountain torrent,
The storm's whistling and howl of winds
Secretly blended in my dark reflection,

56. E. J. Simmons, *op.cit.*, p. 166.

With unquenchable yearning;
And the grief was a delight,
A blessed remnant of the earlier days:
In my torment, it seemed to me,
I was not wholly parted from her.

Where the heart suffers and where it loves,
Our merciful God is there:
He gives us the cross, and in the cross
He also sends us hope.
For seven wearisome, awful years
The comforting light gleamed for me.
Once, in a night time,
I sat gloomily above a river.
And heaven's vault of fiery stars,
And the calm shimmering of the moon,
And the sound of leaves and the plashing
Of waters that the moon silvered –
Involuntarily, all captivated my soul,
All summoned me into a world of bliss
With its mysterious beauty.
My crushed spirit awoke . . .

Kozlov was the last Russian poet of standing to reflect the powerful influence of Young and Ossian in the sentimental manner of Karamzin and his followers. His verse has more than its fair share of bloody hands, moonlit harems, swords, shrieks and tombs. But Kozlov was a sentimentalist before he was a Romantic; it is of obvious significance that much of his thunder and lightning was borrowed from Western poets. The peaceful, church-studded fields over which Byronic storms would break, however, were wholly and only his.

CHAPTER FOUR
THE ORIGINAL VERSE

For Kozlov, poetry was a God-given escape from physical disease and spiritual malaise; so he always regarded it, now emphasizing its divine source (in "My Prayer," "Two Barques," "To the Unfaithful Girl"), now dwelling on its function as a means of escaping blindness, as a source of movement and gay colour. It is tempting to divide all his poetry into two parts – those in which the motif of *escape* predominates, as in the three narrative tales, each filled by strange and dramatic events; and those in which *religiousness* of temperament determines both mood and content. But the clear-cut distinction hardly corresponds to the reality; there are religious elements in *The Monk*, as the title plainly suggests, while no poem, no matter how exalted in tenor, is without the occasional dramatic simile or image. So, in "My Prayer," God becomes "the Destroyer of evil, the supreme Judge," "Always burning in the night's stillness/ With glow of fiery stars"; so in "Stances" (1838), the Creator gives rise to a mighty storm, "And lightning flashes in a stream,/ Like a wild white-maned steed." It would be wrong to claim that it was not the colourful, even the violent aspects of Byron's Eastern tales or Moore's exotic verse that appealed to Kozlov the translator. As blindness and creeping paralysis brought him seriously to ponder questions of man's salvation and immortality – implicit in the prayer-like poems is the certainty that in a second life his own lot would be a happier one – so illness and isolation opened his inner eye to the stirring, the wild, the colourful and grand, in short, to Romantic literature and to the hackneyed Romantic heroes of Byron's time.

Nor can it be denied that he expressed personal feelings and impressions in his original idylls and elegies. As the tales reflect his frustrations and the unspoken but insistent urge to enter "normal" life once more, but as a passionate, resourceful man, so, one might argue, one sees acceptance of his fate, the solace to be found in faith, a serene, easy benevolence in such original poems as "To Svetlana" and "To V. A. Žukovskij." But again, such a schema over-simplifies the question. It was all but inevitable that admiration for Byron's techniques, subjects, attitudes towards both verse and life find echoes in Kozlov's own poetry; Byron could not be kept in one carefully sealed compartment, Christ in another. The paeon entitled simply "Byron" is an original poem, but concerns, and even imitates the English poet.

But whether Christ and the Christian life or the monk and the life of passion predominate in any given poem, one thing is constant: it is the life itself that interests Kozlov, not the minutiae of its description. Intent on the evocation of arresting scenes or moods (the one complements the other almost of necessity, such is the strength of Ruskin's "pathetic fallacy" in all that Kozlov wrote), he had no interest in formal experimentation. And technically there is little of interest in his poetry, which is, formally speaking, highly conventional.

Kozlov wrote approximately one hundred and eighty pieces, excluding the narrative tales and three short poems written in Italian or English.[1] Of these, no less than eighty-five are free or literal translations of works by Western authors. These were, in order of quantity, Byron, Mickiewicz, Moore, Dante, Petrarch, Burns, Ariosto, Scott, Chénier and Lamartine. In addition, there is the small group of poems composed of epistles to these poets ("To Walter Scott," "Byron" and others). Of the total one hundred and eighty-six pieces, more than one hundred and fifty are composed in iambic tetrameters. Kozlov followed a general trend among contemporary Russian poets; more than 80 per cent of Puškin's verse is written in that metre. Well might he have echoed Puškin who declared roundly in *The Little House in Kolomna*, "The four-foot iamb has wearied me:/ Everyone writes in it. . . . "

1. See *Stixotverenija I. I. Kozlov*, ed. I. D. Glikman (Leningrad, 1956), pp. 431-34.

In metrics, as in other branches of technique, Kozlov brought little new to Russian verse. Professor B. O. Unbegaun's remarks concerning Baratynskij and Puškin, that "though marking the beginning of modern verse in attitude towards poetry, they still obviously look towards the eighteenth century,"[2] are no less applicable to Kozlov. Not only did he carefully conform to the late eighteenth-century pattern in such minor matters as the use of the caesura (after the second or, possibly, third foot in five- or six-foot iambics or trochaics – in "From Dante" (1832), for example, and "The Bride: an Elegy" (1835)), as strophe length (never less than four, rarely more than eight lines); even to such details as stress-distribution in the iambic tetrameter he accepted the opinion and practice of his contemporaries. It is most clear from the statistics provided in L. I. Timofeev's *Problems of Verse Study* (*Problemy stixovedenija*)[3] that, where matters of verse technique are concerned, Kozlov stood squarely in the mainstream of cautious conservatism.

Kozlov's first published poem, "To Svetlana," appeared in *Son of the Fatherland* in the late summer of 1821. It is, essentially, an apologia in the guise of an epistle to Žukovskij's niece and Kozlov's close friend, Aleksandra Voekova (1795 – 1829) – the Svetlana of Žukovskij's ballad of that title, written in 1808. An unresolved mixture of elegiac sentiment, religiosity, simplicity and imitation of those neo-Classical French poets popular in Russia while Kozlov was himself still young,[4] the poem's very title shows plainly under whose influence it was written. No doubt hoping to echo Žukovskij's enormous success with "Svetlana," the middle-aged apprentice drew judiciously on an established reputation. The piece was received well enough; its weaknesses were not expounded mercilessly in literary periodicals, nor was Kozlov the subject of a rash of hostile epigrams – as well he might have been, such was the rising confidence of the vociferous anti-Žukovskij

2. B. O. Unbegaun, *Russian Versification* (Oxford, 1956), p. 55.

3. L. I. Timofeev, *Problemy stixovedenija* (Moscow, 1931), pp. 208-19.

4. See my paper, "Eighteenth-Century Neoclassical French Influences on E. A. Baratynskij and Pushkin," *Comparative Literature Studies*, vol. 6 (1969), no. 4, pp. 435-61.

group in 1821 – 22.[5] Instead, critics chose to dwell on the poem's virtues. "The air of gentle resignation," M. T. Kačenovskij told readers of *The Messenger of Europe*, was "pleasing"; so, too, were such images as "sail-less barque/ Smashed by a savage wave," and children subject to "The seas' formidable caprice,/ Without helmsman, without sail."[6] But it is best that the piece speak for itself:

So much do you bring gladness with you
That the heart seems to burst out laughing;
Something in it responds, part of itself,
To your welcoming voice;
My grief is subject to your power –
You know how to delight it;
But for me, Svetlana, you feel
Too much pity.
True, my life is poisoned,
And my heart has beat in vain,
My spring faded early,
The sun setting at noon;
Though inexorable fate
Has burdened me with yearning
And my sail-less barque
Is smashed by a savage wave;
Though I am predestined to darkness
And fields are not green for me,
And the moon's stream does not silver
Nor do roses longer show red,
Still what is to be done? In this life

5. V. K. Kjuxel'beker headed the group by virtue of two highly lucid articles of 1824, "On the Direction of Our Literature, Especially Lyrical, During the Past Decade," *Mnemozina*, No. 2, and "A Conversation with F. V. Bulgarin," *ibid.*, No. 3. Both show the strong influence of Etienne Béquet, whose articles (for example, in *Journal des débats*, April 23/4, May 1, 1821), bear direct relevance to the "semi-Russian Jeremiads" attacked by Kjuxel'beker and A. A. Bestužev, and strike Puškin's Lenskij squarely: "Vous pouvez être sûr d'avance qu'il y a un vague indéfinissable dans leurs figures, du vague dans leurs mouvements, du vague dans leur conduite .. " ('L'Elegie contemporaine,' May 1). Puškin, however, added his own comment, in "The Nightingale and the Cuckoo" (1825) – which is *not* directed against Kozlov.

6. *Vestnik Eyropy*, 1822, vol. 2, p. 33.

I have not lost everything,
And in my burning breast
The fire of feeling is preserved yet.
Let grief oppress me
And tears be often shed –
But oh! my day is not yet finished,
Still I love, still I dream.
My soul well knows how to converse
With wife, with children,
Nor do I need eyes
To admire them in my heart.
(ll. 1 – 32)

Of course there is a good deal of banality. Springs had been fading, suns sinking, tears flowing for many years in Russia, as in Western Europe, by 1821. Nor does Kozlov improve on Millevoye's or La Fare's use of this neo-Classical stock imagery. But there are positive aspects also – a piquancy and a directness that stem from the poet's blindness, a lack of technical affectation. The poem, in fact, contains a number of the main characteristics of Kozlov's maturer verse. Rebellion is conspicuous by its absence, nor is there even a suggestion of true violence or turmoil. Somehow the "sail-less barque/ smashed by a savage wave" is too consciously wrought, too literary; yet this very craftmanship does much to save the poem from an excess of self-pity. Still, it is apparent that blindness does not in itself make a poet.

In one other respect the piece, which is the work of a competent amateur, not of a poet who has found his key, typifies Kozlov's verse: it introduces God, the poet's comforter. God is continually in his thoughts and often, as in the third quarter of "To Svetlana," in his poetry also. Remembering his Maker, the poet's terrors for his future and for his family vanish:

In my soul I soar to that place
Whence the stars gleam for us:
And our merciful Father
Shall hear the prayer of an unhappy man,
And for my thorny crown's sake

Give blessing to the innocent!
Horror quickly vanishes,
A prayer warms the heart
And suddenly hope soars with faith
On iridescent rays . . .
(ll. 43 – 52)

God is omnipresent in Kozlov's original poetry, and in the very texture of his thought. From God come all gifts that make life delightful: friendship, love, and poetry. In its simple expression of Kozlov's personal history and of his attitude towards his past, present and future, "To Svetlana" foreshadows the epistle "To V. A. Žukovskij," written in February, 1822 but not published until 1825.

It is significant that the only other poem of some length written and published by the author of "To Svetlana" before the epistle to Žukovskij, "Night on the River," was a translation.[7] Already the pattern was being determined by which one half of his energies would be channeled into translation work, the other into original verse.

Those three interconnecting thematic elements which together form "To V. A. Žukovskij" also lie at the base of all Kozlov's poetry. For this reason the epistle occupies a central place in any study of his work, no matter how brief or detailed. Those elements are reflections on or recollections of the past, resultant thoughts on a less happy present and hopes for a better future, either on earth or beyond the grave. As thoughts of the (generally unsatisfactory) present stem from reflections on a happier past, so hopes for another, better life counterbalance and contrast with that present. Both future and past, in other words, spring from and complement a black present. The result is that the present serves only as a starting point – a springboard to more cheering memories or hopes. And can one blame Kozlov for choosing, by this simplest of techniques, practically to annul the present? For him, it had less to offer than the future, and no more than his

7. Published in *Son of the Fatherland*, 1821, vol. 49, pp. 127-30, the poem did not satisfy Kozlov, who omitted it from the 1833 collection of his verse.

sociable, military, above all, successful past.

Something of the same pattern has been seen already in "To Svetlana." There, memories of a happier past lead not to thoughts of a miserable present (though "grief oppresses" and "tears are often shed"), but rather to an understanding of the fact that all could be far worse. Nevertheless, it is the three-part structure that grows so familiar to all who read more than a few poems by Kozlov. Like most of his pieces, it ends on a note of measured optimism.

On these three elements rests the whole structure of Kozlov's original verse. Past and future offer escapes; thus he abandons the nineteenth century for the Middle Ages (in "Kiev" and "The Plaint of Jaroslavna"), Russia for other, warmer lands (in "To Italy" and "A Venetian Night"). So, too, he embraces the *fuoco* of Byron, Ariosto, Schiller. But the present can never be destroyed, and serves to remind the poet both of God, who creates life and death, pain and delight, and of his own potential freedom from blindness. Thus the religious element grows ever stronger in his verse, now springing from sublime faith in the afterlife, in "My Prayer" (1833), "Stances" (1838) and "A Prayer" (1839), now from moments of agonizing doubt, in "An Elegy" (1830). What, he demands reasonably, if grief is the common human lot, and not that of only an unhappy few? Still more appalling, what if there is nothing beyond death, or if one enters a life of worse anxieties than on this earth? It is inevitable, in these reflections springing from Kozlov's thematic trinity, that an elegiac tone prevail throughout; for what is elegiac verse, if not verse of a mournful, reflective nature? Nothing is more obvious from a casual reading of Kozlov's original verse of any period than that it is reflective and that his memories of the past tend to be melancholy.

One final point must be made in connection with Kozlov's past, present and future, and this is that it is precisely his *own* past, present and future, not that of all mankind, that concerned him. Kozlov does not universalize, in the manner of Baratynskij or Karolina Pavlova, on the basis of a personal misfortune; the fact is remarkable, for he surely had ample grounds for viewing life in a sombre light. The disaster remains his personal disaster. But all men may enter his heaven ("My Prayer"). At the last, Kozlov was always charitable, and his verse reflects his charity.

Like "To Svetlana," the epistle to Žukovskij is an apologia, at first covertly, later openly so. Contemporaries applauded it as such. Memories of a happier past, despair of the present, hopes for a celestial future, all is familiar but handled with greater subtlety than in the earlier epistle; here there are no sudden transitions, no leaps from the past to the present. Instead Kozlov moves easily from tense to tense, now dwelling on the present, now glancing ahead only to rush back to the past. Here, one feels, is a firm grasp of time sequences which had earlier controlled the poet; no longer a rigid framework, the themal trinity has become a tool or vehicle, governed, not governing.

The epistle may be schematized crudely as follows: Žukovskij is far away, but the poet's thoughts follow him south; who does not live in the imagination? All men have memories; the poet reflects on his past; reflections lead to thoughts of his misfortune (l. 103, "Five whole years . . . "), and so to the present. The poem then follows the familiar pattern. Here, now, are four extracts, chosen to illustrate the interlocking temporal components of the piece and, by direct extension, of all Kozlov's original verse:

O, you have long extended your stay
In distant parts, good traveller!
And this mournful year of separation
Has been a dark year for me, my friend!
But I have not forgotten how to love
Or forgotten my friends,
But ever kept apace with them
And often travelled in thought
With you, above the clouds,
In the land where spring shows
Green luxuriantly among the snows,
Where glows the fragrant grape,
Where peaceful oak-groves murmur,
Meadows are bedecked with flowers
And ancient glaciers sparkle
With the fires of a heavenly rainbow.
And often, often have I heard with you

The howling of Alpine winds
And the sullen sound of stern pines,
And their secret midnight whispering;
Seen how a torrent breaks out from the mountains
There, its thunder echoing in the groves . . .
(ll. 7 – 28)

And who indeed can forget his spring?
Who does not live in recollections?
I, too, by their enchantment,
Am less dismal, and
Meet a smile sometimes
And, lost in the past, forget
How fate knows how to punish me
In its inexorability.
And the memory of earlier, bright days
Moves me with a delightful yearning:
I, my friend, I also have dreamed!
I saw a dream of love and happiness,
Piously I set my hopes that these
Might not be clouded on this earth;
Entranced by a beloved dream
From the dawn of my young days, you know,
I strove for it alone,
And without it the wide world to me
Seemed merely an empty steppe;
My soul filled with fire,
I did not fear waves or storms
But boldly set forth on the sea
In my slight barque . . .
(ll. 52 – 74)

And I . . . I had to part
With my last joy.
In vain for me, in vain
Even the sun gives life to the earth,
And the clear moon breathes her sweet delight
And the currents' ripples gleam silver!
I shall not see the green fields,

The light azure of pure waters,
Nor day's triumphant beauties
Nor stars alight in night's darkness.

Time, you know, changes
Children's features,
Gives them a new appearance with the years;
Tremble: their look shall change
And their form not be that
Which the heart preserves!
And with a desperate yearning
I strained my dimming sight at them,
Feared to leave them for an instant,
Pressed them to my breast,
From grief forgot to think,
Looked at them . . . but already
Dear forms were vanishing from me in a darkness:
They vanished, blended with the mists,
And all that was seemed to me
A dream of long before.
Day's clear light faded, faded out
And my heart expanded,
All in the future seeming to me
An abyss of perdition.
(ll. 126 – 35, 156 – 75)

O friend! Believe, only God,
In His workings incomprehensible,
He alone, almighty, helped me
To bear that unbearable blow.
Already my spirits were failing,
Already I languished in despair;
Though I did not dare to complain,
Oh, I feared to have hope!
Already in that savage grief
All my thoughts had grown dark:
And, in my lot, life and death
Seemed equally terrible.
But suddenly . . . glory to Thee, the Creator!

Thou didst not forget Thy creation!
Thou seest the depths of hearts,
Thou hearest the secret prayer,
My fear vanished, glory to Thee!
(ll. 189 – 205)

With such lines, Kozlov introduced a fresh note to Russian poetry. That his verse could be cheerful, filled with memories of old friendships, young girls, distant countries and towns, seemed to contemporaries remarkable; but that he should himself be gay and cheerful, as visitors unfailingly recorded, struck them as admirable and wonderful. It is not easy to say where memories end and the imagination starts in the two poems cited above; for one faculty so complements and strengthens the other that it seems to become the other. It is an imagined Switzerland, not a remembered one, that introduces the epistle to Žukovskij – yet so concrete are the details, so firm the description of a torrent, an oak-grove, particular glaciers (nothing is generalized in Kozlov's natural scenes), that the poet might himself have been there. So it is also in the ode "To Italy," a country Kozlov never saw. The ode is inspired by Canto 4 of Byron's *Childe Harold*, and one may demonstrate that this or that image is borrowed from the English; yet the total effect is to convince that he, Kozlov, and not Byron, once roamed "Torquato's land."[8] In his blindness, Kozlov empathized with men and women long since dead, with Princess Jaroslavna of Putivl, Princess Natal'ja Dolgorukaja and Desdemona. To do so was a feat, not of memory, but of imagination. Such is his skill, however, that it is difficult to bear the fact in mind.

As apprehensions of the future or hopes for a better life dominate many poems of the period 1833 – 39 (though even in the ballad "The Bride's Dream" (1824), the theme of an after-life looms large, as the drowned fiancé appears), so memories of spring, morning, "earlier bright days" set the tone of many pieces from 1823 – 36. Stylized and consciously modish in earlier years, in "To Joy" (1823), for example, or "Morning and Evening"

8. "K Italii," l.6; from *Childe Harold*, 4, 42.

(1828), those memories grow more personal in "The Reapers" (1836) and, in a curious way, in "The Oak" (1836).

It was inevitable that Kozlov pay his respects to neo-Classical traditions which were strongest in Russia when his literary apprenticeship was in its earliest stages. "Each of us," remarked Baratynskij, "has drawn his opinions from his age. And this is a question not only of opinions, but also of feelings. Our organs have been formed in accordance with those notions by which our minds have been fed."[9] No early letters by Kozlov have survived, and so it is not possible to know whether or not they were composed in an artificial, supposedly literary style of French origin; but one may reasonably think so.

Kozlov was born into the Europeanized, French-speaking Russian gentry. Perhaps, as his daughter claimed, he did care for all things simple and Russian; but it is certain that he chose to correspond with Puškin, Vjazemskij and Baratynskij, among others, in an immaculate French.[10] Since Petrine times, Russian literature and the liberal education of members of the gentry had lain in the western Classical tradition – a tradition based on attitudes deriving from, or seen as deriving from, Greco-Roman antiquity. By the time of Kantemir, however, the Classical tradition had already passed its golden period in France. It was a long and tired, as well as essentially foreign, tradition of neo-Classicism that Kozlov inherited. That tradition had two faces, in Russia as in France. Coupled with an elegance, in art and life, far lighter than the elegance of Louis XIV's time, were philosophical tendencies. Those tendencies, by undermining the religious and political foundations of the old régime in France, ended in revolution. Elegance and wit thus failed to contain the ideas propagated in their framework. From the revolutionary aspect of the neo-Classical tradition – the branch of Voltaire – sprang the Russian civic verse of Ryleev, Bestužev-Marlinskij, and Raevskij.

9. E. A. Baratynskij, *Stixotvorenija, poemy, proza, pis'ma* (Moscow, 1951), pp. 523-4; letter to I. V. Kireevskij of 4.12.33.

10. *Ibid.*, p. 481. "I am very glad," Baratynskij wrote from Kjumen', (a village and fortress on the southern edge of Finland), in April 1825, "that, by starting to write to me in Russian, you allow me to do the same. You and I spoke mostly in French, for which reason I began our correspondence in that same language. . . . "

But from the formal aspect came the verse of Vjazemskij, Del'vig and Kozlov.

Kozlov's education was based less on the ancient literatures than on their echoes and reflections in French and Italian letters, less on Greek mythology than on Chénier's, Millevoye's and Ariosto's often confused record of it. Indeed, there are no grounds for thinking that Kozlov knew Greek at all, or was a better classicist than Onegin, who "knew enough/ To speak of Juvenal,/ And to place *Vale* at his letter's end."[11] He was a modernist. If oaks were "centennial," Phoebus "glorious" and the sky invariably "azure," it was because he and his contemporaries chose to accept indulgently a venerable tradition. Small wonder, then, that Chénier, not Catullus, was the presiding spirit behind pieces that he wrote with an eye to the past. Consider, first, the early elegy, "To Joy":

O joy, joy, why dost thou
Quickly deceive us,
And so soon take away
The heart's fair dreams!

Why, heavenly one, dost thou fly
Like a feathered arrow
And glow in misfortune's darkness
Like a distant star!

And why dost thou pour out enchantment
With thy delights
And leave . . . only the recollection
Of bright days!

(ll. 1 – 12)

"O jours de mon printemps, jours couronnés de roses," cries Chénier, "Beaux jours, quoique souvent obscurcis de mes pleurs,/ Vous dont j'ai su jouir même au sein des douleurs,/ Sur ma tête bientôt vos fleurs seront fanées."[12] "Tu vis," responds Voltaire, "la calomnie/ Des plus beaux jours de mon printemps/ Obscurcir

11. *Evenij Onegin*, Chap. 1, VI, 4-6.

12. A. Chénier, "Elégie première," *Oeuvres de Chénier* (Paris, 1826), p. 16.

la naissante aurore."[13] Kozlov took a metaphor – youth as springtime – that belongs to the poetry of all nations.

Still bolder are the French accents of "Morning and Evening" (1828). Here, Chénier passes into Russian through the mirror of Mickiewicz; the piece is a translation of "Ranek i Wieczor":

The sun gleams in a crimson crown,
Scarce shines the timorous moon,
Under the dew a violet trembles,
And the young rose is languorous.
Ljudmila stands by her window,
Around her snow-white neck carelessly
Twine golden locks.
I fell on my knees in the silence.
She said to me:
"Why is everything mournful so early –
The violet, the rose, my sweetheart?"

But the day flashed by; the horizon
Burns with an evening glow,
And the fragrant meadow is silvered
By the soft full moon.
The violet was revived by dew;
Ljudmila appeared at the window;
Still finer is her attire,
Still brighter her cheerful glance –
And once more I am on my knees
Before my beloved . . . and sad.
I grieved early in the morning,
I grieve now in night's darkness.

Little wonder that Ljudmila seems familiar – she is the Lileta of ten songs by Del'vig, sister to those Chloes and Daphnes whose roamings through a stylized neo-Classical landscape form a bond between de Parny ("A Eléonore," *Poésies érotiques*) and Russians of Puškin's generation.[14]

13. "Epitre XIV" (1719), pp. 8-10.
14. See note 4.

Kozlov cast off such shadows with ease. Here, as an illustration of the fusion of personal memories and descriptive skills of a high order, is an extract from "The Reapers" (1836):

Once a fine summer day was turning to evening,
The shadows breathed the sweetness of green groves.
I was wandering alone where, streaming beneath Filjami,
The Moscow river rushes its blue waves from Kuznetskij
Hills; and my spirit was caught by the blessed simplicity
Of rural occupations, by the rich harvest
In a quiet, fragrant meadow,
And by the songs of reapers, content in their humble lot.
Everywhere among the cornfields their sharp sickles gleam
And yellow ears lie all around them.
Gathered by the young wives of the reapers
They are already bound in golden stooks;
And the labour is useful to all, and far from care,
And blessed by God with a father's smile.

Already the sun had set, casting its crimson glow;
Work had ceased on the stubble of the fields,
The hearty reapers going to their homes.
One, in the flower of his life, stood before me.
His wife amazed my sight in her beauty:
The happy woman played with her joyful child,
And she plaited cornflowers, yellow ears
And small red flowers into her dark curls.
The reaper looked at these . . .

. . . .

And much time, many years have passed since then,
My life has grown dark – but my feelings are not weakened.
Oppressed by langour in night's severe darkness,
That field, those reapers are always in my heart;
And I, deprived of legs, even I, deserted by sight,
Reach for them in my heart, and fly in imagination.
(ll. 1 – 23, 39 – 44)

It is a peaceful, colourful scene that Kozlov retains in his blindness; epithets of colour abound – "green groves," "red flowers," "yellow ears," "golden stooks," "crimson glow." In the background sickles *gleam*, shadows *breathe*, the day *turns* to evening. Nothing is static, everything moves or changes. The corn is quickly *gathered, bound* by young, energetic and attractive women, whose voices, blending with their husbands' cheerful songs, merge with the rushing river. So it is in all Kozlov's extended descriptive passages. Not motionless but changing scenes attract him – a wood before, during and after a sharp shower, in *The Monk*; approaching dusk, late evening and then darkness, in *Princess Natal'ja Dolgorukaja*, Part I. Was the Moscow river truly blue, even in 1820, when Kozlov last saw it? One must doubt it; the Kuznetskij Hills, whence it flows southward, are clay-filled, and the river still carries its grey sediment. For Kozlov alone, whose eyes could not contradict him, it not only seemed but *was* blue. Once more imagination and memory combine.

These three moments, of movement, colour and sound, occupy an increasingly vital place in Kozlov's verse. Significant even in 1821, they loom large indeed in "The Oak" (1836), "Erminija on Jordan's Banks" (1836), and "A Legend" (1839). Nor are the colours the pastel shades of "To V. A. Žukovskij" – even in 1824, with "A Venetian Night," a predilection for bold, striking colours was plain. Neither small nor insignificant to start with, Kozlov's eponymous oak, "the mighty son of the groves," "both strong and tall," is felled, not by a single flash of lightning, but by "a wild hurricane" – and so grows still mightier in the poet's eyes:

The glory of its native hill, a young oak stood
Both strong and tall, with shady branches;
Green bushes and fragrant flowers
Grew round it.

. . . . .

And the oak-groves' mighty son looked
Far across the field with a certain boldness.

In the bloom of youth, he did not fear storms –
Spring was the livelier for them, the azure between clouds
Clearer – he feasted his eyes on lightning's flash

And thunder, delighted in the storms' whistling.

Country maidens and youths loved walking
Beneath his shade, and there the midnight nightingale
Sang sweetly, and the red glow of the dawn
Caught them in soft delight.

And seeing nature's beauty in everything around him,
The oak thought nature would not deceive him,
And insolently felt that wind and foul weather
Would not come to him.

But suddenly the heavens were clad in black,
And rain beat down in showers, and a wild hurricane,
Swirling, catching up flying dust, flew down,
And mist covered the dale.

The hurricane tore from his roots
The green bushes with sweet flowers, and the gay stream was filled
With earth and stones and stumps,
And the comforting current vanished.

The thunder groaned, and lightning scorched the firm oak;
The oak split, but was not destroyed by storm:
Though doomed to wither
Strength for a straitened life remained in him.
(ll. 1 – 32)

Once more, it is the immediacy, the concreteness that strikes one. Kozlov is not writing of storms and oak-glades in general, but one oak, one fearful storm. It has a photographic clarity. Overcast by the hurricane, the tree's colours are not as evident as those of the cornfields in the sun; "shady branches" seem to prefigure the "black cloud," "wild hurricane," and "flying dust." It is to the ear, not to the eye, that this piece is addressed, and Kozlov fills it with sound. Storms whistle, thunder roars, even a nightingale sings in a moment of calm. And again, all is movement – rain beating down, dust flying, maidens strolling. For Kozlov, poetry was a compensation. By 1836 he was chair-bound; through writing, he restored strength to his limbs and lived vicariously:

When I plunge into myself,
As in a dark abyss,
With how magical a shield am I
Protected from black thoughts!
I hear the wondrous sound of a harp,
Hear the singing of the Muses' favourites.
. . . . .
And a new world stands before me;
I live in it, I dream in it . . .[15]

That "new world" contained many countries, and some Kozlov visited but once. Only in the last six months of his life did he "fly above the clouds" to Africa. ("Among the wild African mountains,/ Over the Mediterranean waves,/ A holy cloister draws the gaze. . . . ")[16] Others, like the Scotland of Burns and of Walter Scott – two different, though bordering countries – he visited three or four times (in "A Rural Saturday Evening in Scotland" from "The Cotter's Saturday Night," in "To Walter Scott" and "Beverley"). In Italy and mediaeval Russia he passed long periods returning to each many times.

But all these lands share two common characteristics: all are places never visited by Kozlov; and all are, to a greater or lesser degree, exotic. Kozlov was eclectic in his exoticism – fiery deserts or snow-swept plains, Kiev in the time of the Pečenegs or Venice under the Doges, all served the same purpose. That purpose was release. It was not with details of political or even literary activity that Žukovskij wrote to him from Venice. Knowing well enough what would please his friend "the epistolatory hero" (Kozlov wrote often, missing Žukovskij's company), it was another and poetic Italy that he presented: "Imagine from where I am writing! From Venice! On hearing that word, Tasso, Byron and thousands of gigantic and poetic shades of the past will appear before your closed eyes. . . . "[17]

Many of Kozlov's personal friends were diplomats. Some, like

15. "K V. A. Žukovskomu" (1822), ll. 358-63, 367-8.
16. "Legenda," ll. 1-3.
17. See my paper "Zhukovsky and Manzoni: A Meeting," *Forum Italicum*, vol 5. (1971), no. 4.

Fiquelmont, Paez de la Cadena and D. P. Severin, Vjazemskij's fellow-pupil at the St. Petersburg Jesuits' Institute,[18] were happy to entertain him with accounts of their sojourns in other states. Others, who had been posted to distant and exotic lands, could regale him not merely with tales, but with adventures; and of these, Pjotr Balk-Polevoj, Russian Consul in Rio-de-Janeiro, was closest to him and to literary circles in St. Petersburg.

Kozlov addressed two epistles to Balk-Polevoj, the first in 1828, the second ten years later, three years after the latter's arrival in Brazil. To read the later poem is to know how Kozlov, although fated "never to sail/ The ocean endless as eternity,"[19] and eloquent in the defence of Russia, could envy those who did so:

. . . Not Albion,
Enlightened by a wise freedom,
Nor even that land where fiery mountains
Met your gaze beneath an azure sky –
The wondrous land of sacred antiquities,
The realm of songs and love – so draw me
As the entrancing waves of the Dardanelles.
Oh friend, what a night! boats gleam and dart,
And music wafts from the shores of Stamboul,
And you hear the nightingales of sumptuous Asia;
There, with their daggers, are bold, turbaned
Turks; there young Greek girls dance voluptuously,
More tender than their roses – and the bright moon
Is itself surprised by the night's delight.
And still I like to reflect how, having
Finished a difficult journey, you were captivated
By the beauty of emerald Brazil,
Where the skies' vault gleams with an eternal
Rainbow, and dark forests are gay with the flash
Of wonderful birds; where the pine-apple shows
Red as fire in an open field, and palms are green,
Like gladness, over waves . . .

(ll. 51 – 72)

18. See my article "I. I. Kozlov; Unpublished Correspondence," *Etudes slaves et est-Européennes* (Montréal), vol. 15 (1970), 104-115.

19. "K P. F. Balk-Polevu" (1838), l. 80.

It is unfortunate that none of Balk-Polevoj's letters to Kozlov from Brazil have survived. One can hardly doubt that they were highly coloured, written for a specific reader – Kozlov.

If it was natural that, in his blindness, Kozlov should dwell on exotic and colourful lands, it was all but inevitable that Italy should charm him. Never did a national infatuation with that country reach a higher pitch than among Russians in the third and fourth decades of the last century. As the Russian historian P. N. Sakulin remarks, "the name alone of Italy sufficed to produce poetic dreams in those romantically inclined. All whose souls thirsted for aesthetic pleasures sang Italy, dreamed Italy. . . . "[20] Kozlov's intense interest merely reflected a widespread movement among the educated gentry. Some, like Ivan Kireevskij, simply "built various Italies in the air" – the day of Spanish castles being over.[21] Others, like Zinaida Volkonskaja[22] and Gogol', left to take up residence in Rome or Naples. It was supremely appropriate that, having planned the southern journey for ten years, Baratynskij should die by the Bay of Naples and only his corpse return to Russia.

It was an ideal land of which Russians dreamed – a land where art was the final arbitor of all opinion, "a wondrous land of sacred antiquities,/ The realm of songs and love." There, in Kozlov's conceit as in Baratynskij's, Tasso's octaves re-echoed still; there even the meanest walls in humble villages vibrated with colour while, untroubled by the crude realities of nineteenth-century Europe, gods and goddesses sported in countless splendid frescoes.

Had Kozlov followed Baratynskij to that "land of love, of wondrous harmony," he would perhaps have been sadly disappointed by the modest size and muddy hue of "deep-eyed Brenta." (Byron had much to answer for among Russians!)[23] As it was, nothing could touch the semi-magical name:

20. P. N. Sakulin, *Iz istorii russkogo idealizma: knjaz' V. F. Odoevskij* (Moscow, 1913), p. 5.

21. I. V. Kireevskij, *Sobranie sočinenij* (Moscow, 1911), vol. 2, p. 227.

22. See N. Gorodetzky, "Princess Zinaida Volkonskaya," *Oxford Slavonic Papers*, vol. 5 (1954), pp. 93-106, and Kozlov's two epistles to her of 1825 and 1838.

23. See *Childe Harold*, IV, XXVIII. Almost a century later, the poet Vladimir Hodasevič (1886-1939), also fascinated by Brenta's magical name, would make the same pilgrimage, and find it "a mean, rust coloured little stream."

Fly with me to Italy the delightful,
Aetherial friend, my fancy!
Land of love, of wondrous harmony,
Where the gay family of joys
Is fostered by a heavenly smile,
Italy, Torquato's land,
I have not, and will not, see you,
But how I love you, beautiful one!

Before me blow the midday roses,
Fragrant woods of lemon,
The green myrtle and grapevines,
And skies as blue as diamonds.
I see them . . . and tears flow gently . . .
Italy, your beauty is fair,
Like a first young dream of love,
Like the pure breathing of childhood.

From the heights fly gleaming waters,
Pearl-coloured – they roar over abysses;
Transparent singing choruses of visions
Mysterious, they seethe around your mountains;
Your seas, which know no squalls,
Are green, streaming and murmuring;
Your blessed evening, with its cool,
And aromatic pleasures, is an aerial feast.

The moon has risen, and the horizon glows
With sunset's last purple touch;
Cloudless, the high vault shines,
Quite covered by an iridescent shroud;
Sparkling, the bright ray scatters
A pink hue on the dreamy wave;
But it fades under night's chasuble;
The bay burns, silvered by the moon . . .
(ll. 1 – 32)

It was a glorious, resplendent Italy that Kozlov imagined – a fusion of Africa and Switzerland. Puškin, too, never left the confines of the Russian Empire, and dreamed of southern lands;

nor are there more vibrant or poignant evocations of the Adriatic waves in Russian poetry than in *Evgenij Onegin*, Chapter I, 49. Perhaps it was as well that Kozlov could not see the reality; the sight would have added nothing to his fantasy "A Venetian Night":

A spring night breathed
Light, southern beauty;
Quietly Brenta flowed by,
Besilvered by the moon;
The gleam of transparent clouds
Was reflected by its fiery wave,
And a sweet fragrance arose
From the green banks.

The azure vault, a languid murmuring,
And scarce breaking waves,
The rustle of wild oranges and myrtle,
The moon's beloved light,
Aromatic delights
Of flowers and fresh herbs
And, far off, the melody
Of Torquato's harmonious octaves –

All secretly infuses joy.
The senses perceive a wondrous world,
The heart beats, and youth hastens
To love's spring feast . . .
(ll. 1 – 20)

The pace is an easy *andante*, neither hurrying nor dragging. As in an Eastern print, a picture is created in a few deft strokes; one *hears* the sound of water and the distant singing.

Kozlov was content to use familiar formulae. Moonlit Brenta, gondolas, Tasso's octaves, all were far from original by 1824. But still in that year Russians seized on such information as the awkward Casimir Delavigne offered: "O Vénise . . . tes guerriers/ Ont perdu leur audace/ Plus vite que tes gondoliers/ N'ont oublié les vers du Tasse." Inevitably, Byron had flitted across the ghostly Brenta (see *Don Juan*, I, CXXI and *Childe Harold*, 4, 111), and how could the perspicacious Mme. de Staël not pause for a moment to listen to the Venetian boatmen (in *De l'Allemagne*, 2, 1)? It fell, as by right, to Puškin to sing another city, "where the nocturnal boatman does *not* sing Tasso!"[24] But Puškin was in a very small minority in entertaining such anti-Venetian or, rather, anti-Tassic sentiments. It was Kozlov's distinction, not to have invented the city of his fantasy, nor even to have re-discovered it, but to have given shape and colour to a mild national obsession.

Yet, as a second glance shows clearly, "A Venetian Night" was not without fresh elements. Of these, the most apparent to contemporaries was the fact that, not content with allusions or hints, Kozlov carried his story through. Seldom has the tale of a nocturnal flight to the sea been told with clearer or more pointed detail. One almost smells the warm south, while the plashing of oars is distinctly audible:

Gondolas glide across the waters,
Sparks fly beneath the oar,
The sounds of a tender barcarole
Are borne by a gentle breeze . . .

A girl appears on a flight of iron steps, the moon falling across her face. Her hair hangs loosely about her shoulders, and on her finger, by her slender waist, is an emerald talisman. She hurries into the waiting gondola, and is gone towards the sea. As the torch on the boat grows fainter the poem ends – after a brief salute to Byron. In development it is admirable. The poem moves with the girl's movements, hurrying when she hurries (a single line sees her from the steps into the boat), growing more moderate in pace when she reflects on the night's beauty – a beauty that she cannot admire:

Now the beauty comes out
Onto the iron porch;
Palely the moon sweeps its ray
Onto her sad face;
Among the careless, light-brown locks
Could be seen her slight waist,

24. Letter to M. P. Pogodin from S. P. Ševyrjov of 11.5.31; see V. Nabokov, *op.cit.*, vol. 2, pp. 181-5.

And on her snow-white fingers
An emerald talisman.

Already alone in the gondola
She moves towards that cliff
Where, under a high tower,
Roars the angry sea.
There, the singer's memory
Is sharper in her burning heart;
There, with the echo of earlier days,
Is the enchantment of love.

And in her reverie she heard
How the prophetic, midnight buoy
Mingled its copper sounding
With the waves' ceaseless roar.
Night's delight is not sweet to her,
The light, fresh breeze oppresses,
And her pensive eyes
Languidly gaze to the east.

Clouds stretch out in a bank
And the moon is overshadowed;
The clear vault is covered in mist;
Sudden darkness is alarming.
At once, the gondola is illumined,
And on high a star
Has rolled down to the east
And vanished in the gloom . . .
(ll. 49 – 81)

Deliberately, Kozlov brings into hearing the waves of which the girl thinks grimly (*s večnošumnoju volnoj*) and the hollow echo of her feet on the iron steps by the water (*na čugunnoe kryl'tso*). Like a beast, the sea is made to roar, the smooth "o" – "oi" rhymes of the boat's progress through calms giving way to more hostile rolling "r"s (*More burnoe revjot*). As the darkness and mists close the poem, the refrain – "Night's delight . . . " (*Ne mila ej . . .*) – reaches the reader once again. It is a musical device. And, of course, the poem's opening lines declare it to be song-like, the falling, feminine cadences and endings suggesting a lullaby. Colour and sound combine in a single impression: the fiery tint of waves, green banks, the black and azure sky, silver currents, light brown hair and an emerald talisman. Like a transposed Château d'If, the "high tower" looms above the water. In "A Venetian Night" the arts of painting and of music meet – both based on a sense of measure.

Religious and elegiac in tone, Kozlov's original verse is filled with such controlled flights of the imagination. The Dnieper is a potent source of inspiration; by its banks, "bold warriors" (*Vitjazi udalyje*) search their foes; along its wide, rushing expanses ships bear the goods of Byzantium. Nowhere in Kozlov's verse is the imagery, and the intensity with which he forms it, more striking than in poems that evoke the mediaeval past of Russia. "Kiev" has no parallel. The atmosphere, as in "Jaroslavna's Plaint," is that of a fairytale; only in the concluding lines does the key modulate to produce echoes of Batjuškov. Together with that poet's "On the Ruins of a Castle in Sweden" and Baratynskij's "Finland," certain lines of which it follows almost literally, "Kiev" belongs to the genre, much developed in Russia between 1815 and 1830, of the patriotic ode. Bogatyrs and blossoming princesses, Pečerskij's gleaming dome and cross, the Bayan and high towers, all is splendidly like a children's film. And always in the background is the murmuring of the wide Dnieper. It is as though, for Kozlov, rivers and running water of all kinds embodied sound and movement. Living on Petrovskaja Storona, across the Neva from the Winter Palace, it was a simple matter for him to stroll to the "granite embankment" sung in Puškin's *Bronze Horseman* (ll. 4–8), and listen to the Baltic waves lapping the shallow steps. Kozlov's love of moving water – and of a fictional mediaeval Russia – emerge unmistakably from this version of "Kiev" by Thomas B. Shaw, expatriate Professor of English Literature at St. Petersburg University from 1852 to 1861. The translation appeared in *Blackwood's Edinburgh Magazine*, January, 1844 (p. 80), and is published here for the second time only:

O Kieff! where religion ever seemeth
To light existence in our native land;

Where o'er Petcherskoi's dome the bright cross gleameth,
Like some fair star, that still in heaven doth stand;
Where, like a golden sheet, around thee streameth
Thy plain, and meads that far away expand;
And by thy hoary wall, with ceaseless motion,
Old Dnieper's foaming swell sweeps on to ocean.

The moon her soft ray on Petcherskoi poureth,
Its domes are shining in the river's wave;
The soul the spirit of the past adoreth,
Where sleeps beneath thee many a holy grave:
Vladimir's shade above thee calmly soareth,
Thy towers speak of the sainted and the brave;
Afar I gaze, and all in dreamy splendour
Breathes of the past – a spell sublime and tender.

There fought the warriors in the field of glory,
Strong in the faith, against their country's foe;
And many a royal flower yon palace hoary,
In virgin loveliness, hath seen to blow.
And Bayan sang to them the noble story,
And secret rapture in their breast did glow;
Hark! Midnight sounds – that brazen voice is dying –
A day to meet the vanish'd days is flying.

Where are the valiant? – the resistless lances –
The brands that were as lightning when they waved?
Where are the beautiful – whose sunny glances
Our fathers, with such potency, enslaved?
Where is the bard, whose song no more entrances?
Ah! that deep bell hath answered what I craved:
And thou alone, by these grey walls, O river!
Murmurest, Dnieper, still, and flow'st for ever.[25]

Only the patriotism, which is sustained throughout most easily, is real. Bayan the semi-mythical Slavic bard, the "sunny glances" which enslaved our forebears, even Vladimir's shade belongs to an imagined Russia. But the artifice is supremely apt where one touch

25. Stanza 2 is omitted.

of historical bluntness would break the whole design. The exalted feeling of pride in a lost Russia, like the sweep and colour of the river's "foaming swell," is exhilarating. It is hard, reading such verse, to see how Kjuxel'beker could have erred so grievously as to include Kozlov in his attacks against Žukovskij's "mournful, drawn-out elegies" in 1823 – 24.[26] To be sure, Kozlov was an elegiac. Essentially contemplative, his early epistles to Žukovskij certainly lack that vim which Kjuxel'beker praises in Bestužev's verse. But had Kozlov, like Žukovskij, "Entered into friendship with the German bards[27]?" To pretend any such thing is to ignore his artistic development in post-Decembrist years.

Kozlov had seen no action as an officer. How, then, could he describe, like Raevskij or Lermontov, the bloody realities of war? Nor can we justly blame him if he chose to dwell on other topics than the gore and slaughter of armed conflict. Better, under the circumstances, to accept his "warriors in the field of glory," ephemeral and bloodless though they be.

There are other objections to be made to "Jaroslavna's Plaint" (1825). The introduction of suitably archaic phrasing, the sketchy record of historical events, even the presence of consciously mediaeval figures on the walls of Putivl assure Kozlov of nothing more than a well-told legend. The poem in no way improves on the passage from *The Song of Igor's Campaign* on which it is openly based; why, then, was it written? The answer is easy to find. Žukovskij had translated the entire lay into modern Russian (that is, a Russian of his own making). No doubt he suggested a similar enterprise to Kozlov. Fortunately Kozlov had discretion enough to limit himself to a 65-line extract.[28]

Such moments of bathos are rare in Kozlov's verse. More common by far are the passages in which the reader, as well as Kozlov, escape from tiresome realities to a new world of emotional, if not intellectual freedom. (Kozlov's work is not remarkable for the richness of ideas embedded in it; it expressed no systematic, reasoned outlook on man or human destiny.)

26. See note 5.
27. E. A. Baratynskij, "Bogdanoviču" (1827), ll. 25-6.
28. See I. I. Kozlov, *Stixotvorenija* (Leningrad 1956).

Often, as has been seen, the escape is by water. Occasionally, it is overland, as in "Stances on the Caucasus and Crimea" and the versions of Mickiewicz's "Crimean Sonnets" (1828); and when overland, it is to the south and east.

Oriental motifs abound in Kozlov's work. Plashing fountains in eastern courtyards, dark-eyed odalisques and unseen sultans, nightingales and roses, all belong in a warm country of his own devising – for the description, despite such titles as "The Akkerman Steppes," "Baxčiseraj By Night," and "Harem Graves," fits neither the Crimea, nor the Near East, nor any known khanate or emirate of Central Asia. It was entirely fitting that he invent such a country. It was to answer his personal need; what more proper, then, than that it should wholly match his requirements? Here, to give an impression of its climate and topography, are three short extracts, one from "Čatyrdag," the second from "Baxčiseraj By Night" (both from "The Crimean Sonnets of Adam Mickiewicz"), and a third from Kozlov's admirable version of Moore's *Lalla Rookh* ("Romance," or "The Veiled Prophet of Khorassan"):

Like a Musulman, alarmed
By your lofty fortress,
I kiss your foot today.
You are the mast of the ship
Of Crimea, the universe's minaret
Eternal, O our mighty Čatyrdag!
You are Padishah over the mountains.
From distant cliffs, beyond the clouds,
Like Gabriel, watchman of Eden,
You sit among celestial bodies,
Beneath the gates of heaven;
The thunderclouds you tread underfoot;
Your broad cloak is the slumbering forest;
From clouds your turban is woven
And sewn by streaks of lightning. . . .
(ll. 1 – 15)

Kozlov was liberal in his use of Eastern words and phrases to evoke a desired exotic scene. "The Bajdars," "Alusta By Day," "The Road Above the Precipice of Čufut-Kale," "Aju-Dag," the titles alone sound like a latter-day travel brochure; and such, of course, was their function in 1828 – to lure Kozlov's readers from the cold north:

> *The prayer has passed away, already the* djamid *empties,*
> *The sound of* izan *has died in the stillness of night,*
> *Distance grows dark, and the evening glow blushes*
> *Like a ruby face.*
>
> *The silvery tsar of nights hastens to sweet slumber,*
> *To his delightful concubine in the aetherial silence,*
> *And the celestial harem gleams with an eternal beauty,*
> *Illumined by stars.*
>
> *Here a minaret drowses under a cypress's shade;*
> *And there the ridges of granite cliffs are darkened;*
> *There, in* Evlis's *divan, the inexorable spirits*
> *Do their dark deeds . . .*
>
> *(ll. 1 – 8, 13 – 17)*

(Kozlov provides these notes: *djamid* = mosque; *izan* = a prayer sung by muezzins in minarets; *Evlis* = Lucifer.)

Here, finally, is "Romance," from *Lalla Rookh*. The poem typifies a considerable group, each one of which is heavily ornamented with traditional motifs: moonlight on water or on ancient buildings, roses by towers or chambers (*xoromy*), fresh dew on grass, streams purling, fountains playing and, of course, nightingales. But in no other poem, translated or original, does Kozlov bring these motifs into such perfect harmony:

> *There is a quiet grove by swift brooks;*
> *And day and night a nightingale sings there;*
> *There, clear waters amicably flow*
> *And, in their beauty, red roses bloom.*
> *In that time when youth lured me to dream*
> *I loved often to walk through that grove;*
> *And admiring the flowers in the deep shadow*
> *I would hear songs – and my soul would thrill.*

In my life I shall not forget that green grove!
Places of sweet delight, how can we not love you!
But joy, too, goes quickly when summer comes,
And involuntarily reflection seizes the soul:
"Ah! in the green grove, by the swift springs,
Does the nightingale still sing as before?
And in autumn the red roses bloom still,
Above the clear stream?"

No, the roses have withered, the stream is cloudier,
And the nightingale cannot be heard now in the grove.
When, in their beauty, roses bloomed there,
They were plucked often, and made into crowns . . .
(ll. 1 – 20)

It is a suggestion, not an onslaught, of exotica; it is, quintessentially, the mood of Kozlov's translations of Thomas Moore.

Seldom did Kozlov write poems with contemporary settings. As Byron had little time for the England of dark, satanic mills, so he, too, in his way, averted his eyes from a Russia of serfdom and petty officialdom. Heroes, heroines and events are removed from a modern world of war and railways, contact with which, so Kozlov seems to have feared, would have corrupted or destroyed them. In "Hungarian Forest" and "To Balk-Polevoj" the distance is of space, in "A Venetian Night" and "Jaroslavna's Plaint" both of space and of time. But Kozlov was no less a patriot than Byron; and he was far more willing to give patriotism open expression. It reverberates throughout the introductions to "The Bride of Abydos" and *The Mad Girl* ("Moscow, Moscow, where joys and grief/ Embraced my young spirit, burning –/ Where the alarm of passions, like the sea in storm,/ So often agitated my life!/ You are the cradle of my memories,/ Of heart-felt reveries and bold hopes . . ."). Content with the social order, distressed by thought of change and turmoil, Kozlov felt a patriotism very different from that of Ryleev and Bestužev-Marlinskij – an eighteenth-century sentiment, in origin, as in expression.

Not lack of interest in political reform, however, but a deep and intensely personal interest in God and the life to come marked off Kozlov from his contemporaries and acquaintances. That interest left a profound stamp on his poetry; and it is fitting, many illustrations having been given of his verse as *escape*, that a passage of *God-centred* poetry – a prayer in verse, in fact – should end this brief survey of Kozlov's original poetry. It was composed on December 3, 1839, barely eight weeks before his death:

Forgive me, O God, my transgressions,
And renew my wearied spirit,
Let me suffer my torments
In hope, faith and love.

My sufferings are not fearful to me:
They are the pledge of holy love;
But grant that, with an ardent soul,
I may pour tears of penitence.

Behold my heart's poverty,
Grant the blessed ardour of Magdelene,
Grant the purity of John.

Let me carry my passing crown
Under the yoke of the heavy cross –
To the feet of our Saviour Christ.

CHAPTER FIVE
RELIGIOUS AND POLITICAL CONVICTIONS

To study Kozlov's verse is to study his reactions to a personal disaster; for his verse is formed of changing attitudes towards that same disaster. It is the sum of those attitudes. And blindness and paralysis, which caused him to write poetry in early middle age, also went far to determine its tenor and principal mood. There is no indication that Kozlov was especially pious until misfortune struck him, ruining a promising career; he was known, indeed, as a lion of the *salons*, a fine dancer and wit. Even his dutiful daughter, in her biographical fragment, does not deny that her father was something of a dandy.[1] Hardly surprisingly, blindness, new-found dependence on others and an uncertain but pitch-black future prompted urgent reflections on the nature of life on earth, and on man's relationship with God.

It is an understatement that Kozlov's verse is elegiac. As we have seen (Chapter 4), he was born into an age that developed the elegy as much as any other single genre. Misfortune could not be expected to produce gay or jovial poetry, and sadness, occasionally relieved by cheerfulness that says much for the strength of Kozlov's character, prevails throughout his work of every period. He was fortunate in his time of birth, as in his temperament (others might not have withstood the blow). Attuned to the melancholy of Karamzin and his school, Russians took readily to the gentle reflectiveness of "To Svetlana."

1. Ja. K. Grot, "K biografii, tvorenijam i perepiske I. Kozlova," *Izvestija Otdelenija Russkogo Jazyka i Slovesnosti*, 1904, bk. 2, p. 78.

"Elegy," however, is not a useful term here. In the strict sense of the word, Kozlov wrote no elegies, or poems on the occasion of a death; his "Elegy" (1835) turns out to be merely a free translation of Chénier's "Bel astre de Vénus, de son front délicat," while "A Rural Elegy" is a version of Millevoye's "Priez pour moi." Yet if "elegy" is taken as "a poem of serious, pensive or reflective mood," as lexicographers would have it,[2] then few of his poems are not elegies. Nor could it be otherwise, since elegy is seemingly "the form of poetry natural to the reflective mind."[3] Kozlov's was certainly that and, had not blindness made such a remark almost unseemly, Vjazemskij might well have said of him, as of Žukovskij, "Lord save him from being happy! For happiness would break his lyre's finest string."[4] Elegies occupy a central place in Kozlov's work, even though few pieces go by that simple heading. It is in "To Joy" (1823), "To Filon" (1827), and "Thou Dost not Dwell on Earth" (1828), not in the twelve ballads or the innumerable and often dull epistles, that Kozlov's preoccupations are best and most fully developed. Again, those preoccupations – with friendship's value and passage, with transience and death, with God and eternal life – can only rest on reminiscence; and memory is the theme most central to the elegiac form.

Memory looms large in Kozlov's verse. Few poems do not start or finish in pure reminiscence. But here one at once sees a difference between Kozlov's elegy and that of, for example, A. F. Merzljakov (whose verse he highly respected) or of Andrej Turgenev. How simple was Andrej Turgenev's search for "A sweetness in the memory of days passed happily."[5] For Kozlov, it is not simply a question of recalling sunny days of youth, when girls were always pretty and there were strawberries for tea. Nor is memory's function, as in Žukovskij's case, the vivid recreation of a wholly idealized, personal past. ("I consecrate myself to memory," Žukovskij wrote in 1815, "and truly do not fear the future . . . for the heart, the past is everlasting.")[6] It has, rather, a

2. *Chambers Twentieth-Century Dictionary* (London, 1948).
3. *The Oxford Companion to English Literature* (3rd ed., Oxford, 1946).
4. Letter to A. I. Turgenev of 1.5.19; see M. Ehrhard, *op.cit.*, p. 174.
5. Andrej Turgenev, "Elegija," l. 22.
6. Letter to Mar'ja Protasova of 29.3.15.

function at once more serious and more intimate – the complementing and supporting of imagination. For Kozlov, indeed, memory and the imagination come to fuse in a single, powerful sense; and that sense is prophetic as well as mnemonic. Prescience fills much of his verse – a bringing into focus of events still in the future, of sensations yet unknown. Reflecting on his past and the past of all men, Kozlov feels intimations of the future. This is the essence of his last elegy:

Why does the gentle breeze of spring
Breathe on me so lovingly,
The playful stream rush
And the tender rose glow red?
My heart is given up to worries,
Delight is not to be seized:
In the haze of an oppressive sleep
Joy for me will be – temptation!

To look, knowing my fateful lot,
On a world animated by beauty!.
And to know that I am already
Un-needed, forgotten in it . . .

But suddenly a light gleams at me from
The clouds, my soul hears a certain voice;
It is a greeting to me in moments
When my hair stands on end for fear!
And it seems that this is a heavenly sound,
And the murmuring dies on my lips,
And the languor of torment is sweet to me –
It has its own fascination!

"A light gleams from/ The clouds"; the verb is in the present. But has Kozlov seen that light and heard the voice? Or is this to come in the future? The question is both obscure and unimportant, as the whole passage of time is unimportant in Kozlov's elegiac schema. For in his verse, present and future meet, and the past is present in both. He writes so that this may be so, and, far from concentrating on the past like Žukovskij or Turgenev, he devotes himself to the future, as it were prematurely recalling it. By means of this one device Kozlov effectively annuls the transience of the present, extending it in both directions.

Inevitably, reflecting on the future, Kozlov often recalled the end of all futures, death, and a second, eternal life. For him, indeed (so large does heaven loom by 1830), death is essentially no more than a potential start on another and finer life. But literary fashion made its impress on that verse and, though he did not, like Žukovskij, erect a cult around the tomb (he had no Mar'ja Protasova, and lived with his wife in contentment), nevertheless the tomb, in its sentimental and melodramatic settings, emerges as one of the major *leitmotifs* of his original verse and translations alike. One might name twenty pieces which, like "By the Tomb of Cecilia M.," rest thematically and structurally on death and its results. Yet even that version of strophes 104 – 5 of *Childe Harold*, Canto Four, conveys neither a sense of lasting grief nor a sharp consciousness of death as the decay of living forms:

O grave, it is as though I knew your tenant,
And there breathes above us
A melody of days long gone;
But its sound, like the cry of distant storms
Beneath the clouds, their menaces quietened,
Is mournful, sacred. I sit
On your moss-grown stone . . .
(ll. 1 – 7)

Again, decay and death are *literary* leitmotifs, not philosophical, or even intellectual, concerns, in "Song of a Parrot" (1828); the poet's growing melancholy is the poem's theme, not roses or clouds or distant youth:

Forever, alas, forever the flower of lively
Youth, like a passing day, will dart from us!
Green May will return to the valleys
But there shall be no other spring for us.
Quickly pluck the flower, while morning's
Golden hour is not yet dark . . .
(ll. 9 – 14)

"The flower of youth," "quickly gather the flower," all are old friends, hackneyed expressions of that commonplace of all poetry – that roses are best gathered early. So, too, in "Elegy" (1830) and "To the Faithless Girl" (1835), Kozlov nods amicably to venerable tradition:

Yesterday in the wood, distracted by grief,
I sat alone, my heart broken.
When my spirit is restless from yearning,
I delight to converse with my soul.
Silence drowsed all around,
Fragrant spring breathed by me;
Scarce murmured the lazy rivulet,
And a butterfly settled on the flowers;
A gentle choir of birds, the evening fire of day
And the scent of grasses lulled me . . .
(ll. 1 – 10)

The passage leads, of course, to reflections of grief and illness, and so, by the well-worn path, to (literary) death.

Since the time when I parted with dreams
I have looked at God's world in tears;
Night after night, day after day
Flows by, flows by – and there is no life.
One thing remains in my dejected memory –
How our youth blossomed,
When happy, delightful,
You lived with me and for me.

. . .

But your hopeless glance has spread
A deathly cold around me,
And has poisoned in my troubled breast
All the heat of a celestial fire.
(ll. 25 – 32, 37 – 40)

Occasionally, as in "Yearning" (1835), a free version of Petrarch's second sonnet in the cycle on the death of Laura, death as a literary topos approaches the physical fact so nearly as to produce confusion in the reader:

> *I have already lost my hopes,*
> *And death, without pity, has taken*
> *Both that which I prided in life*
> *And that by which my life blossomed.*
> *(ll. 9 – 12)*

Did one not know that Kozlov or, rather, Petrarch, is speaking of a woman, it would be far from clear whether "death" is to be taken here metaphorically or literally.

There are, in brief, many poems in which Kozlov uses death, waning, fading as those words are employed by Millevoye, Chénier, La Fare – to evoke a mood or impression, not a sense of physical demise.

But there are more poems in which death is precisely that – an end to life on earth; and it is on what lies beyond the grave, not on the grave itself or, still less, the slow process of dying, that Kozlov chooses to dwell. Perhaps because he could not see them, graves were never a potent source of memories for him, as they were for Karamzin; for Kozlov, one must recall, the living and the dead were equally invisible. It was to another stimulus, the sound of living voices and of printed voices, poetry, that he most readily responded.

Beyond the grave lies God, and God, not death, is the dominating presence in the majority of Kozlov's original poems. The fact is as important as it is simple; for Kozlov, death is above all a beginning. What follows it, of course, is no simple question, and Kozlov's verse reflects the dilemma of all thinking men. If God created life, He also ordained its end, but what if peace and happiness do not lie beyond the grave? There is no blacker thought, in the whole of Kozlov's verse or correspondence, than that death may not, after all, herald a time of eternal joy. Žukovskij, indeed, all Kozlov's contemporaries regarded him as a firm Christian, one whose faith was unshakable. That view was not wholly justified by the reality of long but secret soul-searching. Nor is the verse itself devoid of clues to Kozlov's painful periods of doubt. Here in "An Elegy" (1830), as in the later epistle "To the Friend of my Spring, after a Long, Long Separation," doubts are resolved at the last in a faith the more urgent for having been challenged inwardly:

My spirit seethed, I asked myself:
What am I now? What was I? And will be?
I do not know myself, nor is there hope of knowing.
And where is the sage who could give me some answer?
I lay as if in darkness, without aim,
Nor is there a shadow of what I desire.
Having fallen around us, the destructive
Deceit of violent feelings casts its mist.

. . .

And doubt lay around my reasoning;
The years silver my wearied brow.
But do I know why I was born on earth?
What is my life? Those days that once were?
Like a stormy torrent, like running water,
I pass – I rush – I shall vanish forever.
My destiny – a grave; today a man,
Tomorrow dust. And can dust be eternal?
Or is a new life given us in death?
The hope flatters, but for me the secret is terrible.
O, who art thou, breathing eternity,
And whence art thou, incorruptible soul?
You reveal divinity to me within myself;
Leave sin – I will believe in thee.
Who could commit the pure spirit to – a body?
Who ordered you to bear – a corpse?
I am a son of sin – and the divine image!
(ll. 15 – 22, 33 – 49)

One of the basic patterns of Kozlov's original verse, it was earlier seen, is that of the epistle "To V. A. Žukovskij": memories of a happy past give way to reflections on the present; in their turn, those wearisome thoughts, sometimes verging on despair, give way to simple faith and hope in a celestial future. (That future, it may be added, is to be shared by *all* men; Kozlov reserved no special place in heaven for himself or the world's sufferers – an essentially Christian attitude.) Modified in various ways, that pattern re-occurs in numerous pieces of every period. Sometimes, as in "The Reapers" (1836) and "The Oak" (1836), recollections of a happier past loom so large as to overshadow thoughts of a present grief; sometimes, as in "My Prayer" (1833) and "Stances" (1838), gloomy thoughts of personal misfortune occupy no more than a couplet. Always, the emotional effort is to stifle remaining doubts of God's infinite goodness and mercy.

No less than God the merciful, the image of Kozlov himself – the poet shaken by disaster – is omnipresent in his verse. What if disaster is the rule of life?

O dear friend! By what chance
Has suffering met with you,
And the earth's transitory torments
With an aetherial angel of love?
Or do sadness and grief await us all,
As a stormy wind awaits swimmers at sea?
Must she suffer, in whose heart
Breathes paradise?[7]

What if one's life on earth does not merit eternal life? Reading Kozlov's adaptation of four separate passages from Dante's *Divina Commedia*, known simply as "The Dream" (1832), one cannot doubt but that he pondered on "the land of torment":

With Dante I wandered in the land of torment,
One vision gave way to another;
There howls and weeping fly to the dismal
Hearing; flashing, an evil spirit burns my eyes –
And in their sinful glow, in a close passage,
The shades of the suffering appeared before me.
Now I see, alarmed by this wondrous dream,
How Farinat, burning in his grave,
Has raised himself, casting his conceited glance

7. "To – " (1838), ll. 15-22. Addressed to Countess Fiquelmont.

On the horror of torments – haughty rebel!
It is not his fiery grave that crushes him –
It is the shame in his native land.
I see blood, I hear the voice of torment . . .

. . .

And a hurricane roars, like an abyss in a raging sea,
And shades rush by – the fateful hurricane
Blends with the hum of their murmuring: "Grief! Grief!"
(*ll.* 15 – 27, 34 – 6)

Interesting light is thrown on Kozlov's attitude towards the afterlife by unpublished materials preserved in *Puškinskij Dom*, in Leningrad. Among these, in the former collection of the bibliophile and scholar Ja. K. Grot, is a curious prose-poem, written in French, and entitled "A un père."[8] In the same folder is a monologue, note-like in form, consisting of a series of exhortations and a prayer to the Virgin Mary. The poem and the monologue do not appear to have been written at the same time. Here, first, is the prose-poem, dedicated to Lamartine:

O Lamartine! O toi que le Ciel a formé
de tout ce qu'il avait de pur et de suave!
Se peut-il? Se peut-il, ton âme douce et grave
est triste de la vie et pour avoir aimé.
C'est donc triste d'aimer? Quand ta lyre divine
berçait l'enfant joyeux par ton coeur, adoré,
la mort la regardait; de sa piquante épine
elle cherchait le Coeur et l'arbuste pleure.
Père, console-toi! ta fille bien-aimée
est montée ou la mort n'entre que désarmée!
C'est Dieu qui l'a voulu, c'est Dieu qui l'aimera,
ainsi ne pleure plus, père, Il te la rendra.
Une petite fille de onze ans
Ondine Valmore, 1836.

The piece presents two main problems, those of authenticity

8. Preserved under reference *Fond* 88 (*Arxiv Ja. K. Grota*), Op. 2, N. 39.

and of dating. The poem is not in Kozlov's hand; more significantly, it is not in the hand of his daughter either. Nor is it the hand of Ja. K. Grot, in whose archive it remained until acquired for the Academy of Sciences' new literary institute by B. Modzalevskij. Yet Grot was a careful scholar, and plainly had no doubts as to the piece's authenticity. Neither, to judge by the holdings records of *Puškinskij Dom*, did Modzalevskij.[9] And the tone and content of the poem raise no doubts whatever – the invocation of the author of "Le Lac," which Kozlov adapted as "Noč' na reke" (1821), the concern with sufferings to be overcome, the religiosity, all suggest Kozlov. There is no good reason for supposing that Grot made a major error.

Dating presents a more serious problem. There is no mistaking the "1836." Nor is it possible to misread *Une petite fille de onze ans. Ondine Valmore*. But Ondine, daughter of Marceline-Félicité Desbordes-Valmore (1785 – 1859), whose amiable romances and elegies enjoyed a great vogue in St. Petersburg on the fall of Napoleon, was not eleven in 1836. Nor did she die at that tender age, but survived her marriage to a Jacques Langlais, in 1851, by two years, thus reaching the age of thirty-one.[10] The possibility remains, of course, that Kozlov refers to a second Ondine Valmore. The theory, however, is hardly convincing, especially when it is borne in mind that Kozlov certainly knew Marceline Desbordes-Valmore's elegies – "A Délie," for example, and "L'Attente" and "A mes enfants"[11] – and was probably acquainted with her daughter's verse also. Ondine was sickly all her life. Possibly a false rumour of her death reached St. Petersburg where her mother had been a minor literary celebrity. Further speculation is useless.

9. I am indebted here to Professor Marfa Malova, of *PD*.

10. See J. Boulanger, *Ondine Valmore: Les bibliophiles fantaisistes* (Paris, 1909); also *Les cahiers d'Ondine Valmore*, intro A. Caplain (Paris, 1932).

11. See M. Longinov, "Materialy dlja polnogo sobranija sočinenij I. I. Kozlova," *Russkij arxiv* (1864), bk. 2, pp. 230-33; bk. 3, pp. 110-12. "Marceline Desbordes-Valmore," wrote her grandson, Victor Langlais, in the *Grande dictionnaire universelle* (Larousse), vol. 6, p. 529, "avait une fille, mélancholique et gracieuse poète comme sa mère, mais à qui la mort coupa les ailes lorsqu'elle commençait à peine à les déployer." Something of the daughter's work may be inferred from such titles as "La mort d'une fleur," "La mort du papillon" and "Fleur séchée."

Again, the sheer simplicity of the religious attitude reflected in the piece is arresting. Personified, Death walks into a nursery, fatal thorn in hand; but Death is unmanned where Ondine has been taken or, rather, called by God. The father is assured that he and his daughter shall meet in a better world, and the phrasing of the notion, even the tone of its expression, perfectly echo a soliloquy of the monk (*The Monk*, stanza 9):

> *Creator of all! my child,*
> *With my beloved one, not yet forgotten,*
> *Live in Your holy land:*
> *And I, perhaps, shall be with them,*
> *And there they are forever mine!*
> (*ll. 17 – 21*)

God creates life and destroys it, separates and reunites us. As always, Kozlov's relationship with Him is both straightforward and highly personal. There is no shadow in his verse of Jahweh, an angry God; rather is He (as Kozlov informs Žukovskij in his earliest extant epistle) "unseen, mysterious but *comprehensible*." The line is curious, when one remembers that elsewhere in the same epistle God's ways are held to be "beyond the power of human reason"; one wonders in what sense Kozlov found his Creator so comprehensible (*ponjatnyj*). Perhaps the best interpretation is also the most obvious – that he understood God's purpose for himself, which was to suffer gratefully. Kozlov was blessed with ample stores of "negative capability," and one can but envy the confidence with which he could pronounce, "He is my father, not a Judge."

It was, as we have seen, this enviably serene façade that he presented to the world. Contemporaries, it was seen, accepted without hesitation Žukovskij's moving picture of Kozlov the minor martyr, "blind, immobile, continually suffering but deeply touched by a Christian humility. . . . "[12] But was Kozlov's faith truly so simple and sublime, so free from all questioning? Grot's papers show that it was not. Here are a series of notes and

12. Žukovskij's obituary notice on Kozlov appeared in *The Contemporary*, 1840, vol. 18, no. 2, pp. 83-8.

exhortations that, one may be sure, Kozlov had no mind to publish; they are intensely personal:

> Abnégation, détachement, sacrifice et fermeté! Elle accepte tout pour se faire la servante des pauvres et la mère de l'orphelin ... les pauvres, les malheureux ont toujours le même droit sur elle. La charité rend le coeur si bon – Donner sa vie à l'humanité qui souffre – sa religion est tout amour et indulgence, car la veillesse [*sic*], l'enfance et la douleur ont besoin d'être traités aux affections. Et celle qui le donne à des êtres faibles et souffrants doit avoir encore une force qui [--], une douceur inaltérable. Porter au mourant, à l'affligé une parole de consolation et d'esperance. Elle n'est pas retenue que par la pensée de ses devoirs. Détachement de tout! Tout est à Dieu, tout est aux pauvres. C'est que pour accepter cette vie de privations d'une part et de devouement de l'autre il faut tant de force d'âme, de simplicité et de Coeur!
>
> . . . . .
>
> Oh! Marie! Concue sans péché, priez pour nous qui avons recours à vous! 1836 9 decembre. Bénie sois, grâce à toi, ma Délivrance! Débris du *passé* qui ne *troubleront* plus *l'avenir*; restes du [--] homme naufragé ds. la soirée du 8 decembre par excès de faiblesse subite et sauvé pour renaître à la force, au calme, aux idées *tranquilles*. Sur le même sujet qui pouvait jadis bouleverser. – Toujours à des idées d'un amour pur de toute personalité, de dévouement et de constance.
>
> Liberté! Amour pur et guérison complète. Grâce à Marie!

There is one more item in the same folder – a single sheet of dark brown paper, torn at the centre. On it are written the following words: "L'amour c'est le Ciel, l'harmonie c'est l'amour, la pensée c'est l'harmonie, la vie c'est la pensée!" There is also a pen-drawing of an Orthodox cross placed on a boulder and, beneath: "Oh! Marie! Concue sans péché, priez pour nous qui avons recours à vous!"[13]

Together, the notes, the prayer and the prose-poem give us

13. *PD., Fond* 88, p. 2, N. 39.

Ivan Ivanovič Kozlov (1779-1840)

Byron, 1818

A setting for Kozlov's walks

A. S. Puškin

N. A. Karamzin

Admiralty Building, St. Petersburg

E. A. Baratynskij

Prince P. A. Vjazemskij

V. A. Zukovskij

K. F. Ryleev

The Winter Palace and the Old Admiralty, St. Petersburg

good reason to question the idealized creation of Žukovskij's making – Kozlov the perfect Christian. Of course Kozlov "sincerely believed in a world beyond the grave," as Professor I. Glikman gallantly admits.[14] It was precisely because he so desired and counted on that world that he knew moments of awful doubt. Perhaps it is to one such long moment, that of December 8, 1836, that he alludes in the passage above; straining for perfect faith, Kozlov achieved the opposite of what he had intended. Nor is it difficult to understand why he should need such a perfect faith. His disease was incurable, and wasting paralysis gained gradually on all his limbs. He had good reason and no lack of opportunity to ponder the questions of immortality and personal salvation. Heaven and love might be synonymous for him, but harmony and thought most certainly were not. As to the grand equation by which thought balances life, one can merely remark that had *thinking* brought Kozlov unclouded faith (or even harmony within himself), then an element characteristic of his verse would have been entirely missing. That element is the tension of uncertainty. Reflections on the past and present, tensions produced by these, dispersal of all doubts and tensions – such is the pattern underlying no less than a half of all Kozlov's original poems. The equations are as quixotic as the prayer is, in its way, pragmatic.

One might name twenty poems in which faith, having been questioned either rhetorically ("Stances," 1838) or with no view to literary effect ("An Elegy," 1830), emerges at the last triumphant. The images are used repetitively: the "bark of hope" that has been smashed, the "earthly chains" that shall be broken, "God's world" and "the light of God" (*Božij svet*). Three examples may suffice to illustrate the triumph of belief. Here, first, are "Stances." Literary effect is sought no less openly than in Puškin's "The Prophet" or Venevitinov's "The Poet"; "fire flashes" in "th'aetherial gloom," birds tremble and Kozlov himself senses "a holy fear." Christianity, he seems to wish to emphasize, can be a dramatic affair!

Yesterday, surrounded by darkness,

14. "I. I. Kozlov," *Poln. sob. stix.* (Leningrad, 1960), p. 25.

I lay reflecting on my couch, all sleep forgotten;
Silently a fire, to me inspiring,
Burned in my breast with poetry.

Meanwhile a storm had gathered
In th'aetherial gloom – fire flashed from the clouds,
And lightning fled by in a stream,
Like a wild, white-maned steed.

And the crash of the celestial chariot
Threw a holy fear on all,
And wild beasts hid themselves, and birds,
Trembling in nest and den.

And I . . . my spirit flies to the Maker,
Burning with lightning's fire,
While my mind, troubled, reflects
More freely, when the thunder roars.

Moved by a heavenly delight,
I was not the slave of earthly chains
But a wondrous and tuneful organ
In the spheres' enormous harmony.

And God prophesies by me with more might
And in my flaming thoughts,
Than by the roaring storm around,
Or in divine horrors of night.

On a calmer plane, the same message is to be found in "To the Friend of my Spring, After a Long, Long Separation":

My Friend! Perhaps the mournful shade
That has darkened my life
Alarms you – but it has illumined my soul
With a secret strength.
I am not wholly destroyed by fate –
The indestructible is with me:
My sad lot is dear to me,
I have learned to accomodate grief;
Suffering sanctified feeling,

Which misfortunes cannot poison.
All that it loved my heart still loves,
Wishing to live by what it lived.
And it entrusts itself, as before,
To a hope that does not deceive.
Love is far removed from earthly alarms –
A Beatific beauty; and in love is God Himself.
(ll. 68 – 83)

Here, finally, is "The First Meeting." Again, the joys and rewards of pain are deemed worthy of emphasis, not the pain itself. In no other poem does Kozlov speak so openly of patience, his "blessing in misfortunes"; it is, he implies, no less a virtue than love – for it, too, is the instrument by which angels can move us:

There is a delight in the sad darkness,
And there are two secrets, by the power
Of which suffering on earth can blossom.
One of these is in sacred love:
To love what makes the earthly world good for us
Is for the heart a celestial dream:
The other secret drives out horror:
Patience *is a blessing in misfortunes . . .*
(ll. 26 – 33)

Perhaps it is best to allow Kozlov to speak for himself on the question of religion. It is, after all, the matter that most deeply concerned him and on which, therefore, he most wished to be clear in his verse. To comment on verse that is prayer-like in form adds little to that verse, if it is adequate, while the dangers of misinterpretation do not need labouring. To read the poem entitled simply "My Prayer" (1833) is to grasp much of the essence of that verse by Kozlov where Byron's spirit plays no role:

O Thou whom I dare not praise,
Maker of all, my Saviour;
But Thou for whom I burn
With my whole heart and soul!

Who, by Thy heavenly will,
Hast overcome sins by love,

. . . .

Hearken, Christ, to my beseeching.
My soul illumine with Thyself.
And, like the sea's swell, calm my stormy
Agitated heart;
Receive me into Thy abode –
I am the prodigal son, thou my father;
And, as over Lazarus, my Saviour,
O, shed tears over me!

It is not my cross that appals me –
By faith, suffering blooms,
Crosses are sent by God Himself
Our cross gives God to us;
Ready to follow thee, I pray
That my spirit may be strengthened;
I wish to wear the crown of thorns –
For Thou Thyself didst bear it, Christ.

Grant that by holy faith
I scatter passion's mists
And, with a soul unclouded,
Forgive my foes and love my friends;
That hope's comforting light
May always penetrate my heart;
That I remember kindly actions,
And forget insult.

For Žukovskij, the link between the true faith and proper government was never open to question. The French revolution of 1830, "excluding God from life,"[15] had lowered human dignity; what more natural than that Russia, the true tsardom, should also be the land of the inner Church? Echoes of the "third Rome" theory, propounded in the sixteenth century by the good monk Filofej, resound with startling clarity in Žukovskij's correspond-

15. Letter to A. I. Turgenev of mid-January, 1833; see Ehrhard, *op.cit.*, p. 199.

ence of the revolutionary *annus mirabilis*, 1848. This time, he and his family were obliged to flee from Europe, "a volcano that may now erupt at any minute."[16] Politically and religiously, Holy Russia stood as a bulwark against the mounting tides of anarchy; such, after Münchengratz, was the official Russian view.

Kozlov accepted this political position, and concurred with those opinions so pellucidly expressed by the now ageing former tutor to the Tsar. The fact is the only starting point for any just assessment of his views on politics. Kozlov was a royalist and, despite humanitarian instincts that blindness only strengthened, a most reliable supporter of the social status quo; he was a gentleman but also, and more apparently, a *dvorjanin* – a member of the landed stratum of Russian society.

But there is one more basic point where the question of Kozlov's political conservatism is concerned, and it is one that Soviet commentators have not cared to emphasize. Kozlov did not *consciously* link autocracy with the Orthodox Church. Nor, indeed, does he appear to have given serious thought, after the early 1820s, to the rightness or wrongness of tsarism. Rather did he connect the two instinctively. No less unconsciously, he later chose to pass in silence over controversial topics, and political topics in particular, when writing poetry. It does not suit Soviet scholarship that this should be the case (for to have chosen to ignore political issues clearly demonstrates Kozlov's deplorable political and civic "immaturity"). Efforts were therefore made, earlier this century, to stress the poet's sympathies with radicals of the years 1820 – 25; all Soviet editions of his verse have made the point with some finesse. Issue will be taken, later, with the notion that Kozlov was ever more than temporarily interested in theories of revolution, as with the yet more curious idea that he regarded the prospect of approaching social turmoil and political upheaval with anything but deep distaste. First, however, we may usefully consider that sphere in which Kozlov's political activity was most apparent – the sphere of literary and journalistic groupings.

It is a commonplace of literary history that in Russia literary and political polemics have always tended to fuse; only in writing

16. Letter to the Tsarevič of mid-September, 1848; *ibid.*

of a spiritual nature, indeed, has Russian literature ever been free of what we, in the West, term "political undertones."[17] There, literature is part of politics. Thus Del'vig's and Baratynskij's attempted neutrality in literary polemics of pre-Decembrist St. Petersburg at once reflected – and was seen to reflect – a political *prise de position*. It was quite in vain that Kozlov sought to avoid, in the twenties, social and political commitment *as a writer*. In all events, neutrality was enmity to such as Bestužev-Marlinskij and Ryleev;[18] but how could Kozlov hope to be neutral – he, a former assistant to the Commandant of Moscow, the close friend of Žukovskij and so of the Establishment? The impossibility grew clear soon after he had joined the literary society now known as The Learned Republic.[19]

In influence, in membership and by virtue of the sharpness of the struggle that took place between their members, two literary societies stood out in pre-Decembrist St. Petersburg. Until the founding of the Northern Society in 1821 – and until long after that date for many whose interests were primarily literary, not political – the twin cultural centres of the capital were the Petersburg Society of Lovers of Letters, Sciences and Arts (PSLLSA) and the Free Society of Lovers of Russian Letters (FSLRL). The first came increasingly to represent reaction, the latter, political radicalism. Kozlov became a member of this last, "progressive" society on December 15, 1824.[20] Jazykov, Polevoj and Griboedov, poet, journalist and dramatist, also became members on that day. To belong to either society was plainly to forsake pretensions to political *or* literary neutrality. Kozlov does not seem to have weighed the consequences of his joining or, if he did so, left no written indication of his reasoning. At one stroke he became involved in rivalries extending both to literary journals (where he might soon wish to place his work) and to those St.

17. Kozlov's religious poetry, it must be stressed, placed him in the camp of the conservatives, almost of the reactionaries; so it seemed, at least, to radicals.

18. See M. V. Nečkina, *Russia in the Nineteenth Century* (Ann Arbor, 1952).

19. V. G. Bazarov's excellent study *Učonaja respublika* (that is, the FSLRL) can only be recommended. It appeared in Moscow in 1964.

20. *Ibid.*, p. 444.

Petersburg *salons* where he might care to pass an evening. Evenings could only be less tranquil, even if blindness saved him from personal insult; for personal rancour and professional rivalry flourished in unison, epigrams often verging on plain calumny.[21]

At least it was a flourishing society to which he had sacrificed his time and as it soon proved, his peace of mind. Having once, in Radiščev's day, been a progressive force, by 1824 the PSLLSA was nothing if not a centre of reaction. Small wonder that Kozlov chose to join the rival group, the PSLLSA being, in the words of a Russian critic, "merely . . . an archaic assembly of third-rate littérateurs-cum-dilettantes."[22] Yet it was not quite this. In 1817 the ailing society enjoyed a brief *risorgimento*, Krylov, Žukovskij and Batjuškov all joining in that year. Such spirit of reform as these introduced, however, was soon enough stifled by A. E. Izmajlov, in whose journal *The Well-Meaner*, so justly mocked by Puškin,[23] there was "no space for the darling-poets . . . the Romantics."[24] By 1824 the FSLRL was among the most progressive of Russian literary societies.

Kozlov played an active part in the society's functioning. Together with pieces by Puškin, Baratynskij, Del'vig and Vjazemskij, his verse appeared in *Son of the Fatherland*, the journal that was the society's main literary organ. At the meeting of March 17, 1825, his "Imitation of Tasso" was read, probably by the obliging Del'vig, and approved unanimously.[25] And within two months his name was firmly connected (by members of the rival group) with those of Del'vig and Baratynskij.

21. On "Figljarin"-Bulgarin's vicious innuendoes against Puškin, whose Negro ancestor, so Bulgarin claimed, had been bought by a merchant seaman for a bottle of rum, see V. Nabokov., *op.cit.*, vol. 3, pp. 435-6. Puškin, needless to add, retaliated splendidly.

22. V. N. Orlov, "Istorija Vol'nogo Obščestva Ljubitelej Slovesnosti, Nauk i Xudožestv," *Poety-Radiščevtsy* (Moscow, 1935), p. 143.

23. "I know: some would make ladies
Read Russian. Horrible indeed!
Can I imagine them
With *The Well-Meaner* in their hands?
My poets, I appeal to you!"
Evgenij Onegin, chap. III, XXVII.

24. *The Well-Meaner* (*Blagonamerennyj*), 1823, no. 21, p. 16.

25. V. G. Bazanov, *op.cit.*, p. 434.

With each successive month of 1824 – 25, the FSLRL became more consciously a centre of political planning. Few of the secret or semi-secret societies that opened in Russian cities in the months following the wars against Napoleon were either purely literary or wholly political in nature.[26] And FSLRL, like others, encouraged the discussion of both topics, but the emphasis moved steadily towards practical politics in 1825. Some premonition of that move was the appointment, nine years before, of Fjodor Glinka as an active member (*dejstvitel'nyj člen*). The consequences of his presence were predictable. A member of the Union of Welfare and virtual controller of the Lodge of Chosen Michael,[27] from which came numerous future Decembrists, he seemed to embody FSLRL's growing political significance. Kozlov remained on amicable, though not intimate terms with the man at whose instances, and under whose direction, the literary society took on a political colouring.

That colouring, however, was not made obvious to those outside. Considerable efforts were made, indeed, to preserve the society's literary respectability, as is suggested by the early history of *The Emulator of Enlightenment*, a literary journal founded and supported by its members. Scrupulously legal in their actions, the editors first sought permission from the censorship department of the Ministry of Justice. Permission was granted; and only then, in June, 1821, was the journal set to press. "In the beginning," Pletnjov records, "there were almost no writers. But after the Minister for Popular Enlightenment had managed to obtain a special statute we, that is Del'vig, Baratynskij and I, were elected members too."[28]

Such, then, was the society of which Kozlov became a member twelve months before the revolution of 1825. Glinka remained the chairman. Kozlov was certainly acquainted with his poems advocating regicide.[29] It is of note, indeed, that Kozlov was elected on Glinka's personal recommendation. No matter how luke-warm

26. On this subject, see A. G. Mazour, *op.cit.* pp. 64-6.

27. V. G. Bazanov, *op.cit.*, pp. 57-74.

28. *Perepiska Ja. K. Grota s P. A. Pletnjovym*, 3 vols. (St. Petersburg, 1896), vol. 2, p. 254.

29. "Opyty dvux tragičeskix javlenij," "Otryvok iz Farsalii" (1817-18).

his own radical inclinations, then or later, it cannot be denied that of his own free will he came into a dangerous proximity of those who were shortly afterwards exiled or hanged.

What, then, of those inclinations, so plain, in the view of I. Glikman, in "The Captive Greek in A Dungeon" (1822)? The radicals' case rests chiefly on Kozlov's known meetings with N. I. Turgenev from 1817 to 1820. Nikolaj, second of the four Turgenev brothers, was an acquaintance of Kozlov of long standing. Having been two years at the *Pension Noble* of Moscow University, it was to that institution that he repaired in 1808. There followed three years in Göttingen, where he acquired a taste for German literature, law and political economy. On his return to Russia, in 1812, he was offered a post in the Chancery of the Minister of Finance. 1813 – 16 he spent in the occupied West, where his concern with legal matters, and legal reform in particular, grew strong. He continued his career in the Ministry of Finance, then (1821 – 24) in the Ministry of Law. Moscow, an interest in Western literatures, common connections in the service, such were the links between Kozlov and one who escaped arrest and exile for his part in the Liberal movement only because he chanced to be abroad in December, 1825.[30]

It is clear from Kozlov's diary for 1818 that the two met not infrequently, and discussed literature and politics. It was in vain that Turgenev, "a fine, cultured fellow . . . of broad intellect and broad ideals,"[31] attempted to interest him in his *Essay at A Theory of Law*, on which he was then working. Nor does Kozlov record his opinion of Turgenev's plan of reform – a plan that was to extend over twenty-five years or more, and counted, for its implementation, on the Tsar's cooperation.[32] (Turgenev was a

30. Nicholas I personally wrote to Metternich, "the old king of Saxony," and to the British Foreign Office in an attempt to have Turgenev extradited; but Turgenev found a safe refuge in England. See *Meždutsarstvie 1825 goda i vosstanie dekabristov v memuarax i perepiske členov tsarskoj sem'i*, compiled by B. Syroečkovskij (Moscow, 1926), pp. 181-2. It was to visit his exiled brother that A. I. Turgenev came to England in September, 1828, so establishing a link between Kozlov and Thomas Moore; see chapter 7.

31. "Dnevnik Kozlova," *Starina i novizna*, 1906, no. 11, p. 39.

32. *Dnevniki N. I. Turgeneva za 1811-1816 gg.*, ed. E. Tarasov (St. Petersburg, 1913), vol. 2, p. 333.

"gradualist," as he himself put it, in 1818.)

It would be pleasant to be able to suggest that Kozlov was inspired to embrace those "broad ideals." The facts, however, prompt one to accept an opposite opinion. There is no reason to suppose that his interest in politics was ever serious enough, in a practical way, to make him think of joining such secret societies as the Unions of Welfare and Salvation, even, that is, if he had been invited to do so.[33] Certainly he was happy to discuss with Nikolaj Turgenev, and perhaps others, "revolutions English, French, American, happy and unhappy. . . ."[34] But it by no means followed that he also supported revolution. And while sympathetic towards Bestužev's and Ryleev's cause, he played no active part whatever in the radical and ever more practical movement that led to Senate Square. Liberal "to the extent that this is required of every enlightened man,"[35] Kozlov made no move to transform ideals into effective action. Even had he wished to participate in the events of December 14, blindness would not have allowed it.

Soviet commentators, notably E. Medvedeva, E. Kuprejanova and I. Glikman, have done the best they can with the few poems by Kozlov with any real political significance or content: "The Captive Greek in a Dungeon," "The Young Singer" (1823) and possibly "Good Night!" (1824). A somewhat hopeless case is well reflected in Glikman's suggestion, in an otherwise admirable outline of the poet's activity, that Kozlov "left the subjective" and "approached the political" sphere in the post-Decembrist years. Not only do all three pieces named above date from before the rising; even in them, political radicalism is noticably absent. Interest in the fate of Ypsylanty and, later in 1821 – 22, in the Greek cause in general, was widespread among the educated Russian gentry. Ypsylanty, after all, had been a Colonel in the Russian army, and gathered his forces, before marching south to the Morea, in the Southern Headquarters of the Imperial Forces.

33. Puškin remained in ignorance of the Northern Society, being held by I. I. Puščin *inter alia* to be too garrulous.

34. *Dnevniki i pis'ma N. I. Turgeneva* (Petrograd, 1921), vol. 3, p. 312; under January 8, 1822.

35. B. N. Čičerin, "Iz moix vospominanij," *Russkij arxiv*, 1890, bk. 1, p. 515.

Were not the Greeks "co-religionaries"? Alexander hesitated in Laibach until Metternich reminded him of his exalted duty – to maintain order in Europe. In his Kisinjov diary for April 2, 1821, Puškin recorded his sorrow and disgust on learning of Ypsylanty's defeat at Dragašan. Like many others in both Russia and the West, he had been sure, when the rising broke out in Patras and the islands, that soon "the Turks would leave the flowering land of Hellas . . . to the rightful heirs of Homer and Themistocles."[36] If Kozlov was slightly disgusted by Ypsylanty's treatment at the hands of Austria-Hungary (the hopelessly defeated general was kept in prison for seven years), that feeling was by no means unusual, or even remarkable, among his class and generation. Here is Kozlov's response to that imprisonment:

Holy motherland,
O my lovely land!
Constantly dreaming of you,
I long for you in spirit.
But alas, in captivity
I am constrained here,
And on the field of battle
Do not fight.

Night and day I have tormented
Myself over your fate,
The sound of your chains
Has rung in my heart.
Can those alike
Forget their brothers?
Oh, either to be free
Or not to be at all!

And boldly, with friends,
Like a destructive storm,
We flew into battle

36. Puškin typified his generation in enthusing over Ypsylanty's ill-conceived campaign; of the details of the Hetaeria, as of the true situation in the Balkans, he was wholly ignorant; see his letter to D. Davydov of mid-March, 1821, *A. S. Puškin*, vol. 9, p. 26.

For a sacred cause.
But alas, in captivity
I am constrained here,
And on the field of battle
Do not fight.

In confinement I do not know
How the war rages;
I await news –
News flies past.
Rumour of murders spreads,
The sign of terrible revenge;
My native blood is shed,
But I am not there!

Ah, Freedom, your fruits ripen
Amidst the storm!
Like a flaming dawn,
Your bright day glows!
Let me suffer,
An unknown prisoner;
Only let me see you free,
Lovely land.

Sustained oratory complements and confirms the exalted subject matter. Straightforward and declamatory in tone, the piece achieves its end – to present the pathos of the prisoner's situation. But who is this "unknown prisoner"? Ypsylanty has undergone a sea-change. Nor are immediate, contemporary political events in Greece easily recognizable from Kozlov's idealized description. Turkish garrisons were massacred, Phanariots killed in Constantinople; there were murders and "terrible revenges." But these and other happenings are seen through distant eyes, and somewhat generalized by poetic diction. Greece is "the holy motherland"; Ypsylanty's ill-trained and poorly disciplined columns "flew into battle . . . like a destructive storm!" Under Kozlov's gentle touch, the bloodiest of issues become at once less real and more simply colourful. Nonetheless, the message of the final quatrain is unmistakable, and is nobly expressed – it is hard to capture in English the terseness, almost the curtness of Kozlov's staccato lines.

It remains to consider the versions of Thomas Moore's "The Minstrel Boy" (translated as "The Young Singer"), and of strophe 13 of the first canto of *Childe Harold* ("Good Night!"). Revolutionary pathos, if there is any, is borrowed from the British. Historical events can, of course, be highly relevant to modern questions, and it was with that thought that Ryleev undertook his *Reflections* (1824). But is one to see in the tale of "The Minstrel Boy" even covert allusions to the Russia of Arakčeev, the Russia of "military colonies," serfdom and drudgery? If so, it must be said, the connections are not obvious; Kozlov added a footnote to the piece, on its first publication in *Literary News* (1823, no. 43). "In the time of the Normans' onslaught on Ireland," he remarked simply, by way of explaining the setting. Again, it was a fabulous, dramatic world of "sharp swords" and "golden harps" that met his readers' eye – a "melody" (*melodija*), not a rallying call:

To the conflict flies the young singer,
He has cast off the sweetness of peaceful days;
With him he has his father's sword, Kladenets,
With him he has his harp – his life's delight.
"O native land of ringing songs,
Sacred land of my forefathers,
Here in tribute to you is my sharp sword,
And my golden harp!"

The singer fell victim to fearsome battles;
But, as his young life ends,
He casts the sharp sword into the waves
And breaks the tuneful strings.
"O strings, with you I would sing
Love, freedom and my native land!
And how are you now to sing in that land
Where the slave clanks his chains?"

It is significant that Kozlov introduces the magical sword of Russian folk literature. The sum effect is no more realistic, in

Belinskij's sense of the word, than if Wellington were shown on the plains of Waterloo, Excalibur in hand.

"Good Night!" is a tolerably accurate literal translation of the English text. It seems appropriate, therefore, that Byron should inform us why the Childe sets forth from England:

Childe Harold bask'd him in the noonday sun,
Disporting there like any other fly;
Nor Deem'd before his little day was done
One blast might chill him into misery.
But long ere scarce a third of his pass'd by
Worse than adversity the Childe befell;
He felt the fulness of satiety:
Then loathed he in his native land to dwell.

. . . .

His goblets brimm'd with every costly wine,
And all that mote to luxury invite,
Without a sigh he left to cross the brine . . .
(ll. 28 – 35, 96 – 8)

Far from leaving to fight for freedom, Childe Harold leaves – because he is sated with pleasure! Far from hastening to scenes of black oppression, he proposes to "cross earth's middle line," and view the splendours of India! It comes as no surprise, on reading Kozlov's paeon to Byron entitled simply "Byron," to find that, like Ypsylanty, the English poet has undergone a wondrous change. There are no flaws in the Promethean figure who "first at the sound of Freedom's swords/ flies to bring deliverance,/ Who in the fateful struggle/ Sustains the great deed with a mighty soul –/ The saving of holy Hellas!" (ll. 105 – 10). Kozlov, it must be plain already, saw many sides of human life in a heightened, idealized manner. On those few occasions when political realities cast shadows on his work, Kozlov seemed not so interested in the resulting darkness itself, as in the nuances of chiaroscuro that politics created.

His conservatism served him well in the months following the arrest of those implicated with Ryleev and Pestel', for it was known to Benkendorf. He was not troubled by the Third

Department. Anxious to make his position doubly clear, however, he addressed a slightly fulsome "dedication" to the Empress Alexandra Fjodorovna; it served as an introduction to the separate edition of *The Bride of Abydos* (1826), and is one of the less glorious pages of his work and life. A brief extract suffices to demonstrate its general tenor:

And I have not seen him! . . . the victim of dark night,
My eyes, alas! now dimmed do not see
The blessed beauty of the young tsaritsa,
Nor the Russian Tsar, the love of his native land,
The first day of whose reign was a day of
Eternal glory . . .

(*ll.* 57 – 61)

"Him" of the opening line is the Tsarevič. Alexandra Fjodorovna was twenty-eight in 1826, and of no outstanding beauty. The first day of Nicholas's reign, "le joli commencement de règne," as he referred to it,[37] was the day on which grapeshot dispersed the mutinous regiments on Senate Square.

To make sure, doubly sure, Kozlov later repeated what he sincerely felt – that the Decembrist rising was unfortunate. This time, however (in "To the most Blessed Filaret," 1830), a fresh note enters. Kozlov had personal friends among those exiled to Siberia for life:

When our Tsar so piously fulfilled
A sacred duty, a terrible duty,
And you, our inspired pastor,
Met him, cross in hand, –

You pronounced the heavens' good will
To him in the name of the Maker . . .

. . . .

And bright days shall again show forth,
Given according to an ardent faith;
And the half-dead shall arise,
Saved by the Tsar's kindness.

37. See A. G. Mazour, *op. cit.*

Still Nicholas performed a "sacred duty" in quashing a revolt against despotism, but now the question of forgiveness had arisen. Not until 1856, however, would those able and willing be granted the (new) Tsar's mercy, and be permitted to return to European Russia. Kozlov did not live to see it.

Kozlov's involvement in the literary polemics that centred on those two societies earlier named and their respective journals came to a climax in the years 1824 – 5. Consistently he supported the opponents of Izmajlov's *The Well-Meaner*, and so became Izmajlov's literary enemy. Increasingly, he let his name be linked with those of Puškin, Del'vig and Vjazemskij, the moving spirits behind *The Northern Flowers*. A curious letter from A. A. Bestužev to the patient Vjazemskij of late September, 1824 casts interesting light on the rifts then opening between Bestužev and Ryleev, on the one side, and Del'vig and Pletnjov. No longer content to collaborate on the increasingly radical *Polar Star*, Del'vig intended to edit his own almanac and, with the support of Puškin, Baratynskij, Žukovskij and Kozlov, succeeded in doing so. Naturally enough, Bestužev looked askance at *Northern Flowers*, a new and powerful competitor for readers, always too few in the summer months.

Others did their best to embroil Del'vig with Bestužev and Ryleev, and of these A. F. Voekov played the most insidious part. Voekov, editor of *The Russian Invalid*, a government publication which was leased to private persons for operation, was unscrupulous in his transactions with writers. His decision to pirate the beginning of Puškin's *The Robber Brothers* (which was to have appeared in *Polar Star*, and for which Ryleev had even received clearance from the censors), was merely one of many similar actions. Bestužev not only suspected Voekov of having encouraged Sljonin, a successful St. Petersburg publisher, to start an almanac to compete with *Polar Star*; more, he believed that he was trying to undermine his own journal, encouraging its regular contributors to withdraw their works. "If you knew the base motives that impel him," Bestužev wrote to Vjazemskij, "you would be even more astonished by such despicable envy and avarice. The plan for *Northern Flowers* was devised by him and not without reason; he says this himself. Trouble is being brewed between us and Puškin by means of Lev (Puškin's brother – GB). Verses by him and Kozlov, designated for the *Star*, are being reprinted . . . In a word, they are making a kind of flea-market of literature . . . Rescue us, Prince, and ask Ivan Ivanovič to do the same."[38] Kozlov was deeply involved with Del'vig, as his own correspondence confirms.

Since contact between one literary group and another was close, between members of various cenacles – those of Sophie Ponomareva, Pletnjov and Vjazemskij, for example – it was difficult, knowing members of one, not to know many. And Kozlov could not avoid contact with men whose first concern was not with literature, but with political reform. Nevertheless he refrained from the least emulation of the Bestuževs and Ryleevs. Dedications to the Empress and to women in Court circles, the Princess S. D. Radziwill, Countesses Pototskaja and Zavadovskaja, Fiquelmont and Laval' to name but five, are one manifestation of his unswerving conservatism. But that attitude reveals itself in other, subtler ways – in bucolic verse, for example. Fourteen lines from "The Country Life" (1837) would seem to demonstrate sufficiently for every purpose that, whatever else he might be, Kozlov was no ally for any committed radical:

Blessed is he who calmly lives
In his forefathers' unknown hamlet
And knows of white-walled Moscow
Only from passers-by.

Unchanging in his quiet lot,
Blessing the skies,
He ever sees the one field,
The same forests and cornfields.

O you, sacred customs!
Love of domestic life!
Your golden delights
Soothe this earth's bustle.

For the soul it is entrancing
To preserve traditions of the past and what is close . . .
(stanzas 1, 3, 10)

38. Cited in *Literaturnoe nasledstvo*, vol. 60 (1964), pt. 1, p. 228.

Sensitive though he might be to political oppression and cruel inequities of other, no less obvious kinds, Kozlov could by no means bring himself to identify the Tsar as the true source of that oppression. For the Tsar was not merely the mainstay of some social, most religious and all political traditions in the land: he was the very corner-stone on which rested the structure of Russian life as Kozlov recognized it. In Kozlov, as in no other Russian poet save Žukovskij, religious and political conservatism blended; only the Byronic verse remained outside this combination.

CHAPTER SIX
THE NARRATIVE POEMS

No genre was more consciously developed in Russia during the third and fourth decades of the last century than the verse tale, or *poema*; and Kozlov followed a general trend in turning to narrative verse with *The Monk* (1825).[1] It is a commonplace of Russian literary history that, begun in 1821 – 22 by Puškin's "southern tale" *The Captive of the Caucasus* and by Žukovskij's version of *The Prisoner of Chillon*, the wide vogue for tales in verse was precisely contemporaneous with the period of Byron's greatest influence in Russia (1822 – 27). Ending only when poetry itself lost its pre-eminent position to the "historical novel," one of the earliest of which, Faddej Bulgarin's 1086-page *Ivan Vyžigin*, appeared in March, 1829 and was sold out within a week, the fashion never returned in its original guise.[2]

There were great popular successes among the more than eighty verse tales published in Moscow and St. Petersburg during the years 1823 – 33, and of these Puškin's *The Captive of the*

1. For details of the editions, see I. Glikman, *Stixotvorenija* (Leningrad, 1956). Reviews of *The Monk* appeared in the following journals *Moskovskij telegraf*, 1825, no. 11, p. 313 (Vjazemskij); *Severnaja pčela*, 1825, nos. 47-50; *Novosti literatury*, 1825, vol. XIII, p. 101; *Poljarnaja zvezda na 1825 god*, p. 15 (A Bestužev); *Moskovskij vestnik*, 1827, vol. 6, p. 206 (S. P. Ševyrjov). Assessments of *Princess Natal'ja Dolgorukaja* were no less numerous, and included: *Moskovskij telegraf* 1828, no. 9, p. 537 (N. A. Polevoj); *Severnaja pčela* 1828, no. 8; *Moskovskij vestnik*, 1828, no. 8, p. 314; *Syn otečestva*, 1828, no. 1, p. 314; and *Severnyje tsvety(na 1829)*, p. 42 (O. Somov).

2. "Figljarin" Bulgarin (russified Bulharyn, 1789-1859), founder of the St. Petersburg weekly *Northern Bee*, which enjoyed the favour and furthered the work of the secret police, met with a second great success in March, 1830 with *The False Demetrius* – a historical romance of 1551 wearisome pages.

Caucasus and *The Fountain of Baxčiseraj*[3] were unquestionably the most resounding. But with *The Monk*, Kozlov had a success nearly equal to Puškin's.

Alone among poets of his day (he was approaching twenty-one, it must not be forgotten, when Puškin was born), Kozlov was doubly able to reap the benefits of that national infatuation with Childe Harold and the Giaour to which he, too, was subject: he not only found most of Byron's work extremely sympathetic but was able, after a six-month period of intense study in 1819, to read it in original. The strength of his position is clearly, albeit unconsciously, reflected in Vjazemskij's correspondence with A. I. Turgenev for that year. Žukovskij, Turgenev informed Vjazemskij, had been sent a copy of *Mazeppa* from London. Vjazemskij replied at once, from Warsaw, where there already existed a Byron cult: "I read and reread Byron . . . Do you know his *Pilgrim*, four cantos? But why doesn't Žukovskij, who knows English, and the still more difficult language of Byron, turn it to his gain? Who in Russia reads English and writes Russian?"[4] Kozlov's forthcoming version of part of *The Bride of Abydos* furnished the answer.

At first (1818 – 21), as Soviet scholars have shown,[5] it was Byron's shorter poems – *Darkness*, for example, and *Hebrew Melodies* – that proved most popular in Russia. Kozlov, it will be seen (Chapter 7), did not fail in his duty by these. Short pieces, however, soon gave place, in St. Petersburg journals and almanacs, to what were described as "lyrical epic poems": *The Giaour, The Corsair, Lara, The Bride of Abydos, Parisina*. Bestužev-Marlinskij stated a simple fact, recording that "these works . . . turned every head."[6] Such critics as Orest Somov, Vjazemskij and Nikolaj

3. *The Captive* was written in 1820-21, published in 1822; *The Fountain* written in 1822, published in 1824. The latter, a "Byronic poem" of 578 iambic tetrameters composed in Kišinjov, in the Crimea, deals with the "Garden Palace" (*Baxči Saraj*) of the Crimean khans. Its ruins survive, sixty miles from the Black Sea coast and in the very centre of the Crimea.

4. From a letter dated 11.10.19, cited by V. I. Maslov, *Načal'nyj period bajronizma v Rossii* (Kiev, 1915), pp. 4-5.

5. See esp. V. Žirmunskij, *Puškin i Bajron* (Leningrad, 1924), chaps. 4, 6; also N. K. Kozmin, "Puškin o Bajrone," in *Puškin v mirovoj literature* (Leningrad, 1926), pp. 99-112.

6. "Neizdannyje pis'ma Bestuževa-Marlinskogo," *Russkaja starina*, vol. 32 (1881), p. 629.

Polevoj were not slow to discover in them a new type of poetry.

Traveling through Switzerland and staying within walking distance of the castle of Chillon ("The very traces of this last," he wrote to Kozlov, "are eloquent for me; in Chillon, his name is carved on Bonivar's column and in Claran, right by the roadside, there is a simple peasant's cottage in which he passed some days"),[7] Žukovskij did not spurn to translate Byron's "fable." Published in 1822, the version was received by Puškin and Kozlov alike as a tour de force.[8] Yet, despite the urgings of these two and, especially, Vjazemskij, Žukovskij translated nothing else from Byron with the single exception of *Stanzas for Music*,[9] a poem on a theme congenial to his sentimental nature. The truth was, as Vjazemskij put it, that Žukovskij was apprehensive of the "Byronic poison";[10] and, in another letter to Kozlov from Switzerland, the gentle author of *Ljudmila* revealed his true attitude: "Many of its pages (of *The Prisoner of Chillon* – GB) are immortal, but there is in it a most terrible, depressed spirit. It does not belong to a poet whom life has solaced."[11] Žukovskij could only feel the impact of Byron's verse tales; but it was left to Puškin and Kozlov to transfer this impact to Russian literature.

The Monk, on which Kozlov worked for two years, painstakingly correcting his corrections, redrafting whole passages, losing the scraps of paper on which he made trial versions,[12] is essentially a reworking of Part 2 of *The Giaour*. It was all but impossible that Byron's influence, as strong on Kozlov's original poetry as on his translation work, should not impinge also on his verse tales. Both in its form and in its central motif, the confession of a monk once involved in a disastrous love affair, *The Monk* closely resembles its

7. Letter of May, 1833; taken from *Russkij arxiv*, 1867, bk. 1, p. 6, where it is given in full. François Bonivar (1530-86), patriot and republican, lives again in Byron's tale; Žukovskij mingles fact and fiction.

8. See Puškin's letter to N. I. Gnedič of 27.9.22; *A. S. Puškin*, pp. 50-51.

9. "Pesnja" ("A Song"), 1820.

10. See A. N. Veselovskij, *V. A. Žukovskij* (St. Petersburg, 1904), pp. 325-6.

11. *Ibid.*, p. 327.

12. Kozlov continued to use – and lose – scraps of paper: "I would have sent you my princess (i.e. *Princess Natal'ja Dolgorukaja* – GB), dear Mixail Evstaf'evič, but it is not written out, and, in my usual way, I have thrown down a few extracts on flying scraps of paper (*letučix listkax*)." Letter to M. E. Lobanov of September, 1827, preserved in *Puškinskij Dom*, Leningrad, under reference: *Fond* 93, Op. 4, N. 46.

progenitor. Even the hero's dark, morose appearance and long cloak recall those of the Giaour. Yet Kozlov's tale is also an original work. The statements are not incompatible, for, touched by the melancholy, softening air that is so peculiar to Kozlov's verse, even an undisguisedly Byronic content is subtly transformed. In *The Monk*, two spirits meet – those of Byron and Karamzin; it would be difficult to think of less likely bedfellows. The presence of these influences, however, goes far to determine the mood of Kozlov's first *poema*. The scenario is one of vales and mountains, night and lowering clouds, a monastery perched on a crag, a dark, tormented, solitary figure. Yet the ending is Karamzinian. Byron's Giaour is rebellious to the last, Kozlov's young monk is submissive, and, as the Giaour greets Satan, the Russian sees his God; the Giaour bows before no altar (ll. 908 – 10), while the young monk sings in the monastery choir; the darkness of the Byronic hero, in short, is scattered by the monk's repentance and submission to God's will! *The Monk*'s opening strophes suggest that action will occur in the open, in the wild, in a storm; but the action unfolds in the calm air of a monastery. Beyond a certain point, it will be clear from the above, Kozlov was unwilling to follow in Byron's footsteps and, indeed, unable to do so. Here, in his private diary, he reveals part of his character that would always restrain him from uncritical admiration of the English poet: "I have read Byron a great deal. Nothing can be compared with him. The gloomy greatness, the tragedy, the energy . . . but he is something of a misanthrope; I only wish that he had more religious ideas, for they are necessary for one's happiness. . . ."[13]

Like the epistle "To V. A. Žukovskij," *The Monk* is an apologia in the guise of another genre. At first it is directly and obviously so:

Like my monk, I have long since buried
All young passions in my breast:
And I, like he, have exchanged
All earthly joys for heavenly hope . . .

13. Ja. K. Grot, *Dnevnik I. I. Kozlova* (St. Petersburg, 1906), p. 7.

Later, Kozlov's relationship both to the monk and to the tale itself grows less apparent and more complex. On one level, it is plainly reasonable to think the monk a dramatic extension of his creator's character or, rather, a reflection of one facet of that character. Yet on another it is no less clear that the monk, gloomy and passionate, sullen and haughty, is quite unlike Kozlov (or that Kozlov presented to the world as a brilliantly sustained persona). Reason suggests that he simply dramatized his past, giving himself a chance to live again, but vicariously; it is better to concentrate on the text.

In its beginning, *The Monk* is economical. Three strophes set the scene and introduce the hero. At once, the landscape is familiar; it recalls the work of Lermontov. Indeed, the mountain might be Mount Mašuk – its atmosphere is that which pervades "Bela" and "Princess Mary" in *A Hero of Our Time*. There, too, there is "a brook of freezing water" and physical outlines are etched with a crystal clarity; as in Lermontov's novel and verse, attention is drawn to concrete detail – an individual wall, a single stream and cell. The point will be developed later. Here, now, is Kozlov's monastery on a mountain:

By a grove, on a high mountain,
There stands a brothers' cloister:
Around it is a wall with merlons,
Four towers at the corners
And, in the centre, God's temple
With gilded heads;
A row of cells, a dark passage,
A chapel by the sacred gates
With a wonder-working ikon.
Beneath, a brook of icy water
Murmurs in a healing stream
Under an ancient linden's shade . . .

Night falls, as the third strophe progresses. Kozlov skilfully fuses dramatic and temporal time, so that the reader's day becomes that of the monks; their evening, his. Because it is night, light and sound travel easily. A single lamp burns in the hero's cell.

From the whole, the focus changes to the particular. Taking no part in the event that he describes, Kozlov also casts off the limits that constrain his characters' movements and thoughts, a privilege that he foregoes only in *The Mad Girl*. Having no body to move with his fancy, he (and the reader) throw aside the tiresome limitations of gravity and time; it is a technique much used by Byron also, and like Byron's so-called Eastern tales, Kozlov's narrative poems are by nature cinematic. *The Monk*, no less than *Princess Natal'ja Dolgorukaja*, seems calculated to delight a film-maker. Colourful, dramatic settings, a single face fading away into a panorama, a plot strong enough to support the piece but not so strong as to draw the eye from the actors – all lend themselves admirably to film. Here is the passage from strophe 2 in which the monk is introduced:

In the distant cell a lamp's ray
Faintly gleams: and in that cell
A monk, a youthful sufferer,
Is ending his dismal life.
Passions, losses and griefs
Have stamped their awful mark
On his gloomy brow;
There is a storm in his heart's depth:
His fate is hidden in darkness:
Whence he came, and who he is,
No one knows. But he is tormented
By a fateful secret, in arms against
Himself. He came one night, in a storm:
Since then, he has remained in the cloister,
Sadly led the life of the monks,
Avoided all, hidden from all:
His wondrous appearance frightened all,
And the monk spoke with no one:
But in the depth of his despondent heart
The Terrible might be sensed.

It is a remarkable and lucid statement of intent. Every line declares that this is to be a *Romantic poema*, with a Romantic hero. It is difficult, indeed, to think of ingredients for the Romantic hero *à la Pečorin* or Childe Harold that Kozlov overlooks. The cell, one is not surprised to find, is distant (and far from the mundane concerns of common men); the overcast (*pasmurnyj*) brow, with the familiar mark (*znak*) of spiritual distinction, betokens exclusive sufferings – sufferings lost in the darkness of the past (*pokrytye t'moju* . . .). The scope for comparison, like the subject itself, is vast. One might be faced with Vojnarovskij, eponymous hero of Ryleev's verse tale of 1824; or with Arsenij, hero of Baratynskij's unsuccessful tale, *The Ball* (1828). All three have pallid brows, stamped by "earlier passions and torment";[14] all three have restless, unfathomable eyes, restless movements, troubled minds; all three are, above all else, singled out from other men, destined for suffering. Unlike René, they do not consciously think of their suffering as the sign of their spiritual superiority; yet can one doubt that the thought, if suggested to them, would seem most just?

The monk, then, stands in the mainstream of Romantic heroes. All such heroes, in Russian as in French, German and British literature of the first three decades of the century, show characteristics that the "youthful sufferer" shares. He, too, is in revolt against restrictions, some of his own making, others not. (And here one senses the modernity of his revolt; for now, as in 1825, "Man wishes to be free from all restrictions placed on him by religious tradition, political absolutism and a hierarchical social system. . . . " Still, in the personal context, "Man is visited by an urge to discover and recover his authentic self and to express it fully and creatively."[15] Kozlov, of course, had no objections to autocracy or religious tradition, still less was he inclined to oppose the social *status quo*; yet it was precisely "to discover and recover his authentic self" that he answered the call of *The Giaour*.) Like René's and Atala's, the monk's passions are extreme. Therefore, like them, he suffers and has caused suffering. He, like them, is his own prisoner, feels himself unique, has an exceptional capacity for both pleasure and pain. Was his year with his beloved not

14. E. A. Baratynskij, *Bal*, Pt. 1, p. 157.
15. J. L. Talmon, *Romanticism and Revolt* (London, 1967), p. 136.

"heaven-like"? "Ces jouissances," he might have echoed Chateaubriand, "sont trop poignantes; telle est notre faiblesse que les plaisirs exquis deviennent des douleurs."[16] Disgusted by himself, he cannot change – until, of course, Kozlov sends him God's grace. Having once enjoyed bliss and, like Amiel and Senancour, found all other reality empty and harsh,[17] he is the natural victim of melancholy which arises from the disproportion between dream and reality. In the Romantic manner, Kozlov's monk is acutely conscious of his individual fate. (For the Russian Romantics, Fate, far from being the disinterested and dispassionate force of the Ancients, was a highly personal matter. Jazykov, for example, in his poem "Fate" (1823) paints a Goya-like apparition, knife in hand!) Finally, and once again in the Romantic tradition, Kozlov's hero betakes himself to the purifying mountains. "Man," it is written, "should flee that false taste for grandeur that poisons his pleasure in nature. It is on the summits of mountains, in the depths of forests . . . that she reveals her most potent charms."[18] It comes as no surprise to learn that, before arriving at the monastery, the youthful monk would often roam deep woods:

I loved to wander through the woods,
All day to chase the game . . .

The monk was happiest where nature was wild ("Oh! She is fairest in her features wild,/ Where nothing polished dare pollute her path").[19] In his beloved, he found that very force of good glimpsed by Chateaubriand, sylph-like, "behind the veil of the universe" – the girl of whom Andrej Turgenev dreamed (" . . . avec tous ses charmes, sa bonté, sa fidélité, son amour"), and who reappears unchanged, in Verlaine's favourite dream ("Et qui n'est, chaque fois, ni tout à fait la même/ Ni tout à fait une autre, et m'aime et me comprend").[20] The Eternal Feminine enters Kozlov's verse tale briefly, before passing on.

It is appropriate that natural descriptions should be splendid in

16. *Essai sur la Révolution*, Pt. 2, chap. 57.
17. See *La Nouvelle Héloise*, Pt. 6, lettre 8.
18. *Ibid.*, Pt. 4, lettre 2.
19. Byron, *Childe Harold's Pilgrimage*, 11, XXXVII, ll. 5-6.
20. "Mon Rêve Familier" *Poèmes Saturniens* (1866).

this tale of a youth who loved nature. Passages of pure description, one may feel, should be inserted into verse tales only with circumspection, for they are the enemies of pace in dramatic action. A balance must be found between descriptive and dramatic elements. Kozlov strikes it admirably in his opening strophes as, for example, here, in the description of valleys near the monastery:

Already the evening glow dies in the sky:
No songs are heard on the meadows:
In the valleys, the herds can no longer be seen
Nor does the horn sound in the woods:
No one will come by, – only, at times,
A little bell will ring
Far off, along the high road:
And lights no longer glow
On fishermens' boats on the Dnieper
The midnight moon has risen,
And bright stars burn . . .

Boats and herds lend movement to the changing scene, as bell and bugle suggest action and sound, yet a spirit of tranquillity prevails. As light fades, the passage draws to an end. Here, by contrast, the hero remembers his happier past:

I loved to swim the wide Dnieper
Loved to play with danger,
Mocking life insolently:
I had nothing to lose,
I had no one from whom to part.

The writing is original, yet in its attention to detail, in the controlling sense of movement, the moving caesura, the enjambements, it recalls Lermontov. The question of influence arises. Lermontov, it is true, was writing verse in 1814; but so plainly, in theme, mood and characterization, does *The Monk* prefigure his novel and, more especially, the long poem *Mtsyri* (a Georgian word meaning "novice"), that it is impossible to dismiss Kozlov's impact on Lermontov. The subject has been pursued in depth by Professor B. V. Nejman, whose findings need not be repeated here.[21] Suffice it to say that *Mtsyri* also has as its theme the confession at the hour of death of a rebellious young man to his spiritual father; that it, like *The Monk*, is full of sharp, dramatic situations and retells past unhappy events – events which torment the hero. It is, however, easy to overestimate Kozlov's influence on Lermontov who, no less easily than Kozlov, could read Žukovskij's "Prisoner of Chillon" (which *Mtsyri* echoes in metre and diction), and even, though with more difficulty, Byron's original. As for *A Hero of our Time*, it is an obvious patchwork, the earliest chapters having been composed the last, and various influences are discernible. Baratynskij has no less a claim than Kozlov to have shaped Pečorin; his narrative tale *The Ball* (1828) was much admired by Lermontov, and Arsenij, its hero, shares much in common with Lermontov's hero.[22]

Still, "Lermontovesque" chords are struck throughout *The Monk*, as, for example, here in strophes 4 – 5, a passage that the patient Dr. Werner might have heard from Pečorin's own lips:

Here is a secret: in my days' spring
Already I knew all the grief of life:
I grew a homeless orphan,
Knew no caress from my own:
Childhood's merriments flew by,
Scarcely touching me:
While my contemporaries were playing
Already I was sunk in thought:
In vain a pure and beauteous flame
Blazed in my youthful breast:
For me there was no one to love,
Alas! fearing cold scorn
From those unfriendly to me,

21. B. V. Nejman, "Otraženie poezii Kozlova v tvorčestve Lermontova," *Izvestija Otdelenija Russkogo Jazyka i Slovesnosti*, vol. XIX (1914), no. 1, pp. 14-29.

22. On this question, see I. Tojbin, "Poema Baratynskogo 'Eda,'" *Russkaja literatura*, 1963, no. 2, pp. 114-29; also L. Semjonov, *K voprosu o vlijanii Marlinskogo na Lermontova* (Voronež, 1914), pp. 24-7.

I was obliged to hide
The ardent agitation of my heart
And the first fire of my soul . . .

Here, further to establish the connection, is Pečorin's summing up of his youth: "I was modest – they accused me of slyness: I became secretive. I felt good and evil deeply: no one caressed me . . . I was sullen, other children gay and talkative . . . I was ready to love the whole world, – no one understood me: and I learned to hate."

Perhaps because his own personal history had been so free from its stain, Kozlov did not hesitate to inject a large dose of melodrama into that of his monk. It is a major element of the *poema*, as of *Princess Natal'ja Dolgorukaja* and *The Mad Girl*. That element, moreover, grows more noticable in the later narrative tales, tending now to the horrific (the appearance of dead Dolgorukov, headless), now the macabre (as in the mad girl's nightmares: pushed into a grave by her lover, she sees "many a gruesome sight" which Kozlov mercifully leaves unspecified). Here, in skeleton, are the early events of the young monk's life:

Once, long before, an "aging warrior" and his beautiful daughter came to the district where he lived. The monk fell in love with her, only to see his happiness and hers tarnished by a foul rival – a distant relative who "had fought in the Polish forces." The rival is astute, and deceives the aging father; the girl refuses to accept him, is roundly cursed and flees with the hero.

Why does the rival, that is, the cad ("The villain, he had betrayed his honour . . . "), arrive at the crucial moment in the hero's courtship? The text provides one answer: it is because there are no more wars to be fought, and the rival is therefore idle. Taken on this level, at least, the tale becomes realistic, and the shades of melodrama are dispelled. The Hussar of Baratynskij's tale *Eda* (1824) also seduces his (Finnish) maid because he has nothing to do. Onegin and Lenskij are *ot nečego delat' druz'ja* – friends because they have nothing (else) to do; later, Onegin switches his serfs from corvée to quit-rent (*barščina: obrok*) – because he is bored by country life, and has a whim to do so. Yet, one is only too well aware, Kozlov's rival enters the scene at the given moment for a second, more basic reason: it is his sole dramatic function in the work to prompt the *dénouement* by his conduct, that is, by his character in action. He arrives, that is to say, on cue.

The monk's rival is not merely a cut-out figure; like the hero himself, he moves convincingly. But the characters of the *poema*, it must be finally conceded, move in predetermined ways, and those ways are the ways that the plot plainly demands. So, in a sense, their life is artificial; but still it convinces because, as by all good tales, one is willing to be convinced. The girl is beautiful – insipid, undeniably, but essentially beautiful. It is her function and *raison d'être* to inspire love in the hero. Mechanically, *The Monk* is not a subtle piece – one seems almost, at times, to hear the sound of cogs and flywheels. Here is the heroine:

Her charms entranced me,
She surrendered her heart to me,
And her father and mother betrothed us . . .

. . . .

With what holy innocence did she,
Her heart aflame,
Pour bliss onto me!

The plot unfolds briskly, after strophe 7. The girl's mother having conveniently died, the rival, sensing triumph, grows bolder, "swears frightful oaths," and deceives the father.[23] Abduction is predictable, and efficiently performed. A child is born to the young couple and the girl dies, apparently in childbirth. Insane from grief, the hero wanders the countryside crying and groaning (strophe 8).

It is at this juncture, mid-course through *The Monk*, that one encounters an extraordinary phenomenon, but one repeated in each of Kozlov's three *poemy*. Without warning, the action slows

23. The heroine "pours torrents of tears," and the rhyme (*očej-ručej*) reappears in *Princess Natal'ja Dolgorukaja*, where the phrasing is almost identical with that used by Puškin in *Onegin*, chap. VII, XXXII, 13-15, and by Baratynskij in "Eda," ll. 264-5. There are no grounds for suspicion, however; the rhyme is a natural one, the situation not uncommon in verse tales of the time.

to a halt. The hero is left to his raving; the rival waits off-stage. And the hero, through the agency of Kozlov's piety, undergoes a conversion to the Christian faith. The incident, like the passage in which it is described, represents a grave miscalculation on Kozlov's part.

God, it was earlier seen, is an ever-present force in Kozlov's work. He is present in "To the Sea," in "A Sonnet to Saint Teresa," even in "To A Meadow Daisy," a loose translation of Burns's poem to a wild flower.[24] Sometimes Kozlov's allusions to his Maker are deliberate, as in "My Prayer," sometimes casual, as in "We Are Seven," based on the English original of Wordsworth.[25] Even his choice of titles plainly reflects a basic religious preoccupation: "The Destruction of Rome and the Spreading of Christianity" springs first to mind. But there are works in which reference to God seems inapposite, and *The Monk*, a tale filled with ungodly actions and irreligious characters, is surely such a one. Not only is it unfortunate from a structural point of view to introduce a lengthy digression immediately after the second thematic turning point – the abduction; it is embarrassing to overhear the hero's (or Kozlov's) private dialogue with God ("God, Creator of all! My little one and unforgotten beloved are in Your holy land; I, perhaps, shall join them . . . ") Religious joy is a private, fleeting thing. It is on dramatic grounds that the religious interval may be deplored.

At last, with a jolt, action resumes. By the grave of his beloved, the hero sees a vision. A youth and his paramour appear, seated on a haywain; the youth has flowers in his hair. These are the figures of Youth and Happiness. Once more, the hero falls prey to a bout of insanity. Clearly a meeting with the rival is required, for the hero must battle with Evil, for happiness or ruin. Now a nominal Christian, the hero tries to forgive his ill-doer, finds it impossible, and kills him with a dagger. So one returns to the monastery, to find the monk subject to horrors of all descriptions. Life, he and Kozlov reflect, is terrible – but does peace lie beyond the grave? Weakened by death, (strophe 13), he

24. "To a Mountain Daisy" (1786).
25. "We Are Seven" (1798).

sees a second vision. Curiously, the girl whom he loved is now described far more circumstantially than earlier, while she still lived. White shroud and unearthly smile are hackneyed, no doubt, to those familiar with Thomson, Gray, Delille, and Chateaubriand; but the burning black eyes and dark curls are the features of an individual woman. The woman carries a child; the monk thinks himself forgiven, grows feebler and, after two nights and days, expires.

For his concluding scene, Kozlov turned to Scott's *Marmion*, adapting it, as he had earlier adapted *The Giaour*, most skilfully to his needs. It is an excellent piece of work. The tolling bell is heard by various persons: a hermit in his cave; a traveller and his wife, singing to keep their spirits up on a dark night; fishermen, whose sleep it troubles; a child, stirring restlessly. As the verse tale begins with a wide panorama, narrowing to the monastery and cells, so, now, focus is shifted from the immediate to the general. It is as if a camera swept from a window to the countryside beyond, selecting certain scenes, dwelling on each for an instant.

Formally, *The Monk*, like the later *poemy*, shows little originality. Like most of Kozlov's work, it is in iambic tetrameters, the favourite metre of a majority of his contemporaries, as well as of Del'vig and Jazykov, Puškin and Baratynskij, Kol'tsov and Vjazemskij.[26] Fourteen cantos are divided, without regard for regularity, into strophes of approximately forty lines, (strophe 1 has fourteen, strophe 10 – seventy-two). Only two points are noteworthy: thirty-four lines long, the dedication is disproportionately massive, while the rhyme-scheme, as a glance suggests, shows quite amazing irregularity. It is in vain that one seeks recurring patterns.

Other failings in the work have been noted: the time sense is blurred, the pace irregular, now slackening, now hurrying, and there is an unpardonable digression. Kozlov's tendency to overstep the limits of the plausible, moreover, and to indulge in visions serves well enough in fairytales, but is hardly acceptable in such a piece as *The Mad Girl* with its pretensions to realism. A blend of careful detail and improbable events first developed in *The Monk*

26. See B. O. Unbegaun, *Russian Versification* (Oxford, 1955).

appears in each successive verse tale by Kozlov, and partially explains the cooler receptions accorded to the later works. (There, too, one finds tales within tales, visions, and distracted heroines.)

Yet, these flaws notwithstanding, the immediate and lasting popularity of Kozlov's first narrative poem is easily explicable. It is superbly readable. As with other works of the so-called Age of Byron, the shade of the critic Belinskij follows all who discuss *The Monk*; for his comments, while often biased and unsympathetic, are almost always pertinent. For example, it is true that, as he notes, the tale marked a stage in both the literary and the social evolution of educated Russians. The swift expansion in the third decade of the Russian reading public which had proven so beneficial to Kozlov has already been mentioned (Chapter 5). It is even true that, as Belinskij claimed maliciously, *The Monk* did for readers of the pre-Decembrist years what Karamzin's *Poor Liza* had done in the 1790s:[27] it attracted many who might otherwise have been indifferent to literature – a tale like a tree from which fruit would drop at the slightest touch. Belinskij could not approve of the work's producing rewards so easily, rightly observing that such guaranteed emotional satisfaction must certainly assure its author's fame.

Belinskij was also among the first to compare Kozlov's *poema* with *The Giaour* (adding, however, that comparison was hardly possible, such was the superiority of Byron's work).[28] The English poem, he remarked, is reflected in *The Monk* "as the sun in a drop of water"; one is as interested in the former as uninterested in the latter, "which hold the fascination, respectively, of a lion and a dove."

It is pointless to deny the many similarities between the English and the Russian works. Critics, however, have done less than justice to Kozlov's original treatment of this borrowed theme. Perhaps mention of other, more slavish imitations of *The Giaour* and other tales by Byron may help to restore a proper balance in the matter. Two such tales, *Love In Prison* (1828) and *Dorošenko* (1830), both written anonymously, spring first to

27. V. G. Belinskij, *Poln. sob. soč.*, 13 vols., vol. 2 (Moscow, 1957), p. 387.
28. *Ibid.*, vol. 5, pp. 68-9.

mind.[29]

Openly based on *The Corsair*, *Love In Prison* also concerns the misfortunes of a heroine named Gulnare (Gjul'nara). At least three scenes recall their Byronic counterparts: the captive standing proudly before Pacha (*The Corsair*, ll. 1329 – 42); Pacha threatening the hero – the very threats are those of Seyd; and the summoning of a doctor to test the hero's pain threshold ("The Leech was sent – but not in mercy – there/ To note how much the life yet left could bear"). *Dorošenko* (concerning a Little-Russian hetman whose end was bloody) was, like Kozlov's tale, based on *The Giaour*. Compared with it, *The Monk* is a wholly original work. *Dorošenko,* like *The Giaour*, rests structurally and thematically on the confession of a man in a monastery cell. Like the Giaour, that man is close to death – or believes so. He, too, turns to a "holy father," a man of innocence; he, too, recalls the passion that brought him to ruin (see *The Giaour*, ll. 971 – 88); the deathbed agony is highly reminiscent of the Giaour's, the recollections similar ("I am burning; my torment is crueller . . . "; see *Giaour*, l. 945). In his raving, he sees a (Byronic) exotic *paysage* of cherry-trees. One might cite further similarities, or compare with Byron's tale V. Litvinov's *Julija* (1832), but the point would seem to be clear. A reading of *The Monk* is vindication enough of all charges of imitation.

Judged by Belinskij's increasingly utilitarian criteria, the work could only fail. Not only did it not castigate the Alexandrine régime; it did not even, as at least Ryleev's *Dumy* had done, succeed in disguising current socio-political problems as "tales of days of yore" (*rasskazy davno minuvšix dnej*). The fact remains, however, that when Russians have honoured Kozlov's memory, it is the author of *The Monk* and of translations of Moore's *Those Evening Bells* and of Wolfe's *Burial of Sir John Moore at Corunna* – all three politically obscure, if not apolitical, pieces – that they have borne in mind.[30]

29. See V. Žirmunskij, *op.cit.*, pp. 317-8.

30. These pieces are praised by A. Vvedenskij in his introduction to the 1892 St. Petersburg edition of Kozlov's verse; and (to mention an émigré historian) by D. S. Mirskij in *A History of Russian Literature* (New York, 1955), p. 99. To single them out is, in fact, a tradition.

Unlike *The Monk*, *Princess Natal'ja Dolgorukaja* was based on known historical events. Kozlov made the decision to write such a tale consciously, wishing both to repeat his earlier success and, simultaneously, to move with literary fashion. For by 1828, interest was quickening, among many who had always ignored it in the past, in the mediaeval history of Russia and of peoples now enveloped by her ever widening empire: Siberians, Crimean Tartars, and Central Asians. Soon, novels by Mixail Zagoskin would sell in thousands, in Semjon's and Smirdin's bookshops,[31] and Puškin would turn his gaze to the steppe and Orenburg, where *The Captain's Daughter* is set. Deliberately written in the style of Scott's early romances, Zagoskin's *Jurij Miloslavskij, or The Russians in 1612* is a story of the Time of Troubles, when Polish forces occupied Moscow, and of the victory of national consciousness.

Something of the flavour of an interest in the past that was by no means the property of the West, more colourful than *Cinq Mars* by de Vigny, no less exotic, in its way, than Western dreams of Otahiti, may be had from this list of a dozen verse tales written in the years 1827 – 36. The titles speak for themselves:

1827	I Podolinskij	*Div and Peri*
1828	F. Alekseev	*Ceka: A Tale of the Urals*
1828	A. Bestužev	*Andrej, Prince Pereaslavskij*
1828	P. Maskov	*The Robber*
1828	N. Murav'jov	*The Kirghiz Prisoner*
1829	P. Maskov	*A Night of Vengeance*
1830	D. Komisarov	*The Prisoner of Turkey*
1830	Baron Rozen	*The Birth of Ivan the Terrible*
1832	I. R.	*Ali-Kara-Mirza; a Circassian Tale*
1836	A. Fuks	*The Founding of Kazan'*

In the jargon of social realist criticism, Kozlov's later *poemy* were attempts "to solve the problem" of "a national Romantic" verse tale. The "problem," of course, was to write one, and many

31. For details of prices and printings, 1824-34, see A. Meynieux, *Pouchkine Homme de Lettres* (Paris, 1966), pp. 580-88.

attempts were made. *Evgenij Onegin* would not serve because it was not, or, rather, was not seen to be, based on Russian history. In the event, Kozlov, too, "failed" to solve the problem because, having laid the foundations in *The Monk* for an onslaught on the Russian feudal system, he declined to carry it through. Nor was the history selected for his second tale particularly pertinent to radical objectives. It did not prompt indignation with the twin institutions of tsardom and serfdom, or even bring into disrepute those who oppressed the people. Serfs play no part in Kozlov's tales, nor are his princes lacking in virtues.

The story of Princess Dolgorukova (1714 – 71) was well known to Puškin's generation. It is a most interesting one – or so Ryleev thought, selecting it as the theme of one of his *Dumy*. (Since those *Dumy*, moreover, were "to arouse feelings of patriotism" in the gentry and peasantry, as Ryleev euphemistically put it, the intention being to disaffect as many as possible towards the throne, Ryleev plainly thought that Princess Dolgorukova might well serve the cause that Belinskij had in mind for her.)[32] The princess was married to a favourite of Peter II, Prince Ivan Alekseevič Dolgorukov. Three days after the marriage, Dolgorukov was disgraced and the couple exiled to his estates (1730). Two sons were born. In 1738, the prince was again seized by Imperial agents, and executed in Novgorod. The princess brought up her sons. In 1758 she entered a nunnery by Kiev. Her memoirs, written in 1767, were published, little by little, starting in 1810.

It would have been surprising, in the context of Kozlov's work as a whole, had he not chosen to treat his historical theme in a sentimental way. And so one finds a young woman, a child by her side, "on the great Vladimir road" (ll. 1 – 5). The Princess is poorly dressed; night approaches as she quickly crosses a dark grove, entering a valley and seeing a mansion. It is deserted, and the court before it is overgrown. Like the monastery of Kozlov's first verse tale, it has a slightly unreal air; somehow, the heraldic devise by the porch is too obviously plastered on:

Beyond the dark grove, in a valley,

32. See A. G. Tsejtlin, *Tvorčestvo Ryleeva* (Moscow, 1955), pp. 237-49.

By the mirror-like plain of a pond,
A nobleman's village blossomed
In welcoming beauty –
Tall lindens in the green shade.
A noble's mansion stands there,
Preserving the look of antiquity:
In the coat of arms beneath a count's
Coronet is a red shield on a field or,
Surrounded by a laurel wreath . . .

Inexplicably, Kozlov is more engrossed in the description of the Šeremetev heraldic devise than in describing the ancient house itself. Only as the eye is drawn from the house to the natural scene around it does an air of conviction settle. Many fine passages might justly be cited here. Of course, it is better to meet them in context; the two given have been selected arbitrarily, and are very different in tenor. The first immediately follows the lines given above, and leads to a description of a small chapel attached to the mansion, its priest sitting placidly by his window – an idyllic scene that contrasts well with the heroine's predicament. The second (from Part 2, strophe 4), depicts a wood after a storm:

But the garden, and waters, and bridges
And fragrant clusters of roses
Had long been forgotten, orphaned.
The honour of his native land
The master had long lain in the damp ground:
His mansion had grown deserted,
Its broad court grown with grass.

. . . .

The storm has quietened: the vault of the skies
Already shows blue between smoky clouds,
And the wood gives a sweet fragrance
And it smells so fresh in the glade!
Flowers, moistened by rain,
Gleam beneath damp pearls,
And tranquilly, brightly,
The evening sun casts a temperate ray.

Puškin was much impressed by the first of these passages, and recollected it when writing Chapter Seven of *Onegin*; canto XV, ll. 1 – 14 and canto XVI, ll. 1 – 7 are almost embarrassingly close to ll. 11 – 13, 24 – 26, and 28 – 32 of Kozlov's opening strophe in *Princess Natal'ja Dolgorukaja*. In both, the heroine, walking through the countryside, espies a mansion with a garden and a placid stretch of water; in both, the heroine is much agitated, and hesitates whether to go back or advance. Nor, on this subject, is this the only passage in *Onegin* that recalls Kozlov's second tale; one may mention the similarity between strophe 14 of *Princess Natal'ja Dolgorukaja*, ll. 16 – 19, and ll. 5 – 7 of *Onegin*, Chapter Seven, canto 29. Kozlov's lines are given first:

The pond, the trees and flowers
Like unforgotten friends
She met again.

. . . .

As with old friends, she
Hastens to talk with
Her groves and meadows once more.

Similar echoes of Kozlov's work are to be heard in the verse of other poets of the time – in Vjazemskij's "Travelling Reflection" (1830), for example, or N. Kobylin's verse tale *The Hermit* (1831).[33] But such echoes deserve a separate study.

The tale of the princess, like that of the monk, unfolds in fits and starts, but not, as in his case, from her own mouth. Patiently, as she sits and warms herself by his fire, the priest (who, with "an ancient gardener," seems to be the sole inhabitant of the Šeremetev mansion) addresses himself to the reader. Again, Kozlov's technique is not subtle; it is implied three times that the heroine is the daughter of the old Count Šeremetev, not least by her recognizing the mansion and its grounds. Will the priest, in his turn, recognize the heroine, whom he describes in such detail and who played in his sight as a child? Inevitably so; the newcomer

33. The plagiarized verse tale first appeared in Bulgarin's *Northern Bee (Severnaja pčela)*, 1831, no. 183. It does not seem to have been reviewed.

also has the dark blue eyes, thick lashes and chestnut hair of the Count's daughter. But Kozlov exploits his device until it is exhausted.

From the priest, we learn all that we know of the princess's marriage and lost husband. The bridegroom, it must be admitted, is a shadowy figure; "Among all the boyars he was sweetest to her eyes." Nor does even the priest dwell on him, whose memory causes pain – he treated the old priest well, though handsome and proud. The Tsar and high clergy attended the wedding. Disgraced, the young bridegroom was exiled, and his bride remained with him. Kozlov treats the historical facts of the couple's ill-fated marriage with respect: Dolgorukova did remain with her husband eight years; relatives did advise her, unsuccessfully, to return to St. Petersburg and remarry.

At last the scales fall from the old priest's eyes. Entranced by a portrait of her late husband on taffeta, she kisses her ring ecstatically. Part One ends as she sets out for Moscow.

Part One is fractionally shorter than *The Monk* in its entirety and, proportionately, has less action. It, too, is in iambic tetrameters and is comprised of irregular strophes. Unlike *The Monk* and *The Mad Girl*, it contains considerable portions of dialogue; the ninth and eleventh strophes of Part One are almost entirely given over to conversation. Dialogue, however, lends no sense of urgency to the tale; on the contrary, rather, it steadies an already measured pace – for the priest is not to be hurried in his narrative. Not only does the action not develop swiftly, after the heroine's departure for Moscow; there is, in a tale of considerable length, only too little action that can be developed. In both *Princess Natal'ja Dolgorukaja* and *The Mad Girl*, there is also little opportunity for psychological speculation. Motives are plain, the stories simple.

Both the failings and the strengths of Kozlov's work are clearly visible in Part Two of his second tale. Not until strophe 4, and after interminable scene-setting – with, of course, the saving grace of all Kozlov's tales, fine natural descriptive passages – does the princess catch her first glimpse of the spire of the campanile of Ivan the Great, "its crown glowing ember-bright."[34] One is

34. "The great campanile of Ivan Velikiy, erected in 1600, rises to a height of 318

accustomed, reading Kozlov's verse tales, to meeting curious conduct – and the princess proceeds to act oddly indeed, seeing Moscow in the distance. She kneels in the dust three times, rises, kisses her son, runs and stops. "Guardian-angel!" she cries, "give me strength,/ Lead me – not to the grave!" So she comes to the Kremlin, where once her father, Field-Marshal Boris Šeremetev, "feasted with Peter," and hastily enters Spasov Cathedral.

At once, there is a change of atmosphere. Once more, Kozlov's hand is firm, and it is plain, within five lines of the princess's entering the church of his imagining, that here is a setting of which he has perfect mastery. Not that Kozlov's cathedral is precisely a building of stone and mortar; it is, in fact, no more solid than the Šeremetevs' mansion – mysterious and gloomy, too filled with faintly gleaming ikons and the flickering of candles to give a feeling of solidity. But Kozlov does not aim at a sense of concreteness, and the Spasov Cathedral is real in a way that even the monk's monastery is not; it is a building that the heroine can enter without being mere setting (as the praying and singing of monks in the first tale); it is a building in which humans cough, move about and talk. At this point (strophes 6 – 7), various elements of *Princess Natal'ja Dolgorukaja*, as though released from blocked positions, fall smoothly into place. The heroine prays, and as "she seems to hear choirs of angels," one finds that one is not irritated by the fact. Kozlov deals with two of his favourite themes, Moscow and the religious life; small wonder that he conveys his feeling for them well. Strophe 7 depicts the interior of Spasov Cathedral:

Animated by an ardent faith,
She hastens into sacred Spasov's temple:

ft. including the cross, and contains many bells, one of which weighs 64 tons . . . ," P. Kropotkin, T. Bealby, *The Encyclopaedia Britannica*, 11th ed. (New York, 1911). On a calm day, the princess would have seen the spire from six miles, and heard it from twelve; now dwarfed by the Ukraine Hotel, it was in 1730 the tallest structure in Moscow.

In the Kremlin, on the same subject, are the Uspenskij, the Blagoveščenskij and the Arxangel'skij Cathedral – but not the Spasskij. There is, of course, the Spasskaja Tower, through which the princess would have entered the citadel of Moscow, since that tower contains the Frolov Gates; but there is no Spasskij Cathedral.

An ikon not made by human hands
Offers defence to the suffering . . .
With timid steps she passes
Through the dark, echoing aisle,
Behind that golden grille
Where, with the thoughtful fathers,
Daughters of tsars have hidden their lives
In the bright chambers,
And now she falls in tears
Before the wondrous ikon . . .
And it seemed that angels hearkened
To her mysterious sadness.

There is, perhaps, no more blatant weakness in Kozlov's verse tales than his repetition of a few devices. The tale within a tale, the commonest of all these, occurs in all three *poemy*. So also do visions or startling dreams. Yet it is hard to determine if the vision in *Princess Natal'ja Dolgorukaja* is a weakness or a strength, a gratuitous piece of melodrama or a dramatic triumph. It is, moreover, important to decide, because thematically and structurally it forms the apex of the work (the heroine's subsequent actions being entirely the result of her vision; the dénouement, it follows, is no more than a delayed reaction to that vision). On its success or failure the whole work must, to a large degree, depend. Few would deny that it is a spectacular, memorable vision; its strangeness introduces a new note into the tale – one of horror.

The princess sits by Red Square, half-conscious, half-asleep, and sees something approach her. The thing resolves itself into human form, and gazes at her intently. Cloaked, and with flashing eyes, the figure scrutinizes her; seeing the boy, it seems to groan and shudder, then, slowly, removes its cloak to reveal a dark stain on its chemise. By now it is obvious that this is Dolgorukov, or his ghost. Delicately playing chords of horror and suspense (the reaction of contemporaries may be judged from A. A. Voejkova's delighted letters), Kozlov produces a hand from a fold of the cloak. Before the princess's and Voekova's unmoving stare, the prince removes his head like a cap (strophe 18). On his neck is "a purple strip." It is a Gothic touch.

The child grows up and, her duty by her son fulfilled (Kozlov ignores Boris Dolgorukov's second grandson, Ivan), the princess resolves to enter a nunnery. It seems that the tale is about to end, but the impression is erroneous. That action missing from Part One crowds into the final strophes. Again, with a nunnery in the background, Kozlov enters his happiest vein; faith struggles with passion by a suitably wild setting, the shores of the Dnieper. Passion, of course, can hardly win, by the laws of Kozlov's own outlook, but the struggle is a fine one and faith is not victorious until the princess is overcome by a second vision. Again the dead prince appears before his wife: "Leave the earthly! Love is holy, sacred, and in love I am yours!"

So intense is the action in the last ninety lines of the work – the ceremony of profession, the arrival of the son, the drama in the nunnery – that one wonders if Kozlov perhaps intended, while writing Part One, to leave his heroine sooner. The tale might have ended either on her arrival at the nunnery, which she plainly intended to enter from the first, or after the second vision. Neither course would have damaged the work in structural terms. Yet, one may object, Kozlov was plainly adhering to his text, which required a clear acceptance of the nun's life. Moreover, Kozlov was happy in description of religious settings and, forgivably, wished to end in the grand manner. Here is the scene in which the heroine's hair is shorn, in token of the vow of chastity:

. . .The appearance of an ancient painting,
And the dim light of lustres
In the gloom of centennial vaults
And, like sepulchral shades,
A sweet-tongued choir
Of holy monks in black:

. . .

The ikons alone, with relics,
Are bright, as though in celestial fields:
From their mountings, and in crowns,
Diamonds and rubies shine like pearls
And, giving out its heat, the fire
Of ikon-lamps slips, stream-like,

Through the fine smoke.

. . .

The sovereign is here: all is prepared:
Already they are leading her into the
Temple, leading her . . . and on the temple cloth
The cross and Holy Gospel
Lie before the ikon:
Beneath them, the scissors gleam . . .

The son arrives too late; "A new angel is prepared"; faith conquers.

Structurally, *Princess Natal'ja Dolgorukaja* represents no advance on *The Monk*. The entire second half of Part One, it was seen, rests uneasily on pure improbability. First, one must face the priest's improbably delayed recognition of the heroine; second, the fact obtrudes that a dead man is resurrected twice within five pages. (Months pass, in fact, between the two visions, but so little does Kozlov choose to stress this that the interval has no reality; time contracts.) Why is the priest made to relate the hapless past of Dolgorukov, and at such length? One must, of course, accept the improbability attendant on certain conventions in literature – otherwise there is no fiction. In tales that begin *in medias res* as do Kozlov's, past happenings may reasonably be told within the framework of those tales. But so much does this priest reveal artificially that credulity is stretched. It is, in short, bizarre that improbability should loom so large in a work that is not a fairy-tale, and in which realistic description of men and buildings, town and countryside, is also so dominant an element. Yet one encounters precisely that juxtaposition in *The Mad Girl* also.

Such are the negative aspects of the work. There is also a positive picture, and one that deserves to be stressed: there are, in *Princess Natal'ja Dolgorukaja*, wider horizons than in either *The Monk* or *The Mad Girl*. No longer content with two scenes (or three, if one includes the young monk's game-filled woods), Kozlov introduces no less than eight interconnected *loci*, ranging from simple cottages to mansions, valleys and dusty roads to nunneries and mighty churches. Frequent changes of scene, moreover, are well controlled; one is not suddenly jerked, as in

The Monk, from a placid and tranquil present (in the father superior's rooms) to a violent, passionate past (the monk's). And there are, in the second tale, more speaking characters; not surprisingly, there is also more dialogue. The ghost-scene, which has no parallel in *The Monk*, has the disjointed, gripping visual presence of a silent film, while the conclusion, like the beginning, is tauter than much of Kozlov's earlier verse. Like *The Monk*, finally, *Princess Natal'ja Dolgorukaja* is highly readable in an undemanding way, but, like a two-volume sentimental novel, it is best taken in small bites.

The mad girl, too, is wandering alone as dusk falls. She, too, is by "a great road" (the two opening lines are, in fact, uncannily alike). She, like the princess, is given shelter by a well-intentioned man and cared for temporarily; around the conversation that ensues between her and that man (The Traveller), as around the dialogues between the princess and the priest and, in *The Monk*, the abbot and the monk, the action of the work is built. Her past, like the princess's and the monk's, has been filled with unusual grief; like the princess and the monk she has lost her beloved. Like the princess, finally, the mad girl is searching for her lover. True, the princess is not haunted by such wild dreams of him as is the heroine of Kozlov's last tale; but she married her prince, while the mad girl never married. Nor is the princess persecuted as a sinner, and forbidden to enter chapels alone. Yet the similarities between *Princess Natal'ja Dolgorukaja* and *The Mad Girl*, obvious to Kozlov's contemporaries, are no less obvious today. It is unfortunate, however, that *The Mad Girl*'s lack of originality should have cast the princess into obscurity for, as has been shown, Kozlov's second verse tale is not without merit.

As for *The Monk*, it does not stand in need of rehabilitation. It was Kozlov's custom to send autographed copies of his works to many personal friends, among them, Puškin. On Puškin's copy of *The Monk* he wrote a flattering epigraph. Within four days of receiving the book, in the first part of May, 1825, Puškin wrote to his brother Lev: "The epigraph of the blind poet has touched me indescribably. His tale is a delight (*prelest'*) – be he angry or not at my saying so. . . . "[35] "I want to reply to him in verse," he

35. *A. S. Puškin*, vol. 9, p. 155.

concluded, "and, if I manage it, will send the verses with this letter." He did not manage it, but the poem was duly written. It says much of Puškin's attitude towards the author of *The Monk:*

Singer, when before you
The earthly world was lost in gloom,
Instantly your genius awoke,
Surveyed all that was past
And, in a choir of bright visions,
Began to sing marvellous songs.

O dear brother, what sounds!
I hear them in tears of ecstasy.
With his heavenly singing
Genius scattered earthly pains;
For you he created a new world,
And in it you both see and fly,
And live anew, and embrace
Youth's broken idol.

And I, if one line of mine
Gave you a moment of joy,
Want no other reward –
Not in vain, by an obscure path,
Did I cross life's waste,
O no; not in vain were life and the lyre
Entrusted to me by Fate![36]

If, as the Symbolist Valerij Brjusov later observed, there were few persons of any literary standing of whom Puškin did not write at least one paragraph or to whom he addressed not one kindly poem,[37] still the sincerity of this brief epistle seems unmistakable.

36. "Kozlovu" ("To Kozlov"), *ibid.*, vol. 2, p. 75.
37. V. Brjusov, *Izbrannyje sočinenija* (Moscow, 1955), vol. 2, pp. 461-2.

CHAPTER SEVEN
THE TRANSLATIONS: KOZLOV AND BYRON

It was Kozlov's particular achievement to introduce to Russians not Byron "the Promethean ... chained to a cliff, tormented by the vulture" (as in Belinskij's fanciful conceit),[1] nor Byron the Romantic martyr, but Byron the poet. Thanks, in large measure, to his versions of *The Bride of Abydos, Childe Harold* and *Lara*, to mention only three of those especially admired by Andrej Turgenev – one of the earliest Russian acolytes in the Byronic temple – those who "chose to immerse themselves in the surf of poetry, reading and re-reading Byron" were by 1825 no longer condemned "to struggle through *miserable* French extracts."[2] The hold of the Pichots and de Salles, Thiéssés and Letourneurs was broken.

Nor was this the full extent of Kozlov's achievement; few Russians in 1819 had even a passing acquaintance with English literature (unless it were with Letourneur's lamentable versions of Shakespeare, Cowper, Young and Thomson, or other paraphrasts' attempts on Ossian – and even MacPherson was not English).[3] By 1825 Byron was a mighty hero among Russians.

1. V. G. Belinskij, *Poln. sob. soč.* (Moscow, 1948), vol. 2, p. 454, ("Russkaja literatura v 1842 godu").

2. Letter of P. A. Vjazemskij to A. I. Turgenev of Oct. 11, 1819.

3. Among Letourneur's versions that sold in quantity in St. Petersburg were *Les nuits d'Young, traduites de l'Anglois par M. le Tourneur* (Marseilles, 1770), and *Ossian, Poésies galliques* (Paris, 1777). For some years, MacPherson had the distinction of being the "most translated poet" in Russia; Ermil' Kostrov's inimitable *Ossian, syn Fingalov, bard tret'jego veka: gall'skie stixotvorenija* (1792) was followed by the "translations" of Karamzin (*Pesni Sel'mi*), Gnedič, I. S. Zaxarov, V. N. Olin', N. F. Grammatin and six others.

Perhaps it is unnecessary to stress the significance of Kozlov's decision to translate Byron into Russian and not French. The fact would seem to be so plain. It was, with few exceptions, through French versions that the Russian reading public of Puškin's youth and adolescence made what acquaintance they had with English, German, Italian, even Greek literature. Admittedly, Žukovskij's versions of Schiller and Gray were more than adequate – but these were exceptions. "The gentleman author, the St. Petersburg fashionable, the ennuied hussar, the civilized squire, the provincial miss in her linden-shaded château – all read Shakespeare and Sterne, Richardson and Scott, Moore and Byron . . . in French versions, and French versions only."[4]

Yet Russians of Puškin's generation had the examples of several Western literatures before them – those who are backward, as Čaadaev remarks in his "Lettre Philosophique" (1836), are well placed to observe and avoid the mistakes of those walking ahead. It was a consequence of national and literary backwardness that so many Russians, some poorly qualified to do so, should try their hand at literary translation between 1800 and 1820; neither the precept nor the examples of Žukovskij, A. Merzljakov, Andrej and Aleksandr Turgenev fell upon stony ground. Many, predictably, followed the most obvious course and produced slavic equivalents of the (already extinct) eighteenth-century French novel, pale reflections of the odes and elegies of Chénier, Millevoye, and La Fare.[5] Others, certain that Russian literature "needed" Schiller's tragedies, purchased large German dictionaries. Naturally translators chose works that they themselves most cared for, or thought most "useful" to the waiting Russian public. The result, as V. Kulešov has admirably shown,[6] was an incomparable hotch-potch of Scottish lays, French and Italian elegies, and German drama. Something of the conditions in which Kozlov began to translate Byron can be learned from Vasilij Sopikov's invaluable *Opyt*

4. V. Nabokov, *Eugene Onegin*, 4 vols. (New York, 1964), vol. 2, p. 158.

5. See my article "Eighteenth-Century Neo-Classical French Influences on the Verse of Puškin and E. A. Baratynskij," *Comparative Literature Studies*, vol. 6 (1969), no. 4, pp. 435-61.

6. V. I. Kulešov, *Literaturnyje svjazi Rossii i zapadnoj Evropy v XIX veke* (Moscow, 1965), pp. 19-30.

rossijskoj bibliografii (St. Petersburg, 1813). Sopikov compiled lists of the poems, articles, prose pieces or works in translation by Western authors that appeared in the city's literary journals in that year. By or on Rousseau, there were published thirty items, by Florian – twenty-six, by Gellert – nineteen, by Shakespeare – eight, and by Byron – none.

On one thing, at least, there was general accord: the two Western examples best suited to Russian needs, and therefore most worthy of study and translation, were the literatures of France and Germany. Perhaps Karamzin had once translated Shakespeare's *Julius Caesar* and praised it enthusiastically; perhaps, for his own good reasons, Baratynskij had honoured Richardson at the expense of Rousseau;[7] the fact remains, however, that in Moscow and St. Petersburg for the first twenty years of the century, English literature remained both overshadowed by and, strange to tell, subserviently connected with the recent literature of France. (More than once, between 1826 and 1830, Byron and Victor Hugo, Shelley and Barbier faced one another in the pages of Polevoj's *Moskovskij telegraf.*[8]) Ivan Kireevskij was correct: "In the composition of Russian literature," he declared in 1829, "there entered two elements – the French and German ways of thought."[9] But England was far away. Few followed Žukovskij there. While Italians and Frenchmen came to Russia in great numbers, moreover, *pour être ouchitel*, an English tutor was a rarity. And, as though to ensure that Puškin should continue to the end to make schoolboys' blunders, translating his Byron, Wordsworth and Shakespeare,[10] the perverse convention flourished among fashionable families that only girls should be taught English. Had Ol'ga Puškina's English merely been better than her brother's, the fact would have been sad but understandable; as it was she had an admirable command of the tongue, and he, lacking a Miss Bailey or Baillie, none.

7. See Karamzin's introduction to *Julij Tsezar': tragedija Villiama Šekspira* (1787), and E. A. Baratynskij, *Stixotvorenija, poemy, proza, pis'ma* (Moscow, 1951), letter 30.

8. It was Polevoj, not Belinskij, who coined the phrase *Novoe napravlenie*, speaking of a new awareness of French and, especially after 1825, English Romantic literature.

9. I. V. Kireevskij, "Obozrenie russkoj slovesnosti za 1829 god."

10. See chap. 3, n. 14.

It was to a generation that grew up in time to feel the *Arakčeevščina,* who came to maturity only to know, with each successive month, the growing weight of Nicolaevan oppression, that Byron was teacher, leader and, after Missolonghi, martyr. From the first, he was what he remains in Russian eyes – the embodiment of proud, misunderstood and injured individualism, a seeker after abstract Freedom for all men, the victim of corrupt society. He was a revelation. Byron alone could outshine Rousseau, and in his wake came all the other British poets. "After twenty years of isolation," declared a rapturous Polevoj, "the Continental System having been effective in literature as in commerce, there has come about a Renaissance in England. . . . "[11] It says more of the stability of Byron's reputation in Russia than of fresh literary events in England that Polevoj could write in such terms in 1833; Vjazemskij, after all, had enthused over *The Corsair* in 1819, while Žukovskij, still more conscious now of Byron's importance, had attempted a version of "The Prisoner of Chillon" in 1821.[12] Byron, in fact, by no means entered St. Petersburg only after the Decembrist fiasco; Ryleev and Bestužev-Marlinskij had found ample room for him in the columns of *Poljarnaja zvezda*. It was the reign of Nicolas, however, that brought his greatest glory.

1825 marked a watershed in Russians' growing consciousness of the new Prometheus. Kjuxel'beker's diaries for 1826 – 28 speak eloquently of his interest not only in all that Byron wrote or did, but also in all that he was said to have written and done.[13] Unwilling to wait two months or more before reading the final eleven cantos of *Don Juan*, Puškin sent to Anna Kern in Riga, where she purchased Pichot's and de Salle's *Oeuvres de lord Byron* (4th ed., 1824) on his behalf, and sent him off Vol. VII by *occasion*. It seemed, as Jazykov said, as if all poetry, certainly all

11. N. A. Polevoj, "O sočinenijax A. S. Puškina," *Moskovskij telegraf* (1833, Pt. 49), p. 7.

12. See *Ostaf'jevskij arxiv Knjazej Vjazemskix* (St. P., 1886-1903), vol. 2, p. 245. The translation, according to S. D. Poltoratskij (*Revue Encyclopaedique*, vol. 18 (1823), p. 356), "created an epoch in Russian literature. . . . " Poltoratsky also notes that Žukovskij began, but did not finish, a translation of *The Giaour*, (the *MS* of which is missing).

13. For interesting extracts, in this connection, see *Russkaja starina* (1875), pp. 83-5.

English poetry, were embodied in that gaunt and splendid form. Shakespeare had become a smaller figure (though extracts from *Hamlet, Macbeth* and other plays with adequately Byronic, that is, colourful, dramatic plots and heroes, continued to appear throughout the third and fourth decades, notably in *Moskovskij telegraf*).[14]

Kozlov was not the first to translate Byron into Russian. Essays by Orest Somov appeared in St. Petersburg early in 1818, when Kozlov read a line of English only with the greatest difficulty. Again, M. T. Kačenovskij published translations or, more accurately, paraphrases from five different poems by Byron, to which, during the course of 1819, he added lengthy comments.[15] What, then, did contemporaries know of Byron that they had not learned from Kozlov? (That they were anxious to learn anything is clear from a sustained interest, among St. Petersburg *literati* headed by Del'vig, Pletnjov and A. I. Turgenev, in the works of Thomas Moore, whom Puškin, like these three, always regarded chiefly as Byron's biographer and friend, and only secondarily as the author of *Lalla Rookh* and *The Loves of the Angels.* Moore's decision, approved by John Murray, to burn Byron's private journals in the summer of 1824 produced anger and grief in Russia.)

There were French paraphrases, of course. The first French translator of Byron seems to have been Léon Thiessé (*Zuleika et Sélim, ou la Vierge d'Abydos*, Paris, 1816), but his version was little read, and scarcely heard of outside St. Petersburg. Then there were the fragments of *Childe Harold* and passages from *The Corsair, The Giaour* and "The Prisoner of Chillon" published anonymously in *La Bibliothèque universelle de Genève* from 1817 to 1819 (Vols. V – XI). But even these considerable efforts had been overshadowed, by the time Kozlov translated *The Bride of Abydos* (1819), by the huge bulk of Pichot's and de Salle's *Oeuvres de lord Byron*. (Amédée Pichot and Eusèbe de Salle wisely remained anonymous in the first edition (1819). In the

14. Translations from *Hamlet, Macbeth* and *King Lear*, for example, appeared in that journal on seven occasions between 1827 and 1832; the "translators" were A. Rotčev and V. Vrončenko.

15. A booklet entitled *Vybor iz sočinenij Lorda Bejrona*, edited by Kačenovskij, appeared for sale in Moscow in 1821.

second (1819 – 21) they adopted the joint pseudonym 'A. E. de Chastopalli', an imperfect anagram of their names.) It was from this prose version, which ultimately grew to eight volumes and contained pale shadows of Byron's originals, that Puškin, in Pjatigorsk with the Raevskij brothers, first read the opening cantos of *Childe Harold, Manfred* and *The Corsair* in the summer of 1820.

But there were Russian versions, too. And, as the reign of Alexander drew to a close, opportunities to read Byron in extract form became more numerous. Polevoj both published Russian translations of poems by Byron and, as editor of *Moskovskij telegraf*, praised the hero at length – his note to Scott's "The Character of Lord Byron" (1825, no. 1) is an expression of unaffected homage. The long review of the poet's life and work that appeared in *Le Conservateur Impartial* for 1824, no. 2, typified many published in Russian literary journals and almanacs in the first half of the third decade.[16] The article is a paeon. Byron was (inevitably) a warrior in the cause of "human liberty," the Greeks' true friend, a unique spirit, a "great and original poet." Not even A. E. Izmajlov, so soon to turn Del'vig, Baratynskij and other purveyors of "bacchic, Liberal verse" from his door, could bear to refuse Orest Somov space for three versions of Byron – and this in the respectable *Blagonamerennyj*.[17]

Somov did much to spread his own enthusiasm for Byron among the membership of the Free Society of Lovers of Russian Letters. Vjazemskij, too, was an early convert; having first tried his hand at Canto Four of *Childe Harold* – the canto chosen by Kozlov also for four of his five passages from that tale – he soon acquired a taste for the original of which, however, he cannot have understood more than a half. Vjazemskij's Byronic translations, now in verse and generally of tolerable accuracy, continued to appear for the next eight years, "Stixi, vyrezannyje na mjortvoj golove" in 1820, "V al'bom" in 1823, "Bajron" in 1827.[18]

16. See M. Zdziechowski, *Byron i yego wiek: studya porownawczo-literackie* (Krakow, 1894-7), vol 2, chaps. 2-4.

17. On Izmajlov's refusal, see *Blagonamerennyj* (1821), no. 21, p. 16. Translations by Somov appeared in the journal, in that year, in Pts. 15, pp. 211-2, and 17, pp. 122-6.

18. See *Ostaf'jevskij arxiv*, vol. 1, pp. 326-7 and pp. 330-32.

Finally, there were Žukovskij's versions – it would have been surprising if Žukovskij had not translated one whom even Goethe compared with Homer. Conversing with the greatest of his heroes, in Weimar in the spring of 1820, Žukovskij listened patiently as the English poet was extolled. Soon after, he turned his attention dutifully to the new idol of Europe, and his "Prisoner of Chillon" was immediately acclaimed in St. Petersburg.[19] "What I have read of *Silon'skij uznik*," Puškin informed his brother in September, 1822, "is most delightful"; again (writing to N. I. Gnedič eighteen days later), "Žukovskij's translation is a *tour de force*. . . One must be Byron in order to show the first signs of madness with such terrible fidelity, and Žukovskij, to translate this."[20] And it is true, as Poltoratskij noted in his review of the piece (*Revue Encyclopaedique*, 1823), that nothing of the pathos of the original is lost in the translating.

To this extent, then, Russians might become acquainted with Byron even avoiding Kozlov's work. He had predecessors and rivals in the field of translation from the English, yet by 1828 none were so famous as he. The fact is illustrated by a passage from A. I. Turgenev's private diary, for February 20 of that year. Turgenev, one may note, had no reason to praise Kozlov at the expense of Puškin or Žukovskij. "Nos meilleurs poètes," he remarks, "ont traduit Byron. Joukoffsky a reproduit toutes les beautés du Prisonnier de Chillon dans des vers dignes de Byron. Pouchkine, qui s'est formé sur Byron,[21] et dont le génie s'est essayé dans presque tous les genres de poésie . . . l'a imité dans "La Mer," dans son "Napoléon". . . Mais celui des poètes Russes qui doit la plus belle partie de sa réputation littéraire à Byron, c'est Kosloff qui, devenu aveugle à l'age de 42 ans, a commencé à apprendre l'Anglais et debuta par une traduction de la fiancée d'Abydos. Outre cela, il a traduit les stances de Byron: A la mer; La nuit dans le château de Lara; une nuit à Vénise, sur le tombeau de Cécile, à l'Italie, la chanson portuguèse, la bonne nuit, un fragment de

19. See V. Žirmunskij, *Gete v russkoj literature* (Leningrad, 1937), pp. 22-60; also V. I. Kulešov, *op.cit.*, pp. 26-9.

20. Letter of 27.9.22.

21. On this thorny topic, see V. Žirmunskij's classic study, *Puškin i Bajron* (Leningrad, 1924).

Manfred, The Enchantment, deux épitres à Tyrza, The Hebrew Melody. . . . "[22]

Turgenev's list is not complete, nor does he mention that poems by Kozlov of indisputable originality (among them "K Italii," which Turgenev thought taken from the English), are haunted by Byron's shade.[23] In "K Italii," indeed, Byron is mentioned by name.

Kozlov made nineteen translations from fourteen tales or poems by Byron; of these nineteen, eight are translations of whole pieces, eleven are fragments, generally of two to six strophes, from longer poems. Three, "Ne na zemle ty obitaeš'," "Iz Bajronova *Don Žuan*" and "Iz Dzijaura," are free versions by Kozlov's own estimation. Details of the translations and originals have, regrettably, not been available hitherto in easily digestible form, and so are given here. Kozlov's and Byron's titles are followed by the year of the Russian publication and the number of lines, in the original and in the Russian text. Versions of whole poems by Byron are given first, for the sake of clarity:

1.	"Prosti! (Elegija lorda Bajrona)"	"Fare thee Well . . ."	1823	82	82
2.	"V Al'bom"	"Lines Written in an Album at Malta"	1822	8	16
3.	"Evrejskaja melodija"	"Sun of the Sleepless" (*Hebrew Melodies*)	1825	8	8
4.	"Nevesta Abidosskaja (Turetskaja povest' lorda Bajrona)"	"The Bride of Abydos"	1826	1700	1700
5.	"Portugal'skaja pesnja"	"From the Portuguese"	1828	8	8
6.	"K Tirze"	"One Struggle More, And I am Free . . ."	1828	56	56
7.	"K Tirze"	"Away, Away, ye Notes Of Woe . . ."	1828	32	32
8.	"Evrejskaja Melodija"	"If That High World"	1836	8	8

22. The diary is preserved in Puškinskij Dom, *Fond* 309, N. 637.

23. See I. Ejges, "K perevodam I. Kozlova iz Bajrona," *Zven'ja*, vol. 5 (1935), pp. 744-48. Ejges stresses Kozlov's indebtedness to Byron for his own celebrity, and thinks it proper.

9. "Dobraja noč'!"	*Childe Harold,* Canto 1, XIII	1824	80	80
10. "Obvoroženie"	*Manfred,* Act I, sc. 1 (Incantation)	1827	70	70
11. "Noč' v zamke Lary"	*Lara,* Canto 1, X-XV	1827	114	114
12. "K morju"	*Childe Harold,* Canto 4, CLXXVIII-CLXXXIII.	1828	54	54
13. "Pri grobnitse Tset-silii'M."	*Childe Harold,* Canto 4, CIV-CV	1828	18	18
14. "Ne na zemle ty obitaeš'"	*Childe Harold,* Canto 4, CXXI	1828	9	16
15. "Iz Bajronova *Don Žuan:* vol'noe podraženie"	*Don Juan,* Canto 1, CXXII-CXXIII	1829	16	30
16. "Javlenie Frančeski (Iz *Osady Korinfa* lorda Bajrona)"	"The Seige of Corinth"	1829	171	183
17. "Bajron v Kolizee: otry-vok iz 4 -oj pesni *Čail'd-Garol'da*"	*Childe Harold,* Canto 4, CXXX-CXXXVII	1834	64	96
18. "Iz Džijaura (podraža-tel'nj perevod)"	*The Giaour*; "As Rising on its purple wing . . . Except an erring sister's shame."	1838	34	40
19. "Stansy"	*The Corsair,* Canto 1, XIV, i-iv	1838	16	16

Three facts at once emerge from the above: first, that of the nineteen versions, fifteen had appeared by 1830; second, that a tendency to render two lines by three, even by four, grew after 1828; and third, that Kozlov chose to translate passages of the most varied lengths, from eight lines (in "Portugal'skaja pesnja," both Hebrew melodies and "V al'bom") to seventeen hundred (in Nevesta Abidosskaja'). Admittedly, five pieces are of "medium" length, of between eighty and one hundred and fifteen lines; but no overall pattern emerges – a work of 1700 lines balances the three paired quatrains.

It may be seen, however, that the extracts taken from tales or lengthy poems fall into two main groups: those comprising a single scene or, at most, two essentially connected *loci* ("Ne na zemle

. . . ," "Pri grobnitse Tsetsilii M.," "Iz Bajronova *Don Žuan*," "Dobraja noč," "Obvoroženie"), and those of six or seven strophes ("Noč' v zamke Lary," "K morju," "Bajron v Kolizee"). Four of the six in the former group, moreover, had been distinct and separate scenes in the English. Strophe XIII of *Childe Harold*, Canto 1, for example (which becomes "Dobraja noč"), is the Childe's "last Good-Night" – there are no others; again, "Obvoroženie" translates *the* incantation scene, *the* words spoken on one occasion (over Manfred's senseless body). Kozlov, in other words, tended to choose passages that not only attracted him particularly (because of Italian associations, perhaps, in 15, or religious sentiment, in 13) but which could also stand as independent poems. Plainly, extracts containing the description of a single scene or incident and which, therefore, draw or seem to draw to conclusions, commend themselves well in this respect.

Metrically, the translations are unremarkable. Kozlov conformed unwaveringly to the iambic tetrametric norm of his period.[24] Well might he have echoed Puškin (*Domik v Kolomne*, ll. 1 – 4) that four-footed iambic lines had wearied him – eighteen of the nineteen versions are in iambics, and fifteen of these tetrametric. More than 80 per cent of Kozlov's total output, as of Puškin's, Baratynskij's, Batjuškov's and Vjazemskij's, is in iambics – a fact that becomes more remarkable when it is borne in mind that nothing like the same high percentage obtains in the case of Byron's verse. Specifically, Kozlov preserves the original (iambic) metre in eleven of his versions, alters it slightly in one (in "Nevesta Abidosskaja" – Byron's fluctuating iambic and anapaestic rhythms are not reflected accurately), and changes it radically in seven. Only once, in "Evrejskaja melodija" (1825) did Kozlov presume to change a binary metre to a ternary. Nor, in this connection, are liberties taken with the English rhyme-schemes, which are faithfully echoed.

Kozlov's translations from the English were, of course, not strictly limited to Byron. He also made versions of Robert Burns ("To a Field Daisy" and "A rural Saturday Night in Scotland," the

24. See L. I. Timofeev, *Problemy stixovedenija* (Moscow, 1931), pp. 210-78; also B. O. Unbegaun, *op.cit.*, under "Binary Metres."

latter from "A Cotter's Saturday Night . . . "), as well as from the work of Wordsworth ("We are Seven" and "A Sonnet") and Charles Wolfe. It is no doubt significant that for more than forty years Russians persisted in believing not only Kozlov's "On the Burial of the English General Sir John Moore," but also his version of Tom Moore's "Those evening Bells . . . " (from *Irish Melodies*) to be translations from the English of Byron![25] It was, moreover, only as a friend, collaborator and biographer of the mighty poet that Moore was known at all in Russia, at least until 1850. "The Twopenny Postbag" (1813) might enjoy considerable success in London, but for Russians of the 1820s and 1830s Moore's satirical pieces were of small account if, indeed, they were read by anyone. But many would have sacrificed careers to have been given, as Moore was given, Byron's private memoirs. And as many again saw something fine and romantic in Moore's subsequent decision with John Murray to burn them.[26] Through Kozlov's efforts, *Irish Melodies* (1807 – 34), *Lalla Rookh* (1817) and *The Loves of the Angels* (1823) enjoyed a considerable and steadily increasing popularity among the Russian reading public. Kozlov first, among Russians, translated Moore in a methodical and careful manner. A. Podolinskij, V. Olin', P. Redkin and a dozen other paraphrasts might follow, but it was Kozlov whom Andrej Belasoglo, speaking for his whole generation, hailed as "the Russian Moore, of the sphere of Ireland."[27]

Interest in Moore grew in Russia as a result of Kozlov's work. But had Kozlov never been born, Moore's place in literary histories of Russia would have been assured by his intimate connection with Byron. Russians could not long remain indifferent to a poet who, as well as having flatteringly alluded to themselves in his *National Airs*, was the author of *The Letters and Journals of Lord Byron* (1830).

25. Wolfe's elegy first appeared anonymously in 1816. Since an Englishman like Thomas Medwin (*Journal of the Conversations of Lord Byron*, London, 1824) could believe Byron to be the author, A. I. Turgenev cannot be blamed for making the same error (in his diary for February 20, 1829). Nekrasov needlessly repeated the mistake in 1842 (see *Literaturnoe Nasledstvo*, vols. 53-4, p. 17).

26. In August, 1824.

27. "A.N.V.," *Poety-Petraševtsy*, ed. V. Komarovič (Leningrad, 1940), p. 16.

Those traits which characterize Kozlov's translation work are typical of all parts of that work. For this reason, heavy emphasis is placed here on Kozlov's most distinguished and best known pieces – the versions from Byron; for what is true, technically speaking, of "Nevesta Abidosskaja" or "Dobraja noč," is true also of the translations of Mickiewicz's *Crimean Sonnets*. For this reason, too, it seems superfluous to analyze any particular version or versions from Moore's English original. Nonetheless, two pieces may most justly be mentioned in passing. Few, if any, parts of Kozlov's work became more popular in Russia during his own lifetime than "Večernij zvon," a brilliant translation of Moore's "Those Evening Bells," and that piece known as "Ect' tixaja rošča" ("There Is a Quiet Grove"), Kozlov's paraphrase of "The Veiled Prophet of Khorassan," from *Lalla Rookh*. Here, first, to suggest the accuracy with which Kozlov captures the easy lilt of Moore's rhythm, are the first two quatrains of the air.

Those evening bells! those evening bells!
How many a tale their music tells
Of youth and home and that sweet time
When last I heard their soothing chime.

Those joyous hours are pass'd away;
And many a heart, that then was gay,
Within the tomb now darkly dwells
And hears no more those evening bells.

Večernij zvon, večernij zvon!
Kak mnogo dum navodit on
O junyx dnjax v kraju rodnom
Gde ja ljubil, gde otčij dom

I kak ja, s nim navek prostjas',
Tam slušal zvon v poslednij raz!
Uže ne zret' mne svetlyx dnej
Vesny obmančivoj mojej!

I skol'ko net teper' v živyx
Togda vesjolyx, molodyx!

I krepok i mogil'nyj son –
Ne slyšen im večernij zvon.

Kozlov takes certain liberties with his text, rendering eight lines by twelve. By so doing, he gives himself the patent obligation to expand Moore's meaning or, at least, to make that meaning doubly clear. Moore, in the event, says little, and says it in commonplace terms; but much is implied by the simplest couplet. Insofar as he cannot leave a great deal unsaid, Kozlov is more pedestrian still. Like Moore, he is content to deal in banalities. Of course Kozlov could, had he chosen, have translated four lines in four. It is plain that his expansion of the theme is a deliberate one. Lines 5 and 6 of his version are, in literal terms, gratuitous additions; so, too, are lines 7 and 8 of the second strophe. Matters are still more complex in Moore's final quatrain and Kozlov's equivalent six lines: lines 1, 3 and 4 of the English text are given accurately enough in Kozlov's first, fifth and sixth lines. Closer inspection, however, shows that the Russian fifth line only half translates "While other bards shall walk these dells." Similarly, Moore's sixth and seventh lines ("And many a heart that then was gay/ Within the tomb now darkly dwells") are only half rendered by Kozlov. Only in conjunction with lines 10 and 12 do they translate the English. Thus the sense of the original is expanded naturally. Additional lines contain no unexpected or discordant images; on the contrary, all is organically connected with the rest. Even the strong personal element that Kozlov chooses to introduce (deliberately mentioning his blindness), blends with the whole. Since the personal element is present, it would be disconcerting if the poem did not expand to something a little larger than the English text, and in this lies Kozlov's justification and, some might claim, success.

The poem had a curious history in Russia. An article appeared on Kozlov's translation of it in the journal *Teleskop*, early in 1831.[28] The article was entitled, extraordinarily enough, "A Translation of a Poem by Kozlov into English by T. Moore."

28. "Perevod stixotvorenija Kozlova na anglijskij jazyk Tomasom Murom," *Teleskop*, 1831, no. 8, pp. 567-70.

Having known Kozlov's translation since 1828, when it appeared in Del'vig's *Northern Flowers*, and meeting "Those Evening Bells . . . " only in the 1829 (Galignani) edition of Moore's works, the anonymous reviewer plainly supposed that Moore's piece, which was, after all, headed "To the air: 'The Bells of Petersburgh'," was simply translated or adapted from Kozlov's Russian! In fact, "Those Evening Bells . . . ," as part of *National Airs*, was published no later than April, 1818 (by a certain V. Power, esq.).[29] Kozlov composed "Večernij zvon" only in 1827. But Russians remained confused as to its date and origin, and that confusion was doubled by the curious decision of the editors of two editions of his collected verse, of 1832 – 33 and 1840, to publish "Večernij zvon" without reference to Moore. It was, in the circumstances, excusable that Andrej Kalinovskij should later assert that "Vecernij zvon" was nothing less than a literal translation from the mediaeval Georgian of Georgij Mtatsmindeli (1014 – 65) – "of which," Kalinovskij concludes aggressively, "those curious may convince themselves by examining the manuscript in the library of Gelatskij Monastery, seven versts from Kutaisi"![30]

Here, now, are the opening lines of "The Veiled Prophet of Khorassan," together with Kozlov's version:

29. Power's London edition of April 23 was quickly followed by a Dublin edition (July 6); see S. Gwinn's notes in *Thomas Moore* (London, 1904), p. 194. The Galignani edition, printed in English in Paris, was entitled simply *The Complete Works of Thomas Moore*, and was imported by the St. Petersburg booksellers Plavil'ščikov and Smirdin. Moore's *The Letters and Journals of Lord Byron*, which appeared in the following spring (1830), was banned by the Moscow and St. Petersburg censors (!) Kozlov was obliged, therefore, to wait until Louise Belloc's French translation came out, six months later. The translation, which is barely adequate, was announced in *Literaturnaja gazeta* (St. Petersburg) for March 6 (no. 13, pp. 104-6), suggesting that whatever her faults, Mme. Belloc was not guilty of sloth.

30. A. Kalinovskij, *Gde pravda? (Istorija Afonskogo-Iverskogo Monastyrja)*, (St. Petersburg, 1885), pp. 12-13. The theorem was supported by the erudite A. Xaxanov in his "Očerki po istorii gruzinskoj slovesnosti," Čtenija *v obščestve istorii i* drevnostej *rossijskix* (Moscow, 1892), bk. 2, p. 71. It was a common belief, among Kozlov's contemporaries, that the monasteries of Georgia and Armenia were crammed with valuable ancient manuscripts. V. Grigorovič-Barskij attested as much (*Putešestvie k svjatym mestam*, St. Petersburg, 1819, vol. 2, pp. 222-24), and so did D. V. Daškov ("Afonskaja gora; otryvok iz putešestvija po Gretsii v 1820 godu," *Severnyje Tsvety*, 1825, p. 95). Small wonder that many who never came within 1000 miles of the sacred mountain were outraged on learning that precious, fragile MS lay scattered about in thick dust!

There's a bower of roses by Bendemeer's stream,
And the nightingale sings round it all the day long;
In the time of my childhood 'twas like a sweet dream
To sit in the roses and hear the bird's song.
That bower and its music I never forget,
But oft when alone, in the bloom of the year,
I think – is the nightingale singing there yet?
Are the roses still bright by the calm Bendemeer?

Est' tixaja roščа u bystryx kljucej:
I dnjom tam, i noč'ju pojot solovej:
Tam svetlyje vody privetno tekut,
Tam alyje rozy, krasujas', tsvetut.
V tu poru, kak mladost' manila mečtat',
V toj rošče ljubila ja často guljat':
Ljubujas' tsvetami pod ten'ju gustoj,
Ja slyšala pesni – i mleka dušoj. . . .

Again the pace of the original is slowed and, in keeping with that *rallentando*, the poet's reflections are broader and more leisurely. Of Azim and the maid who sings "in the pathetic strain of Isfahan," as of the Bendemeer that flows by the ruins of Chilimar, there is no trace. All is vaguer. Yet the movement of the poem is not inappropriate to its oriental theme, and Moore's Turkish overtones are preserved in the scenario of roses, clear waters and the inevitable nightingale. It is, to conclude, a poem based on *Lalla Rookh*, not a true translation. There are many such pieces in Kozlov's work, some of them standing on the very point where it is difficult to ascertain whether originality or skill in echoing another text predominates – whether the piece is a free rendering, or an original poem.

Thomas Moore, then, was seen by Russian *literati* first and chiefly as Byron's friend and biographer, and only second as a poet in his own right. Hardly surprisingly, therefore, Kozlov's translations of his poems were seen as in some way forming an appendix to his versions of the greater poet's work. It is not an exaggeration to state that, by 1840, Kozlov's name suggested Byron first, second and third, and Thomas Moore a poor fourth.

Nor did Tom Moore succeed in igniting Kozlov's imagination as, to judge by his epistle "To Walter Scott," Childe Harold could and did:

Suddenly Childe-Harold appeared before me!
Oppressed by a spiritual storm,
Darkened by weary yearning,
He sang hearts' sufferings to me,
And his secret, grievous fate –
And I trembled, I burned with passion,
I heard the voice of torment in my heart.

. . . .

Now I blazed up, now I fainted,
Alas! I myself loved, suffered.
He awakened my dreams . . .
(ll. 20 – 26, 28 – 30)

Each line of "K Val'teru Skottu" (1832) speaks volumes. Kozlov, as both this epistle and his earlier "Bejron" make plain, understated the case, in declaring to Žukovskij " . . . the singer of passions/ Draws me above all others" ("Drugu V. A. Žukovskomu"). Byron, it cannot be over-emphasized, fulfilled for Kozlov an immediate and urgent need. The point is made obliquely in Gogol's essay on Kozlov's verse and translation (1829): "Because the light, clear world of the Greeks . . . had no power to control his poetry, Kozlov . . . sought another encounter in the darkness – and found Byron."

Of itself, the fact that Kozlov learned English chiefly to read Byron in the original is sufficient indication of his admiration for that poet. From the first, he found himself in sympathy with Childe Harold; and always Byron would remain for him "the voice of torment," one who "sang hearts' sufferings." Always, that is to say, he saw only what he preferred to see.

There is a curious detail of his attitude towards the English poet in the "Anecdotes of Russia" of an anonymous Englishman who met him in St. Petersburg in the winter of 1828 – 9. The anecdotes appeared in *New Monthly Magazine and Literary Journal*, published in London, in July, 1830.[31] Kozlov, so the

31. Vol. 19, pp. 73-81.

visitor found, was in the habit of asking his daughter to read him passages from *Childe Harold* to distract him from the pain in his legs, which were paralyzed. The visitor recorded other details. Having learned English, it seemed, "Mr. Kazloff" had translated part of a long poem by Puškin into that language, "which he then sent to His Lordship." He received no reply, for Byron had died within days of the poem's leaving Russia, in March, 1824. Learning that the visitor would shortly be leaving for England himself, Kozlov promptly gave him a second copy of the piece (lines 135 – 154 of *Baxčiserajskij fontan*). So it reached the editor of *New Monthly Magazine*. The first nine lines are given here, following the Russian original:

Oni pojut. No gde Zarema
Zvezda ljuvbi, krasa garema?
Uvy, pečal'na i bledna,
Poxval ne slušaet ona:
Kak pal'ma, smjataja grozoju,
Ponikla junoj golovoju:
Ničto, ničto ne milo ej.
(Zaremu razljubil Girej.
On izmenil . . no kto s toboju,
Gruzinka, raven krasotoju?)

But where is she, Zarema bright,
The star of love, the harem's light?
Alas! she lingers, weeps alone,
Her sweetest dream for e'er is gone.
No jocund tales, no playful songs.
Like the young palm, whose tender bloom
Was blasted by the tempest's gloom,
So stood that fair and lovely maid
Ere yet forsaken or betrayed.
(Yet still in beauty who can be,
Poor Georgian slave, compared to thee . . .?)

Technically, the piece is an improvement on Kozlov's other excursion into English, "To Countess Fiquelmont (In Desert

Blush'd a Rose)." Here there are no awkward inversions, no missing definite articles. Admittedly, Puškin's conciseness proves too much for Kozlov's ingenuity, and the opening rhyme, perhaps, is a little flat; but the palm image is admirable, flexibly but closely rendered. By the introduction of "tender" and "young" – both calculated risks – Kozlov introduces the femininity of *pal'ma*, while *smjataja* is adequately compensated for with "blasted." Above all, the movement of the original is kept. Obviously a more thorough and measured analysis of this, as of each of Kozlov's translations, requires more space than can be given to it here.

Kozlov, to conclude, sympathized with, and felt respect and admiration for an idealized "Bejron." The sympathy was on two planes, personal and literary – the admiration chiefly on the first. But, as was stressed earlier, he felt affection also, and his feeling of affection for his hero was quite independent of Byron's supposed exploits in Greece. It is an abstract, sacred Greece that "Bejron" comes to rescue (ll. 107 – 10): "He is there, in the fateful struggle/ He sustains the great deed with his great soul –/ The saving of holy Hellas." For such Liberals as N. F. Raevskij, Ryleev and Kjuxel'beker, Byron was more a political than a personal hero; for Kozlov, he would have been a hero even had he died quietly in 1823 in Newstead Abbey. It was in feeling a personal closeness to the man, the humanized idea that he most revered, that Kozlov differed in attitude from Puškin.[32]

32. This emerges from Žirmunskij's study, as from N. Polevoj's reminiscences; "O stixotvorenijax I. I. Kozlova," *Moskovskij telegraf*, 1833, no. 10, pp. 323-4.

CHAPTER EIGHT
CONTEMPORARY TRANSLATING PRACTICE AND KOZLOV'S VERSIONS OF BYRON

Few of Kozlov's translations from Byron are literally accurate renderings of the English texts. Of those three or four that might lay claim to such accuracy, none sustains it from the first line to the last. Neither fact is surprising, for Kozlov began his literary activity when precise literal accuracy was by no means the main objective of Russian verse translators. Rather was there a tendency, among the followers of Karamzin and V. I. Lukin, whose examples had been forceful in the last two decades of the previous century, to place secondary importance on exact fidelity to an original text. As Žukovskij put it, summing up his own views on the matter and those of Aleksandr and Andrej Turgenev also, "The prose translator is a slave; verse translators are rivals . . . and a poet-imitator may be an original author, though he write nothing of his own. You see two actors, studying the art of declamation in a third. One, with slave-like accuracy, imitates the glances and bodily movements of his model; the other, to the contrary, trying to vie in the excellence of *his* presentation of one and the same rôle, uses methods (*sposoby*) that are his own and proper to himself alone."[1] It was inevitable that such an attitude, expressed with such authority, should weigh heavily with any literary novice.

Nor was this the full extent of Žukovskij's lucid dogma. "Not being an inventor in the whole," he continued (1809), "the imitator must most certainly be one in parts; beauty rarely passes

1. "O basne i basnjax Krylova," cited by Ju. D. Levin in "Ob istoričeskoj evoljutsii printsipov perevoda," *Meždunarodnyje svjazi russkoj literatury* (Moscow, 1963), p. 20.

from one language to another having lost nothing of its perfection: so what must the translator do? He must find such beauties in his own imagination as may serve as substitutes (*služit' zamenoj*) for the original's, consequently creating his own work. . . . " The imitator, Kozlov learned, *must* be an inventor in parts; translators *must* find alternative expressions for those in the original. Against this, the novice reacted. Kozlov was not slow to reject the full, massive implication of this message – that literal accuracy is, in itself, of minor value.

It is quite true that in no single translation of a poem or extract by Byron did Kozlov fail to replace at least ten images, ten concepts, ten expressions by substitutes of his own devising. But he did so not with relish, but with a marked reluctance. Far from feeling obliged to "create his own work," he most obviously felt a duty towards materials with which he worked; and it is in this attitude, this feeling of duty, that Kozlov's verse translations mark the beginning of the end of the Karamzinian period – the time of grand paraphrase. Of course Karamzin and Žukovskij had also felt obligations to their original poets, but these were of another kind and had been adequately met by the conveying of the spirit (*dux*) of a piece. Kozlov helped to open a new period in Russian verse translation. His contribution is best viewed, first, in historical perspective.

When, in 1803, Vasilij Puškin was invited by the editor of *Mercure de France* to contribute "some Russian translation or composition of your own," he did not hesitate to offer four "translations" of Russian folk songs.[2] There were no hostile reviews by other Russians in Paris or by Frenchmen who chanced to know Russian. The fact remains, however, that Puškin's "translations" were, as such, frauds; rhyme, rhythm, phrasing, all were lost. Local colour was deftly removed. What had been matter-of-fact became suitably sentimental. Puškin is saved, by modern standards, only by the fact that a precise rendering of the

2. 1803, no. 3, under the heading, "Chansons Traduites du Russe"; for piquant detail, see N. N. Trubitsyn, "Iz poezdki Vasilija L'voviča Puškina za granitsu, 1803-04," *Puškin i jego sovremenniki*, no. 19-20 (Petrograd, 1914), pp. 239-69.

originals was obviously not his objective.

Far from setting a precedent, of course, the good Vasilij was following one. Had Karamzin, for example, placed an exalted value on literal preciseness? On the contrary, those articles that he translated in such numbers, from 1802 to 1810, from the originals in *Gazette de France, Le Moniteur Universel, Journal des Débats, Die Zeitung für die elegante Welt* – and reprinted wholesale in his *Vestnik Evropy* – had been filled with errors of every shape and size. Nor were his few verse translations any better.[3] Fortunately, Karamzin understood from the first that his readers read French no worse than he – Madame de Genlis, Madame Cottin and many another "mushroom growing at the feet of oaks" (as Vasilij's nephew scornfully referred to Chénier's successors) made their way to St. Petersburg in French attire.[4] Not a literal translation (though this was also admirable), but a rendering of the mood and tenor of original poems was Karamzin's cardinal purpose. And such, as Puškin knew, had been the purpose of translators in Russia for more than fifty years. Tred'jakovskij was explicit on the subject. It was desirable and feasible (he wrote in the lengthy introduction to his verse collection of 1751) "to lose nothing of the strength and beauty of the original, to compete with its heights. . . . " In this, he was more sanguine than later translators would be; but the passage in "K čitatelju" ends on a familiar note: " . . . to give a rendering that is natural to a Russian's ears."[5] Certainly, Tred'jakovskij's own translations of Boileau were far from literal, nor did he scruple to change metre and rhyme schemes when he chose.

V. I. Lukin, too, was quite prepared, "carefully including and

3. Karamzin edited the journal from 1802-07; under the direction of M. T. Kačenovskij (1807-09), the standard even of paraphrasing sank.

4. A. S. Puškin, "O russkoj literature s očerkom frantsuzskoj." Madame Cottin enjoyed an enormous vogue (very briefly) as the authoress of *Elisabeth, ou Les Exilés de Sibérie* – a touching tale copied by Xavier de Maistre, inter alia, in *La Jeune Sibérienne* (1815). As for Madame Genlis, "she hates philosophy, sighs for the past and writes novels while waiting for the future," (Vasilij Puškin informed Karamzin; V. L. Puškin, *Soč.* (St. Petersburg, 1895), p. 147).

5. See "K čitatelju," *Soč. Tred'jakovskogo*, 4 vols. (St. Petersburg, 1849), vol. 1, p. 8. "Nauka o stixotvorenii i poezii s frantsuzskix stixov Boalo-Depreonovyx," also published in the 1751 edition, makes amusing reading.

excluding . . . to incline [the original – GB] to Russian ways."[6] Above all, Lukin believed, the forced and unnatural should be avoided – even if this means sacrificing the semantically perfect translation of a given word or phrase. Karamzin, as we have seen, did not demur. "As far as my translation is concerned," he declared of his version of *Julius Caesar*, "I have most of all tried to translate faithfully, while at the same time avoiding expressions contrary to our tongue."[7] Precisely what expressions he considered "contrary to Russian" one can only surmise after having checked Shakespeare's text for omissions; but here, for the first time, there are premonitions of Kozlov's later attitude – at least Karamzin places fidelity first ("to translate faithfully"), and the avoidance of the ugly second. Karamzin struggled valiantly, moreover, to capture individual differences of speech and style.[8]

Small wonder, these earlier tendencies having been hallowed by Merzljakov, Andrej Turgenev, Žukovskij and Orest Somov, that by 1826 Polevoj should praise Kozlov's Russian version of *The Bride of Abydos* – precisely because it made him forget that Byron was not a Russian. For those conscious of Kozlov's true aim, there is bitter irony in Polevoj's remarks: "An English or French translation can delight me; I read it willingly; but I am gladdened even more . . . if I see a Russian version. Here it is as though you forget that the great author was an Englishman. Of course the translator who succeeds in rendering his (Byron's – GB) work makes it closer to me (*mne bolee blizkim, rodnym*)."[9]

Žukovskij's position has been seen. It is clearly set forth in two articles, "O basne i basnjax Krylova" (1809) and "Radamist i Zenobija; tragedija" (1810). A brief extract from the latter would seem to be sufficient to underline points made in "O basne i basnjax Krylova," cited already: "Of course the original idea on which the verse structure rests, like the plan of that structure . . .

6. *Sočinenija i perevody V. I. Lukina i B. E. El'čaninova*, ed. P. Efremov (St. Petersburg, 1868), p. 112.

7. N. M. Karamzin, *Izbrannyje sočinenija* (Moscow, 1884), pt. 1, p. 24.

8. For his views on the question, see his letters to I. I. Dmitriev of 1798, esp. March 1; *Pis'ma N. M. Karamzina k I. I. Dmitrievu*, compiled by Ja. K. Grot (St. Petersburg, 1866), pp. 92-5.

9. "Abidosskaja Nevesta; sočinenie I. I. Kozlova," *Moskovskij telegraf* 1826, Pt. 12, p. 183.

does not belong to the translator. But having conceded this honorary superiority to the original author, the translator himself remains a creator of *expression* – for he has his own materials for expression, and must use them without guidance and without others' assistance. 'And the expressions of the original author?' He will not find them in his own language; he must create them. And he can create them only when, filled by the ideal presented to him in the work that he is translating, he, so to speak, transforms it into a creation of his own imagination."[10]

Žukovskij, in brief, regarded himself as the rival, not the servant, of Byron, Schiller, and Goethe. Expressing his own personality and "using his own materials for expression," he might well leave an original text on occasion, stressing some aspects of a poem, softening others and omitting others entirely. In his view, translations were to be judged not as shadows or imitations, but as works in their own right and on their own merits. The theory was consistently put into practice. "Orleanskaja deva," for example, scarcely reflects in Russian all that Schiller intended in his drama; not only is the question of Joan's honour heightened and intensified quite beyond recognition – whole episodes are removed and geographical details jettisoned![11] The example was a potent one; Žukovskij's attitudes live on in translations by Lermontov (in whose "Sosna" and "Gornyje veršiny spjat vo t'me nočnoj" Heine's "Fichtenbaum" and Goethe's "Über allen Gipfeln ist Ruh" are scarcely recognizable). It is a short step from loose translation to mere imitation, and Lermontov did not hesitate to take it.[12]

Žukovskij's basic premises, however, were not universally accepted among Russians – not, at least, after his coming to Moscow (1809). By that year an embryonic opposition movement had been formed, under the lead of B.V. Golitsyn. Golitsyn contested the assertion that the spirit of a work, above all else,

10. See note 1.

11. V. Češixin, *Žukovskij kak perevodčik Šillera* (Riga, 1895); also G. Raab, "Die Lyrik Schillers in fruher russischer Ubersetzung," *Zeitschrift für Slawistik* (1956), bk. 1, pp. 40-60.

12. A Fjodorov, "Tvorčestvo Lermontova i zapadnyje literatury," *Literaturnoe Nasledstvo*, vols 43-44 (1941), pp. 161-2.

must be rendered, and that it determines the value of translations; in a closely-argued introduction to his own versions of Rochefoucauld's *Maximes* (which, as he appreciated, could only lose in force through inexact translation), he took a stance very different from Žukovskij's. "The translator," he argued, "must come to know his author well, become acquainted with his thoughts and turns of speech and be able to translate these into his native tongue. . . . "[13] The phrasing is deceptive; it represents a basic change of attitude.

Golitsyn soon found support – some of it in unexpected quarters. Griboedov himself translated little, yet contributed largely to the theory of verse translation. Perhaps his most lucid, certainly his most outspoken article (it attacked Žukovskij roundly), "O razbore vol'nogo perevoda Bjurgerovoj ballady *Lenory*" appeared in St. Petersburg in 1816[14] and provoked an immediate controversy. Not only did Griboedov criticize Žukovskij's "Ljudmila" as an enfeebled, verbose reflection of the original; Žukovskij himself was charged with carelessness and prettification (*priukrašivanie*). Griboedov, moreover, took the unprecedented step of collating the original and translated texts – much to Žukovskij's disadvantage. The path was open to still more extreme censure of Žukovskij the law-giver. P.A. Katenin was merely one of twenty to follow it to the end. "In great authors," he wrote somewhat stiffly in a "Pis'mo k izdatelju *Syna otečestva*" of 1822, "form is not an arbitrary thing, which can be changed without harming the spirit of a work: the two aspects are linked indissolubly, and distortion of the one inevitably leads to the ruin of the other."[15] Of course verse should be rendered in verse and in the original metre! Of course the Russian language, "supple and rich," was equal to any foreign work, were the translator's skill sufficient! It will be seen that this last point bears directly on Kozlov's versions of Byron.

Kozlov, then, participated in a general movement of reaction

13. Golitsyn edited D. Pimenov's *Nravstvennyje rassuždenija gertsoga de la Rošfuko* (St. Petersburg, 1809), and expressed his own views on verse translation in the Introduction.

14. *Syn otečestva* (1816), no. 30, pp. 150-60.

15. *Ibid.*, (1822), no. 14, p. 304.

against "the teacher of harmony" – a movement similar to that in the field of verse composition in which he would have no part. Reaction had come late; but within ten years of the appearance of Griboedov's article, Žukovskij's views were being ridiculed so widely that Puškin felt obliged to defend his old master ("Why should we bite the breasts of our wet-nurse? Because we have cut our teeth?")[16]

"In order to preserve the qualities of ancient poetry," wrote Gnedič simply, – "qualities that are generally so opposed to those that we demand of our poets – the translator of Homer must renounce all servility . . . before that capricious refinement of society whose approbation we seek so timidly."[17] To the modern eye, perhaps, the statement is axiomatic; in the 1820s it was not so.

Kozlov did not follow, but led the newly intensified quest for greater literal accuracy than Žukovskij held wholly necessary. Thus it is in 1827, twelve months after the publication of Kozlov's "Nevesta Abidosskaja," that we find Vjazemskij attempting (in his version of Constant's *Adolphe*) "first, to bring the language as close as possible to the foreign language." Later, Vjazemskij would repeat the effort in his versions of sonnets by Mickiewicz;[18] still in 1825, however, he could bring himself to read Pichot's and de Salle's *Oeuvres de lord Byron.* It is a striking illustration of Kozlov's impact on Vjazemskij and on changing Russian attitudes towards all verse translation that by 1831 the latter could write (as though it were a very obvious thing, and hardly worth the stressing) that " . . . we already have shining examples of *independent* translations, that is, of re-creations and migrations of souls from foreign languages to Russian; Karamzin and Žukovskij translated in that way. But these emigrations do not speak of the soil and climate of the homeland."[19]

16. Letter to K. F. Ryleev of 25.1.25.

17. *Iliada Gomera, perevedennaja N. I. Gnedičem* (St. Petersburg, 1829), Pt. 1, p. 8.

18. *Adol'f: roman Benžamen-Konstana* (St. Petersburg, 1827), pp. 26-7; on the sonnets, see P. A. Vjazemskij, *Poln. sob. soč.* (St. Petersburg, 1878), vol. 1, p. 334; for this quotation, see *ibid.*, p. 90.

19. Vjazemskij seems to allude to Baratynskij's "Pereselenija duš" (1829), a Voltairian *conte à la russe*.

So, too, Kjuxel'beker was soon striving "to capture the distinctive features of the style, the turns of speech, images and allegories of the original" (in his case, *Macbeth*).[20] Soon, that is, after Kozlov's example began to impress itself on his fellow-countrymen; Kjuxel'beker wrestled with *Macbeth* in 1827-8, and was fully acquainted not only with Kozlov's earlier translations from English originals, but also with problems connected with the lengthy preparation of these versions for the press. Kozlov had become an examplar. His attitude towards translation was echoed, not altered, in Belinskij's articles and correspondence. "Who," demanded the critic in 1845, "will guess how Goethe would have written in Russian? To know this, the guesser would have to be Goethe."[21] Essentially rhetorical, the question represented a *volte face* from Belinskij's own earlier position – that "translators . . . should convey the spirit of the original, . . . translate in Russian as if the very author were a Russian."[22] Had Kozlov known to what an extent he contributed to the changing of Vissarion's mind, he would have been content; for Belinskij came to express views on the question of verse translation that he himself might well have uttered: "And who has the right to modify, alter, shorten or expand the thought of genius? What is the object of translation?"

Such were the prevailing conditions and conventions when Kozlov began to translate. His practice, and the gap between practice and theory, will now be considered briefly.

Immediately apparent in each of the seventeen translations given here is a unique blending of independence and loyalty to the original, of exactness and inexactitudes. Plainly enough, the balance reflects the unchanging dilemma facing all verse translators, Russian or otherwise: to strike an acceptable, or at the least judicious compromise between the demands of any given text and

20. Unpublished *MS* in the Lenin Library, Moscow; F. 218, *kart* 362, N. I. It may be noted that Kjuxel'beker put to good account the experience of M. P. Vrončenko, whose *Gamlet* appeared in a 12-page booklet in 1828 (it was a *partial* translation). His own *Makbet* was written in Schlusselburg Fortress, while he was awaiting transportation to Chita.

21. V. G. Belinskij, *op.cit.*, vol. 9, p. 276.

22. *Ibid.*, vol. 2, p. 427.

the linguistic and syntactic possibilities before one. Study of verse translation is, first and foremost, study of the nature of that compromise.

Something of this dilemma was seen in Kozlov's English version of ll. 135 – 54 of Puškin's *Baxciserajskij fontan* (see pp. 181-2). There are passages – lines 6 to 9, for example – that Byron might have written; phrasing, tenor and vocabulary, all are "Byronic." Where there are changes, they are cautious. Twenty lines are rendered in twenty-two – an excusable expansion. (It is of interest, in this connection, that certain nineteenth-century critics headed by Pavel Vejnberg actively deplored Kozlov's attempts to translate original passages in an exactly equivalent number of lines (for such was Kozlov's object); to make such an attempt, Vejnberg argued, was to run the inevitable risk of losing detail – better by far to concede an additional line and render every shade).[23] And yet, despite this care and caution, the mood of *Baxčiserajskij fontan* undergoes a remarkable change in the translating. One is aware, for example, of certain Victorian undertones that have no place in Puškin's plan. Both "The bashful wish of woman's heart" and "warmer kiss" are drastically bowdlerized versions of the originals, which were more fiery. Both mood and literal accuracy are lost.

Obviously, however, the problems of translating Russian into English verse are not precisely those raised by the opposite process. It is these problems that chiefly concerned Kozlov, and will therefore concern us here. Like the essentials of his method of translating, they are best appreciated by practical comparison. Here, first, is the beginning of the hero's monologue from strophe XIII of *Childe Harold*, Canto I, together with Kozlov's rendering of it, "Dobraja noč":

Adieu, adieu! my native shore
Fades o'er the waters blue;
The Night-winds sigh, the breakers roar,
And shrieks the wild sea-mew.

23. P. I. Vejnberg, "*Don Žuan*: poema lorda Bajrona; perevod I. I. Kozlova," *Žurnal Ministerstva Narodnogo Prosveščenija* (1889), no. 8, pp. 437-9.

Yon sun that sets upon the sea
We follow in his flight;
Farewell awhile to him and thee,
My native Land – Good Night!

Prosti, prosti, moj kraj rodnoj!
Už skrylsja ty v volnax.
Kasatka v'jotsja, vetr nočnoj
Igraet v parusax.
Už tonut ognennyje luči
V bezdonnoj sineve . . .
Moj kraj rodnoj, prosti, prosti:
Nočʼ dobraja tebe!

It will be seen at once that the main problem for Kozlov is one of compression. Byron's sustained terseness places a constant strain on the resources of Russian and, by direct extension, on the Russian translator's ingenuity. The problem, in other words, is rather of linguistic feasibility than of Kozlov's command of his native tongue. Byron's "wild sea-mew" reinforces the point; *kasatka* (swallow) is a *pis-aller* – not only do swallows not fly over open ocean, but they are in no sense connected with the sea or ports. Admittedly, *v'jotsja* lends them a certain aerial splendour. They twist, presumably, in strong air-currents of the sort Byron clearly has in mind. But *kasatka*, like *lastočka* (both with their secondary but common meaning of "darling"), lies at the opposite extreme of avian society from wild sea-mews. *Kasatki* are gentle birds, and never shriek. Why does Kozlov not introduce *čajka*? The word does not, it is true, convey the romantically unusual sense of "sea-mew," but does at least mean "mew." An answer presents itself at once: had he done so, there would have remained one syllable in which to translate, or at least suggest, "wild." There are in Russian no monosyllabic adjectives. A compromise is thus struck; since *čajka* cannot be qualified, and there is no suitable monosyllabic bird (for any adjective, be it *dikij, svirepyj* or whatever, will absorb two of the three available syllables), the *čajka* will be dismissed. There is no space here to consider further alternatives for "wild sea-mew," or even ways in which the concept of following the sun, which Kozlov simply abandons, might reasonably have been conveyed in Russian. Nor is it necessary to do so; clearly, it is difficult to match Byron's succinctness.

Two points immediately arise from all that has been said: first, that Russian is less amply supplied with monosyllables than many other languages, including English; second, that it is hard, therefore, to reflect in Russian the sense-cycles that tend, in Byron's verse, to form tight, regular patterns – couplets. The two questions will be considered separately.

It may be seen that in the opening couplet of *Childe Harold* given here there are four elements or units of sense: a farewell; a native land; a vanishing; and an expanse of water. The phrase "unit of sense" is not technical, or meant to be so; it is, rather, a somewhat imprecise term used for the sake of convenience. (Clearly, "my," "native" and "land" might, no less justly, each be called units of sense; but morphemes, adjectives, participles hardly express completed thoughts or images, whereas clauses plainly do.) Comparison of the two texts shows that of these four units two are conveyed unchanged (a farewell, a native land), and two in modified form. "To fade" is not "to be concealed" or "to conceal oneself"; nor are "waves" "waters blue."

Again, Byron's second couplet may be said to contain three elements of sense. (Purists may discover seven, but the point is clear.) Of these, only the last ("shrieks the wild sea-mew") and first ("Night-winds sigh") are conveyed – in modified or expanded form. The second is simply missing. No breakers roar in Kozlov's ear, which is filled by the sound of wind on canvas. To summarize, then, two elements are lost and two gained in the opening couplet – one, possibly two, lost and one gained in the second. These losses and gains, it must be emphasized, are quantitative, not qualitative; questions of merit and liking have no place as yet in this discussion. Every strophe of "Dobraja noč," each one of Kozlov's translations may be viewed in this same manner. Here, for example, is the third strophe of "Dobraja noč":

Come hither, come hither, my little page!
Why dost thou weep and wail?

Or dost thou dread the billow's rage
Or tremble at the gale?
But dash the tear-drop from thine eye;
Our ship is swift and strong:
Our fleetest falcon scarce can fly
More merrily along.

Ko mne, ko mne, moj paž mladoj'
No ty drožis' kak list?
Il' strašen rjov volny morskoj?
Il' vetra bujnyj svist?
Ne plač': korabl' moj nov: plyvu
Už ja ne v pervyj raz:
I bystryj sokol na letu
Ne peregonit nas.

Four elements are lost, five gained. Robert Rushton's tear-drop is missing,[24] and he neither weeps nor wails in Kozlov's version. No doubt, being "swift and strong," the Childe's ship was also of recent structure – but Byron does not say so. Kozlov's alternatives provide semantic substitutes for words and images that he cannot (or does not choose to) convey. But they serve a second, less obvious function in the framework of a strophe (not of a couplet). Not only do alternatives express something of the image, mood and sense of the original English line (Kozlov's line 1 generally reflecting Byron's opening line, but often Byron's second); they also compensate for elements and *nuances* lost in other, earlier or later lines with which, semantically, they have only the faintest link. Alternatives, in other words, have two, interlocking aims: to make good a specific loss and to compensate for all other weaknesses possible. Thus *drožis' kak list* (l. 2), which hardly does justice to the force of "weep and wail," at least goes far to compensate the loss – which is of tension no less than of meaning – of "Or tremble at the gale?" (l. 4). It is not difficult, of

24. The "little page" was the son of one of Byron's tenants, taken because (as Byron informed his mother) "he seems a friendless animal, like myself." The boy missed his parents, and was sent home to England from Gibraltar.

course, to see why Kozlov's fourth line *needs* to be made amends for: this time the problem of compression overwhelmed him. Unable to convey "tremble," the verb is simply dropped. Similarly, *ne peregonit nas* both suggests the import of Byron's last line and does much to reinforce *bystryj* – a word incapable, left unsupported, of conveying Byron's superlative.

Perhaps it is inevitable that the level of losses and gains, that is, the degree of literal accuracy, varies not only from piece to piece but also from strophe to strophe within a single poem. Human factors attendant on translation need not be laboured here. The degree of accuracy, as a glance suffices to show, varies greatly in "Dobraja noč," sinking noticably in strophes 6 to 8. Here, to make the contrast more striking, is the admirable fifth strophe:

My father bless'd me fervently,
Yet did not much complain;
But sorely will my mother sigh
Till I come back again –
"Enough, enough, my little lad!
Such tears become thine eye;
If I thy guileless bosom had,
Mine own would not be dry."

Ne skryl otets toski svoej,
Kak stal blagoslovljat':
No dolja materi moej –
Den' plakat', noč' ne spat'.
"Ty prav, ty prav, moj paž mladoj!
Kak smet' vinit' tebja?
S tvoej nevinnoj prostotoj
Ax, plakal by i ja."

What would a father feel in such a case if not *toska*? And how well the unending vista of the mother's grief is caught in *Den' plakat', noč' ne spat'*. These are gains in more than one sense. Nor can one reasonably deplore the substitution of *smet'* for "become"; for Byron's idea of rightness in the sense of suitability is rendered by a concept of rightness in the sense of justifiable moral correctness. Changes in the Russian text are few and well-considered. Here, now, are strophes 6 and 7:

Come hither, come hither, my staunch yeoman!
Why dost thou look so pale?
Or dost thou dread a French foeman?
Or shiver *at the gale? –*
"Deem'st thou I tremble for my life?
Sir Childe, I'm not so weak;
But thinking on an absent wife
Will blanch a faithful cheek."

My spouse and boys dwell near thy hall,
Along the bordering lake,
And when they on their father call,
What answer shall she make?" –
Enough, enough, my yeoman good,
Thy grief let none gainsay;
But I, who am of lighter mood,
Will laugh to flee away.

No vot i kormščik moj sidit
Ves' polon čornyx dum.
Il' bujnyj vetr tebja strašit?
Il' morja groznyj šum?
– Sir Cal'd ne robok ja dušoj,
Ne umeret' bojus':
No ja s det'mi, no ja s ženoj,
Vpervyje rasstajus'.

Prosnutsja zavtra, na zare
I deti i žena:
Maljutki sprosjat obo mne,
I vsplačetsja ona. –
– Ty prav, ty prav! i kak penjat'
Moj dobryj udalets?
Tebe nel'zja ne gorevat':
I muž ty i otets.

Kozlov could not know, of course, that the "staunch yeoman," William Fletcher, is Byron's valet – temporarily on loan to the Childe; but why is "yeoman" replaced by a (poetic and archaic) helmsman? There is no indication that the staunch yeoman is at the tiller. Nor, admittedly, is there a Russian equivalent of "yeoman," though this is another matter. Again, why does he lose his pallor only to be plunged into "black thoughts"? Why is the "French foeman" dismissed? Here, a new factor enters: Kozlov plainly did not choose to translate with complete literal accuracy – for it is foolish to suggest that he was incapable of doing so. It was a departure from his usual practice.

But perhaps the two explanations are linked to one another. Seeing enormous difficulties, the solution of which, though possible, would contribute only marginally to the success of a whole translation, perhaps Kozlov preferred to avoid the thankless task. The suggestion seems valid, seen in the context of the strophes that were given above.

All this leads to an obvious question and a simple observation. When does the level of substitution climb to an indefensible pitch, (it being assumed that literal accuracy, other aspects of the original being also conveyed, *is* most desirable)? It is when Byron's line contains more short, crisp words than can be handled in a Russian line of equivalent length. The problem, in other words, centres on Byron's habit of using many monosyllables, and monosyllabic verbs in particular. The question is starkly simple. Of course, there exists the expedient of simply extending the line – from five feet to six, for example, as in "Stansy" (from *The Corsair*). A glance, however, shows that Kozlov was evidently loathe to resort to such a measure.

Consider, first, the opening quatrain of "Dobraja noč'." It contains 23 words; of these 18 are monosyllables – 78 per cent of the total. Again, strophe 10 of that poem is comprised of 47 words, 39 of which are monosyllables – 83 per cent. Matters are much the same in complete poems: "Sun of the Sleepless!" formed of 61 words, 47 of which are monosyllables – 66 per cent; "From the Portuguese," 43 monosyllables out of a total of 55 – 78 per cent. Analysis of other poems and long extracts gives comparable percentages. Kozlov's dilemma stands out in even higher relief when it is borne in mind that in Russian monosyllabic verbs are not, as in English, commonplace, but rare.

That Kozlov's essential difficulty is with the English verb is plain from the opening of "Dobraja noč'": "fades," "roar," "shrieks" all fall by the wayside. The pattern is the same throughout the 17 pieces. Here are strophes X and XI of the first canto of *Lara* along with an extract from "Noč v zamke *Lary*":

It was the night – and Lara's glassy stream
The stars are studding, each with imaged beam;
So calm, the waters scarcely seem to stray,
And yet they glide like happiness away;
Reflecting far and fairy-like from high
The immortal lights that live along the sky:
Its banks are fringed with many a goodly tree,
And flowers the fairest that may feast the bee;
Such in her chaplet infant Dian wove,
And Innocence would offer to her love.

These deck the shore; the waves their channel make
In windings bright and mazy like the snake.
All was so still, so soft in earth and air,
You scarce would start to meet a spirit there;
Secure that nought of evil could delight
To walk in such a scene, on such a night!
It was a moment only for the good:
So Lara deem'd, nor longer there he stood,
But turn'd in silence to his castle-gate;
Such scene his soul no more could contemplate:
Such scene reminded him of other days,
Of skies more cloudless, moons of purer blaze.

Nastala noč'. Nebesnyj svod v zvezdax
Izobražon v serebrjanyx volnax.
Edva strujas', prozračnyje begut,
I navsegda, kak radost', utekut.
Bessmertnyje ogni s rodnyx vysot.
Krasujutsja v stekle volšebnyx vod.
Primančiv vid tenistyx beregov,
I net dlja pčel prelestnee tsvetov:

Mogla b' v venke Diana ix nosit',
Mogla b' ljubvi nevinnost' podarit'.

Mež nix reki igrivaja struja
Bežit, blestit, i v'jotsja kak zmeja.
Vsjo tak svetlo, takaja tišina:
Xot' dux javis' – s nim vstreča ne strašna.
Kak byt' vredu? Brodit' ne stanet Zloj
V takix sadax, v takoj krase nočnoj:
Podobnyj čas dlja dobryx sotvorjon!
Tak Lara mnil, i v zamok molča on
Idjot skorej; emu prekrasnjy vid
O prežnix dnjax nevol'no govorit,
O toj strane, gde svod nebes jasnej,
Svetlej luna, noč' tixaja milej.

Comment seems superfluous; of twenty-seven verbs in these two strophes, all but six are monosyllabic. Nor, needless to say, is the problem confined to verbs – in Byron's hands, all parts of speech seem to acquire unwonted succinctness. Occasionally, as in strophe XI, ll. 9 – 10 of *Lara*, that problem is insurmountable; recognizing it as such, Kozlov omits the couplet ("Where history's pen its praise or blame supplies,/ And lies like truth, and still most truly lies"). It must be said, however, that Kozlov's alternative for the preceding couplet, (*Ukor, xvalu – sxodnej*), not only goes far to compensate for the imminent omission, but conveys an idea of consummate subtlety. More frequently, as the remainder of Kozlov's version attests, Kozlov faces an almost, but not wholly impossible task. Here is strophe XI of *Lara*, ll. 11 – 16:

He wandering mused, and as the moonbeam shone
Through the dim lattice o'er the floor of stone,
And the high fretted roof, and saints, that there
O'er gothic windows knelt in pictured prayer,
Reflected in fantastic figures grew,
Like life, but not like mortal life, to view . . .

Tam xodit on i smotrit, a luna
V gotičeskom otverstii okna

Vidna emu, i blesk bežit struej
Na pol iz plit, na potolok s rez'boj:
I obraza na steklax raspisnyx
Moljašixsja ugodnikov svjatyx
V tainstvennyx videnijax lunoj
Oživleny, no žizn'ju ne zemnoj.

It is an excellent attempt, one feels, at the impossible. Where Byron's gothic windows have four syllables, Kozlov's are apportioned no less than ten (l. 2); when the compactness of the English is preserved, as in the second hemistich of Kozlov's fourth line (six syllables balancing Byron's six: "And the high fretted roof . . . "), it is at the sacrifice of the full original sense. Yet much, semantically, grammatically and even in point of mood, is conveyed by the Russian text. If, as Vejnberg observed, it is difficult to render an original passage in an exactly equivalent number of lines, it is often impossible to render every image and idea in the corresponding line of the translation – a clause in the third line in the third, a word in Byron's sixth in the sixth and so forth. Wisely, Kozlov does not make the attempt.

Of all processes in the art of verse translation, none perhaps is more delicate than that of re-arranging the gathered parts of the original. Here, certainly, one sees the force of Gautier's dictum, *L'art sort plus belle/ D'une forme au travail rebelle.* For, plainly, the re-arranging must and can only depend on certain fixed and inexorable demands – those of metre, rhyme and pace. Yet if grammar, which carries sense, bows to these demands unconstrainedly, how can the result be verse? Again one is brought face to face with the ultimate necessity, in all verse translation, of arranging material in ways compatible, on one hand, with practical linguistic possibilities, and on the other with the demands of sense.

This leads to another major point: that the sense-cycles of Byron's English can only with the greatest difficulty be forced into Russian passages of equal length, yet must be forced; for failure tells strongly on the remainder of any given passage. Byron's verse is comprised, for the most part, of couplets: an image or thought, or both, or two of these, are commonly brought to a conclusion after two lines of verse. For all the questions that may be posed or begged in these line-pairs, circles are also closed. The point is clear in these three couplets from *Childe Harold*, Canto 1, XIII:

But why should I for others groan
When none will sigh for me?
Perchance my dog will whine in vain
Till fed by stranger hands;
But long e'er I come back again
He'd tear me where he stands.

I kto že, kto po mne v slezax
Teper' v strane rodnoj?
Čto-z' rvat'sja mne, žalet' kogo?
Ja serdtsem opustel,
I bez nadežd, i bez vsego,
Čto pomnit' ja xotel.

The failure to translate two lines in two is irremediable, given that a line-for-line translation is intended; there is no room in Kozlov's version for dogs, friendly or otherwise. Vital space has been commandeered – and cannot be returned to the rightful canine owner. The alternative, a repetition of the first three lines followed by variations on that theme, is weak.

This and other shortcomings are compensated for by the occasional *trouvaille* – the translation that is so apt that no other seems possible. One thinks of Kozlov's solution to the problem of "So calm, the waters scarcely seem to stray,/ And yet they glide like happiness away." Or again, we have Lara's features "fix'd in horrible repose" (*Otsepenel v pokoe rokovom*), or the "waving banner" in his hall (*zybučij flag*). Not a shade of strength, not a breath of the original mood is lost in these versions, of which many examples might be found. Consider, for example, the lines *Už polnoč'* to *strašnyj krik*, the first quatrain of "Noč' v zamke Lary." Word for word, the translation could hardly be called literal; yet the lines mirror the English. Again, the first five lines of the following strophe seem to echo Byron's thought. Nothing is lost, no detail or nuance.

Yet always one returns to the shortcomings. Kozlov's eighth line is a pale shadow of Byron's "flowers the fairest that may feast the bee;" no assonance remains, nor any drowsiness. Lara does not, for Kozlov, return to his "castle-gate," nor does he brood on "nights more soft and frequent." Finally, on quite another level, it seems uncertain if Kozlov correctly understood the last three lines of strophe X; it is the storm, surely, that is unsparing, not the man (and, in any event, Kozlov seems to have thought "unspared" better than "unsparing," and offers *heščadim*).

So it is also in "K morju" (from *Childe Harold*, Canto 4, 178 – 83). Again there are *trouvailles*: quatrains faultlessly rendered, lines that reflect the brittle mood of the original; and once more one is conscious of something lost. Most flaws are minor – misunderstanding of "society" in Byron's third line, for example, which is quite lost in *beseda*; or a crude translation of the crucial line, "I love not Man the less, but Nature more." At most, one half of this idea is conveyed by *Mne blizkij mil*. Here, as in *Lara*, there are phrases that defy translation: "Spurning him from thy bosom to the skies," with its close-meshed associations of scorn, spitting and restless, irritable movement – all is lost in the bland, *Vostaneš'ty*. Nor could any man hope to deal with "thunderstrike the walls" (l. 25) or the grand, Miltonic lines of Byron's fourth strophe. The vigour of the last quatrain, most would agree, is sadly sapped by Kozlov's refusal to face up to slime and monsters.

But in this, as in each of the nineteen translations, there are fine touches; were there not, all later generations of Russian and Soviet critics would surely not have accepted the view of Kozlov's contemporaries – that he was the most distinguished of Byron's Russian emissaries. Failure is always near. The fact hardly needs labouring. Are translators to work only with feeble poems, selecting those pieces that they feel they can improve in the translating? The dilemma is insoluble. Translation of poetry is a quixotic undertaking. *How* Kozlov sometimes fails to do full justice to his models has been suggested here; precisely in what the loss consists is a matter of personal judgement.

CHAPTER NINE
KOZLOV'S CHANGING LITERARY FORTUNES

During his lifetime, Kozlov enjoyed varying literary fortunes, from the triumphs of "A Venetian Night" (1824) and *The Monk* (1825) to the muted success of *Princess Natal'ja Dolgorukaja*, the gradual decline of the years 1835 – 39 and the last, unexpected *coup* of the collection of his works published in 1840. Since his death in that year his fame, both as a poet and as the translator of Byron, Moore and Wolfe, has been subject to less dramatic oscillations, yet still has not come to rest at one, steady level. Only during the years 1855 – 90 and 1948 – 68, indeed, was a consistent attitude towards his total work maintained, in both cases because of the appearance of editions of his verse (those of A. Smirdin and the *Biblioteka poeta, bol'šaja serija* edited by E. Kuprejanova), with large and favourable prefaces. Needless to add, the attitude was very different in each case, Smirdin unconsciously reviving Žukovskij's emotional conceit of Kozlov the Christian Sufferer,[1] Kuprejanova insisting rather on the friendship with Puškin, the historical context of Kozlov's narrative tales and versions of Western Romantics. The last three years have witnessed a new interest in Kozlov's verse and, especially, his translations from the English, both in the West and in the Soviet Union.[2]

Kozlov's rise to fame as an original poet, as B. Mejlax rightly stresses in the 1953 Academy *Istorija russkoj literatury* (*A History*

1. For details of Smirdin's 1855 edition, and of subsequent editions, see I. I. Kozlov, *Stixotvorenija* (Leningrad, 1960).

2. To my knowledge, two postgraduate dissertations on Kozlov have been written in Leningrad State University (Philological Faculty) since 1968.

of Russian Literature), was the direct result of his extraordinary personal circumstances, loss of the use of a leg, then of his eyes, then of other limbs.[3] Although rapid, however, his rise to celebrity in the two capitals was not remarkably so. He had been Žukovskij's friend, and been seen as such, for ten years before his French translation of *The Bride of Abydos* was circulated in manuscript form. Two more years passed before the appearance of the epistle to Žukovskij that was his literary début.[4] By 1824, it may be said, Kozlov occupied an assured but modest place in Russian literary circles. Most leading poets and critics of Puškin's, as of his own generation, were his personal acquaintances. From a letter written by Del'vig to Puškin in the September of that year[5] it is plain that Del'vig, like P.A. Pletnjov, visited Kozlov regularly. In the following year, Kozlov became a reliable contributor to Del'vig's almanac *Northern Flowers*.[6]

It was *The Monk*, however, that caused such men as Griboedov and Baratynskij, neither Muscovites nor city-lovers, to write to him in the tones of purest enthusiasm, then to call on him. Baratynskij's letter from Gel'singfors (Helsinki) of January 1825, bears citing here; it throws interesting light on the reaction of informed contemporaries to Kozlov's first tale:

> So we live to see another year, my dear Kozlov; I hope it may be *happy* for you, and full of fine inspiration. I have received your *Monk*, and read it through with particular pleasure; certain passages touched me deeply. You call it "your favourite child" and have good reason to love it: it is, in my view, a beautiful work. The situations in it are distinguished by their strength, and the style is full of life and glows with colour; you have poured your soul into it. The places where you imitate Byron excel his own, so far as I can judge. The quatrain from *The Giaour*:

3. p. 334.
4. See *I. I. Kozlov*.
5. Letter of 10.9.24 Kozlov was also visited, between 1824 and 1829, by Krylov, Gnedič, Baratynskij and Tjutčev.
6. See J. Mersereau, *Baron Del'vig's Northern Flowers* (Ann Arbor, 1967), pp. 81-4, p. 214.

I clasp – what is it that I clasp?
No breathing form within my grasp:
Alas, around a shadow prest
My arms sink on my lonely breast

> comes out beautifully in Russian. But where Byron would have wished to imitate you is in the conclusion of your tale. It, in particular, speaks to the imagination, and breathes a special, national Romanticism – which, it seems to me, you are the first to have caught. Continue on the same path, dear poet, and you will accomplish wonders. I will return your notebook next week; I am transcribing it for myself, for I wish not only to read you but also to study you![7]

It was the strength of the situations, the style "full of life" and "glowing with colour" that appealed to Kozlov's first readers. Baratynskij's remarks are closely echoed by those of Polevoj, Vjazemskij, Puškin. . . . Small wonder that Kozlov, ranked with Byron and among Russia's Romantic poets (it is the drama, the *brio* of which Baratynskij speaks, not the structure or form), was also seen as the enemy of the conservatives, or *klassiki*. From Baratynskij's tone, it is clear that he counts on Kozlov's sympathy and agreement with such a position as this: "Our journalists have become simply literary monopolists; they create public opinion, and set themselves up as our judges with the help of their usurious machinery. They are all of one party, and have, as it were, formed an alliance against all that is fine and honourable. This Greč, Bulgarin and Kačenovskij form a triumvirate, which directs Parnassus. You will agree that this is rather sad. So we should support *Mnemozina*, and help Polevoj's journal on its way; otherwise the reputation of our works will directly depend on how the above-named gentlemen are feeling disposed towards us."

Baratynskij was disappointed as far as V.K. Kjuxel'beker's and V.F. Odoevskij's radical *Mnemozina* went. Hostile though Kozlov might be towards Nikolaj Greč (1787 – 1867), once the enemy of autocracy but now, after the fateful Decembrist uprising, the conservative editor of *Son of the Fatherland*, still he did not

7. E. A. Baratynskij, *op.cit.*, pp. 473-4.

choose to take an openly aggressive attitude; and Greč continued to receive his work.[8] Faddej Bulgarin (1799 – 1859), however, was another matter, and Kozlov came to regard that arch-entrepreneur of Russian publishing with real aversion. Kozlov's position in the literary polemic centred on A. E. Izmajlov's *The Well-Meaner* has already been considered (Chapter 5).

It is of particular interest that Baratynskij saw in Kozlov the natural ally and supporter of Nikolaj Polevoj. The link between the two, it is clear from another letter (of April, 1825) was strong in his mind. "I have seen Polevoj only once," he informed Kozlov, who had seemingly mentioned him in an earlier, unfortunately lost letter,[9] "before he left for Moscow; he seemed to me an enthusiast in the manner of Kjuxel'beker. If he raves, it is with a good heart, and at least he is honest."

Nikolaj Polevoj (1796 – 1846), was a self-made man, the son of a merchant. He could never "become a gentleman," and gentlemen, as opposed to aristocrats such as Vjazemskij and Odoevskij, always despised him.[10] But his enthusiasm did much to spread "the new literature," that is, English and French Romantic literature, and to intensify Russian literary life. His magazine, *The Moscow Telegraph* (1825 – 34), was a committed, if undiscriminating propagator of Scott, Byron, Hugo and Barbier. In 1834 *The Telegraph* was banned for having printed an unfavourable review of an ultra-patriotic blank-verse drama *à la Schiller* by Nestor Kukolnik, a superficial and justly forgotten playwright. Polevoj was financially ruined.

Polevoj's journal was founded three months before *The Monk* appeared, and was in the flush of its editor's Byronomania. Small wonder that the review, written by Vjazemskij at Polevoj's request, was enthusiastic.[11] The tale, declared Vjazemskij roundly,

8. See *I. I. Kozlov; stixotvorenija* (Leningrad, 1960), p. 445.

9. E. A. Baratynskij, *op.cit.*, pp. 481-2.

10. Neither Prince Vjazemskij nor Puškin declined to drink champagne in Polevoj's well-appointed rooms, and treated him with bonhomie (see the diary of Franciszek Malewski for Feb., 1827, publ. in *Literaturnoe nasledstvo*, vol. LVIII (1952), pp. 266-72). What rankled with some was that Polevoj not only *drank* champagne but knew who imported it and at what cost. (In 1818, according to Polevoj's *Moscow Telegraph*, 1830, no. 14, p. 229, 158,804 bottles were imported from France, at a cost of 1,228,579 roubles. Such knowledge was thought vulgar).

11. *Moskovskij telegraf*, 1825, no. 11, p. 312.

was "an unexpected phenomenon in the realm of poetry" – the more delightful because its existence was only dimly suspected. (Here Vjazemskij showed himself unusually out of touch with literary developments; *The Monk* was no secret to Puškin or Pletnjov, his close informant.) The author's age and personal destiny were remarkable; Vjazemskij therefore remarked upon them at length. As to the work itself, it was excellent both in point of style and of content. "The richness of Mr. Kozlov's talents," concluded the critic, "promises us a major poet in the near future. . . . "

Princess Natal'ja Dolgorukaja, too, seemed to Polevoj a worthy representative of "the new direction" in Russian verse. Less inclined to abstract theorizing than his journalistic rivals (and fellow-plebeians), N.I. Nadeždin, Schellingian editor of *The Telescope* (1831 – 36) and M. P. Pogodin, son of a serf, historian, businessman and founder of *The Muscovite* (1841 – 56),[12] Polevoj was acutely sensitive to fresh currents in European literature other than German. And were not Kozlov's tales obviously English in flavour and inspiration? It followed that they should be given all praise.

Polevoj proved a useful friend to Kozlov; he would have been an awkward enemy, as was discovered by "those stupid people and journals" less conscious than himself of "the new direction": "Literature is not limited now by codices, which halted it for so long; it has expanded its territory and, showing an *enlightened* respect for the ideas, works and education of the ancient, has added the experiments of *new* times to its intellectual store. This transformation has occurred, not in the imagination, not in the fancy, as stupid people and stupid journals believe. The constant advance of the new tendency is the proof of its existence."[13] Kozlov's verse found a ready welcome in *The Moscow Telegraph*, where, between 1825 and 1828, Byron remained the spirit in residence. Readers of the opening issue, apprised of Polevoj's opinions on such matters, were not surprised to find an enormous tract from Walter Scott's *The Character of Lord Byron* therein.

12. For a thumb-nail sketch, see D. Mirskij, *op.cit.*, pp. 161-2.

13. "Vzgljad na nekotoryje žurnaly i gazety russkie," *Moskovskij telegraf*, 1831, no. 7, p. 49.

Polevoj himself added a "supplement" to that article ("Pribavlenie k *Xarakter lorda Bejrona*"). Nor did England soon lose its dominant position in his journal. Twenty-eight cantos of *Don Juan* appeared in its pages in 1829 (Pts. 25 – 26); Scott's *Clorinda*, also in 1829 (Pt. 29); Moore's *Loves of the Angels*, in 1828 (Pt. 24); and translations from *Hamlet, Macbeth* and *King Lear* on seven separate occasions from 1827 to 1832. Kozlov benefited from that position in a way that he neither deserved nor chose. To Polevoj, as to many of his countrymen, he always remained Byron's and Moore's agent in Russia.

"After twenty years of isolation," declared Polevoj in 1833, "the Continental System having been effective in literature as in commerce, there has come about a renaissance in England – a renaissance completed alone."[14] It was England, and so, by extension, Kozlov who showed the way; and what was the distinguishing mark of Byron's, Scott's, and Kozlov's verse? It was an awareness of individuality, of the virtues of their own, but also of other national literatures and peoples. "The effort to translate into the French tongue the great works of English, Spanish, German Romantics has reached a high pitch of accomplishment . . . the time has now come to render these works into our native, Russian tongue."[15] Kozlov, who had been doing so for nine years, deserved the gratitude of Russians.

"Ce n'est point à la surface de l'art que doit être la couleur locale, mais au fond, dans le coeur même de l'oeuvre, d'où elle se répand au dehors, d'elle-même!"[16] Hugo's remark might have been written by either Kozlov or Polevoj; both sought the development of passion in the Russian tale, of colour, action and, above all, the arresting quality of unexpected drama; both sought to exalt the grandiose and striking in Russia's own national past; both, finally, believed, and tried to demonstrate in verse or criticism, that "passions burn brighter in a few . . . when cold has chilled the hearts of all."[17] For precisely those reasons that Polevoj con-

14. "O sočinenijax A. S. Puškina," *ibid.*, 1833, no. 1, p. 7.

15. "Dramatičeskie proizvedenija 1828-ogo goda," *ibid.*, 1831, no. 4, p. 86.

16. Cited by G. Brandes in "Frantsuzskaja literatura, romantičeskaja škola," *Literatura XIX-ogo veka v ejo glavnyx tečenijax* (Moscow, 1911), p. 259.

17. N. A. Polevoj, "Inostrannaja literatura na 1833 god," *Moskovskij telegraf*, 1833 Pt. 49, p. 69.

demned Baratynskij's *Bal* (1828) – its concentration on the trivial and mundane, its lack of colourful, dramatic happenings[18] – he could only praise Kozlov's second *poema*.[19] And, of course, the blindness of the poet moved him, as it moved Vjazemskij and Orest Somov also.[20] "Speaking with him," Polevoj informed his readers in 1828, "I forgot that he was blind, that the burden of sickness riveted him to the couch of suffering. . . . "[21] The metaphor is confused, perhaps, but the sentiment plain; it was echoed by Puškin.

Kozlov and Puškin first met in 1819, but the friendship had not time to develop before, disgraced by his own epigrams and ode "To Freedom," Puškin was transferred to Ekaterinoslav, now Dnepropetrovsk, and thence, taken suddenly ill, to the Caucasus. Nonetheless, it was as to an old friend that Puškin referred to "the dear blind men" in the years 1823 – 4. Puškin was generous in his praise of others' work and complimented many authors over a period of twenty years as he complimented Kozlov. Nor was that praise always, in retrospect, wholly justified, save on the grounds of kindliness and friendship. Yet Puškin's admiration for *The Monk*, and for Kozlov the man, does not appear to have been forced or unfounded. As in the cases of other friendships with contemporary authors, Puškin made no attempt to separate the man from the creator,[22] and it is plain, from his several references to Kozlov in letters to his brother Lev, Pletnjov, Del'vig and Vjazemskij, that he admired him both personally and as the author of *The Monk*, "A Venetian Night" and certain original elegies. Personal and aesthetic merits mingled, sometimes inappositely, in Puškin's assessments of contemporaries and friends.

Puškin and Kozlov found an extraordinarily reliable intermediary, for personal and literary matters. Pjotr Pletnjov (1792 – 1862), a gentle scholar, weak poet and skilful critic, as well as

18. The charge is, of course, spurious. Is the sudden appearance of "a dry, withered hand" from the dark (90 ll. from end) not dramatic?

19. "Knjaginja Natal'ja B. Dolgorukaja; sočinenie I. Kozlova," *Moskovskij telegraf*, 1828, Pt. 19, pp. 537-9.

20. Somov reviewed the tale for Del'vig, *Severnyje tsvety na 1829*, p. 42.

21. *Moskovskij telegraf*, 1828, no. 4, pp. 549-50.

22. See *A. S. Puškin*, vol. 9, p. 155.

Puškin's literary agent, Imperial tutor in Russian literature and history (1826 – 32), editor of Puškin's journal *The Contemporary* and, finally, Rektor of St. Petersburg University, lived in that part of St. Petersburg, Petrovskaja Storona, where Kozlov also lived. It was entirely natural that he should see Kozlov often.[23] And it is clear, from two letters to Puškin of early spring, 1825, that he kept Puškin well informed as to Kozlov's activities. "I shall see Kozlov tomorrow," Pletnjov wrote conscientiously, "and will read him your letter. He values your opinion more than any noisy acclaim. His 'Byron', it seems to me, is better in parts than in the whole. You cannot chop up a tale into a lyrical poem."[24] Again (on March 3), "Kozlov's *The Monk*, you know, is coming out soon. . . ."[25]

Puškin did not forget to enquire after Kozlov, as after other St. Petersburg acquaintances, when writing to his brother and sister in December, 1824. Had *Evgenij Onegin* been read to him? Was he well?[26] He had, in fact, no chance to forget Kozlov's existence. A. A. Bestužev wrote from St. Petersburg within days of his writing to his brother: "The literary news at this end is meagre in content, and no less boring. I will only say that Kozlov has written *The Monk*, and they say it's not bad. He has flashes of poetry, but the livery of poetry has not yet been fitted to him, and pray God that Byron will not be judged by his versions."[27] In the same terse letter, Bestužev condemns Baratynskij's "Eda"; it, like other works of the time, totally failed to meet his new, and increasingly stringent, utilitarian criteria.

Bestužev, of course, was not the only one whom *The Monk*, and Kozlov's work as a whole, failed to please. N. N. Raevskij's grounds for dissatisfaction were quite different. "Il y a de la véritable sensibilité," he informed Puškin in a letter of May 10, 1825, "de l'observation, (j'allais dire de la connaissance du coeur humain), une intention heureuse et bien éxécutée, enfin un style

23. The fact emerges from A. A. Voekova's correspondence with Kozlov; see N. V. Solov'jov, *Istorija odnoj žizni*, 2 vols. (Petrograd, 1916), vol. 2, pp. 24-55.

24. Letter of 22.1.25; see Puškin, *Poln. sob. soč.* (Moscow, 1937), vol. 13, p. 133.

25. He, Pletnjov, circulated *MS* of the tale in Vjazemskij's *salon*.

26. *A. S. Puškin*, vol. 9, p. 126 (letter of 4.12.24).

27. A. S. Puškin, *Poln. sob. soč.* (Moscow, 1937), vol. 13, p. 149.

pur dans le *Shernets*, tant que Kozlov parle d'après lui-même; mais pourquoi a-t-il pris pour cadre une parodie du *Giaour* et finit-il par une longue paraphrase d'un passage de *Marmion*?"[28] Raevskij's charge is considered in Chapter 6. Suffice it to say here that Bestužev and Raevskij formed a minority in censuring Kozlov's first tale. To censure the third, many were willing.

On Puškin's copy of *The Monk*, it was seen, Kozlov wrote a brief, flattering epigraph. Puškin's indirect response – to his brother Lev – bears mention. "His tale is a delight," he wrote, "and 'I Wished to Forgive, But Could Not Forgive' worthy of Byron. The vision and the conclusion are beautiful. Perhaps the epistle is better than the tale – at least the frightful place in which the poet describes his going blind will always remain a model of anguished poetry. I want to reply to him in verse and, if I manage, will send the verses with this letter."[29] In the event, he did not manage it, but the verses, "To Kozlov," were written, and have been cited.[30] Kozlov's reply, dictated to his wife and dated May 31, 1825, casts a bright light both on his working method and on his attitude towards Puškin, man and poet. Here it is in entirety:

St. Pétersbourg, le 31 mai

Mon cher Pouchkine,

Il m'est impossible de vous exprimer l'extrême plaisir que m'ont causé vos charments vers; ce fut vraiment un moment délicieux dans ma vie et je vous en remercie chaudement. Ce n'est pas le peu de talent que je puisse avoir, mais mon admiration pour le vôtre et le sincère attachement que je vous porte, qui justifient le premier hémistiche du 7-e vers; encore une fois merci et grand merci: il a été droit à mon coeur.

J'ai lu le deuxième chant d'*Onéguine*; c'est un charme; j'ai lu aussi les poésies fugitives; parmi celles que je ne connaissais pas encore, j'en ai trouvé qui me paraissent inimitables: la fille de Czerni-Georges, les versets du Coran et deux élégies m'ont tourné la tête. Quand je fais des vers, je lis mon Byron, Joukovsky et vous, et tant bien que mal mon

28. *Ibid.*, vol. 13, pp. 172-3.
29. Puškin did, however, write the epistle within ten days.
30. Pp. 162-3.

imagination fermente et je me mets à chanter. J'espere que votre triple imagination ne m'abandonnera pas dans mon nouveau petit poème – c'est la Princesse Dolgorouky-Chérémetieff: je trouve que ce sujet est infiniment touchant. Je n'ose pas dire que la *Douma* de Reileeff, qui porte ce nom, soit sans mérite; mais il me semble qu'elle n'empêche pas de tenter un petit poeme de 7 à 800 vers. Mon plan est fait et quelques fragments aussi, mais avant tout c'est ma fiancée d'Abydos qui viendra se présenter à votre porte.

Je vois votre frère et tous nos amis très souvent; Baratinsky nous arrive dans quelques jours, ainsi que Viazemsky, mais en revanche Tourgénieff part; c'est une perte irréparable. Si vous lisez nos journ-aux, vous verrez que Boulgarine ne se rappelle plus qu'une seule chose, concernant Tourgénieff, c'est qu'il prend beaucoup de café et gobe des mouches en avalant ses craquelins. Nos journalistes deviennent de jour en jour plus plats. Vos deux epigrammes contre celui de Moscou font mourir de rire, surtout *Basile* et *Michel*; ceux d'ici en mériteraient de semblables; mais si vous voulez du verbiage français dans un autre genre, lisez le nouveau poème de Lamartine sur *Harold*. Malgré quelques beaux vers, c'est de ce galimatias double dont parle Beaumarchais. Je finis cette lettre peut-être beaucoup trop longue: pardonnez si j'ai osé vous traiter comme une ancienne connaissance – je vous demande votre amitié, cher Pouchkine, et fais des voeux ardents pour votre bonheur. Je vous embrasse de tout mon coeur, et suis à jamais tout à vous,

Jean de Kasloff[31]

It was, in the context of his own aesthetic, not surprising that Kozlov admire Puškin's *Imitations of The Koran* (*Podražinija Koranu*) and *To the Daughter of Black Georgij* (*Dočeri Karageorgija*). That he should be acquainted with the poems is, in itself, an interesting incidental proof of his rapport with the literary life of St. Petersburg; though the epistle was composed in October, 1820 (in Kišinjov, in the vicinity of which lived the

31. Taken from V. Ja. Brjusov's *Pis'ma Puškina i k Puškinu* (St. Petersburg, 1903), pp. 95-6.

Serbian leader's family), the first work was not written until mid-November, 1824 – and neither piece was published until 1826. It would seem reasonable to think that Pletnjov, who had manuscript copies of both, read them to Kozlov soon after receiving them.

As *To the Daughter of Black Georgij* reflects all the colour and violence of Kozlov's narrative tales, so *Imitations of the Koran*, consisting of nine sections, of between twelve and thirty-six iambic lines, seems steeped in that "sumptuous dreaminess" (to use Baratynskij's phrase),[32] that same religious spirit that prevails in his original elegiac verse. To claim that Puškin's *Imitations* are religious in their content is a supreme diminution; the Prophet and his wives, the Day of Judgement, a seer in his cave, God and his angels, sinners and pilgrims vie for the attention. (Based on Mixail Verjovkin's 1790 translation of *The Koran*, Puškin's pieces are so independent, in phrasing and in spirit, as to defy the literary detective.) Since clear statements by Kozlov as to his personal predilections in contemporary literature are few, it may be well to see what it was that "turned his head" in the April of 1825. Here, first, are the opening lines of section II:

O pure wives of the Prophet,
From all women set apart,
To you the very breath of sin is fearful:
In the sweet shadow of silence
Live modestly: the veil
Of the unwed maiden becomes you.
Preserve your faithful hearts
For sweet bliss that is shy and licit . . .

Again, the concluding quatrains of III:

But an angel shall sound the trumpet twice;
A heavenly thunder shall roar on earth:
And brother shall run from brother,
And son recoil from mother.
And all shall come before God,
Disfigured with fear;

32. E. A. Baratynskij, *op.cit.*, p. 481.

And the profane shall fall,
Covered in flame and ashes.

And the cameo of section VII:

Arise, timorous one:
In your cave
The sacred lamp
Burns until morning.
Prophet, with a heart-felt prayer
Dismiss
Sad thoughts,
Cunning dreams.
Humbly until morning
Make a prayer;
Until morning read
The celestial book!

It is not difficult, bearing in mind such pieces as *To V. A. Žukovskij, Solitude* or *Not While Awake,*[33] to see what it is in such poems as these that attracted Kozlov: the praise of God and warning of punishment to the impious, the exaltation of spiritual modesty, of chastity and purity of heart, all would be quite in keeping in his own original work. So, too, the traits attributed to Black Georgij, indeed, the entire epistle to his young daughter might well have sprung from or, had it been written six months earlier, even have formed Kozlov's monk. The graphic imagery, the light, colour-filled lines all consciously appealing to the visual, no less than to the aural sense, all this is familiar to students of Kozlov's tales:

Moon's threat, warrior of freedom,
Covered in holy blood,
Your wondrous father, criminal and hero,
Deserved both fame and the people's horror.

33. This poem, "Ne najavu i ne vo sne," is one of five selected by N. M. Gajdenkov to typify Kozlov's work; the choice is apt (see *Russkie poety XIX-ogo veka* (Moscow, 1964), pp. 335-9).

You, as a child, he caressed
On a burning breast with bloodied hand;
Your plaything was a dagger
Sharpened by fratricide.
How often, having awakened the fire of savage vengeance
Would he, above your innocent cradle,
Silently ponder a fresh murder's blow,
And listen to your prattling . . .

It is all pleasantly familiar, instantly recognizable, the slightly artificial yet still acceptable *dagger* and *bloodied hand* of Polevoj's "new direction." One learns much of Kozlov the peaceful blind man from his liking for such verse; indeed, it adds another, humanizing facet to his character.

Kozlov's antipathy towards Lamartine's *Le dernier chant du pèlerinage d'Harold* was widely shared in Russia. Lamartine finished his 800-line, 23-canto attempt, so he informed Virieu, on February 28, 1825; he was unable to find an interested publisher. Finally, Dondey-Duprès offered him 9000f, and the work was announced in the *Journal de la Librairie* for May 14 (no. 2741), that is to say, seventeen days before Kozlov wrote to Puškin.[34] With French, as with Russian literature, Kozlov remained more than abreast.

Puškin's ungrudging praise of *The Monk* is the more interesting for a knowledge of comparisons that were being made, certainly to *his* knowledge, between Kozlov's tale and *Evgenij Onegin*. Vjazemskij went so far as to hold, indeed, that *The Monk* was the better work! "Let me tell you this in your ear," he wrote to the ever-attentive A. I. Turgenev: "There is in *The Monk* more feeling, more thought than in Puškin's poems."[35] By curious coincidence, it was on the same day that N. M. Jazykov wrote his bi-weekly letter to his brother. "God grant," he wrote, after a number of acrimonious comments on the state of "the Russian Parnassus," "that *The Monk* be better than *Onegin*." Vjazemskij, at least, later

34. Another French journal that Kozlov is known to have received was the *Revue des deux mondes*.

35. Letter of 22.4.25.

amended his opinion. Jazykov, not atypically, reserved for himself the pleasure of finding Chapters Two and Three of *Onegin* "no better than the first cantos – mere rhymed prose."[36] Few poets have been prophets in their own countries.

Inevitably, *The Monk* was read aloud in various *salons* in both capitals, and parts of it learned by heart by those with time to do so. Its sombre charm appealed especially to women. In St. Petersburg one of the most brilliant, the blue-stocking and beauty Anna Kern, was a mutual friend of the Kozlovs and the Puškins. To Puškin, it seems, she became more than a friend.[37] Anna visited the Puškins at Trigorskoe in July, 1825; to Pletnjov on the nineteenth of the month Puškin wrote: "Tell Kozlov from me that not long ago a certain beauty visited our region, who sings his *Venetian Night* in a heavenly fashion, in the voice of a gondolier's recitative. I promised to let the dear, inspired blind man hear of it. It is regrettable that he will not see her, but let him imagine her beauty and sincerity – and God grant that he at least hears her!"[38] Few of Kozlov's poems had greater success in his lifetime, or better maintained their popularity throughout the nineteenth century, than his "fantasy," *A Venetian Night*.

Like Puškin, Baratynskij held the poem in particular esteem, as he informed the modest author in a letter from Finland of mid-April, 1825. "Our regiment," wrote the semi-exile whose absence was just to end, thanks to the efforts of Žukovskij and A. I. Turgenev *inter alia*, "will be in Petersburg this summer. My heart beats with joy when I think that I shall soon be in the circle of my true friends and that I shall embrace you, dear brother-poet. Without flattery, your *Venetian Night* is a delight! In it a sumptuous dreaminess subtly blends with a sombre reverie. The description of Venice is filled with a particular midday warmth

36. *Jazykovskij arxiv: pis'ma N. M. Jazykova k rodnym za derptskij period* (St. Petersburg, 1913), p. 407.

37. Kozlov admired Anna Kern, *née* Poltoratskaja (1800-79), in a benign, Puškin in a more sexual way; she rebuffed his advances in July, 1825, remaining faithful to Major-General Ermolaj, 35 years her senior. Residing in Riga, Anna was able to procure for Puškin the last eleven cantos of Byron's *Don Juan* in the last week of that year and, had Kozlov asked her, would have done the same for him.

38. *A. S. Puškin*, vol. 9, p. 167.

and delight; but the place where the beauty heads her gondola towards the sea is perhaps the finest in the whole piece. . . . "[39] Anna Kern's success at Trigorskoe was greater than she knew, and for days, as Puškin himself told Anna Vul'f on July 21, "tout Trigorsky chanta *Ne mila ej prelest*"[40] Kozlov would have been gratified. As if to assure his triumph in the year of the Decembrists' uprising, his version of Charles Wolfe's *On the Burial of Sir John Moore* also became widely known in that autumn. It was received with loud acclaim.[41]

By September of Kozlov's year, *The Bride of Abydos* was finished in Russian (*Nevesta Abidosskaja*). Pletnjov duly informed Puškin, adding "Kozlov, by the way, having heard your 'Chénier' asked me to let you know, if you've forgotten, that after Chénier's head had been picked up, they gave his brother an anonymous note: Cain, where is your brother Abel?"[42] By 1825, it is plain, Kozlov felt able to address Puškin as a friend, not an acquaintance.

1825 marked the zenith of Kozlov's popularity. Neither of his two later *poemy* equaled the success of *The Monk* nor, as Del'vig noted, did they deserve it. It would be wrong, however, to think that Kozlov's popularity in Russia collapsed after this; and it was Del'vig, through his almanac *Northern Flowers*, who did much to sustain it in the years between *The Mad Girl* (1830) and the publication of Kozlov's first verse collection in 1833.

Kozlov, it was seen in Chapter 5, contributed heavily to Del'vig's almanac – five pieces in 1825, the same in 1826, two in 1827, 1829 and 1830. Suitably, as Del'vig always regarded Kozlov's translation work as his most important contribution to his native literature, no less than eleven of the eighteen pieces published over "I. K.," "K –" or "Kozlov" (1825 – 31) were translations or adaptations. Although none of his justly celebrated translations of Adam Mickiewicz's *Crimean Sonnets* were published in *Northern Flowers*, one version by Kozlov of an erotic

39. E. A. Baratynskij, *op.cit.*, p. 481.

40. *A. S. Puškin*, vol. 9, p. 168.

41. Kozlov's translation appeared with the title "On the Burial of the English General Sir John. From Moore." The error was noted in the errata (*Northern Flowers*, 1826, p. 121).

42. A. S. Puškin, *Poln. sob. soč.* (Moscow, 1937), vol. 13, p. 234.

sonnet by the Polish poet did appear in the 1829 edition, entitled "Stanzas (A free Imitation of Adam Mickiewicz)." Kozlov's last contribution to the almanac, entitled simply "Desdemona's Song (from the Eng.)," enjoyed no less a success among critics.

Chief poetry critic for *Northern Flowers* was Orest Somov. Orest Somov (1793 – 1833), Del'vig's close friend and collaborator,[43] student of British poetry and, in 1831, publisher of *Literary Gazette* (founded by Del'vig and later edited by Vjazemskij, Puškin and Žukovskij in that order), was given a free hand by his editor. It would, to be sure, have been strange had Del'vig countenanced strong negative criticism of verse by writers whose collaboration he had solicited. But Kozlov could do little wrong in Somov's eyes; his work, like Fjodr Glinka's, D. Venevitinov's, Puškin's, Krylov's and Baratynskij's, was warmly and consistently praised in each of the critic's annual reviews: "A Review of Russian Literature for 1827," "A Review . . . for 1828," "A Review . . . for the First Half of 1829," "A Review . . . for the Second Half of 1829 and the First of 1830."[44] Somov had himself translated Byron[45] and gladly saw Kozlov do so.

The appearance of Kozlov's first verse collection in book form, *A Collection of the Works of I. I. Kozlov* (St. Petersburg, 1833), initiated the second phase in his literary progress – a time of measured, then lessening success; a time during which he came to be revered (always his afflictions preserved him from ridicule), but less often read than honoured among his own people. The collection sold well; a second edition appeared in the following autumn. But Kozlov was a man of more than fifty when the fourth decade began; nor were Herzen and Belinskij wrong in thinking him a representative of other, half-forgotten days when Russian poetry was, in Mirskij's phrase, "a movement of gentlemen." "Socially, the age of Puškin marks the high-water mark of the hegemony of the gentry. Higher literature was completely

43. "Poor Del'vig!" wrote Puškin on hearing of his death in January, 1831; "We will remember him with *Northern Flowers* – but I am sorry if this will be a loss to Somov – he was sincerely attached to him, and our friend's death is perhaps hardest of all to him"; *A. S. Puškin*, vol. 10, p. 16.

44. *Severnyje tsvety*, 1828, pp. 3-82; 1829, pp. 3-110; 1830, pp. 3-114; 1831, pp. 3-100.

45. See Chapter 7.

monopolized by men of that class. At the same time the literary press was almost entirely in the hands of the non-noble class – of pedants, hacks and hucksters. The opposition between the two classes was clearly marked. The plebeians had their revenge in the thirties."[46] Though simplistic, Mirskij's summary is true in its essentials. And Kozlov was a *dvorjanin*. True, he suffered less at the hands of "hacks and hucksters" than many; being poorer than, say, Baratynskij or Jazykov, he also proved more shrewd in dealing with literary publishers, and his verse continued to appear in a wide variety of journals throughout the fourth decade. But the heights of 1825 were no longer to be scaled. Nonetheless, Kozlov maintained his contact with the leading literary figures of the day, nor was it difficult for him to do so, with Pletnjov and, until 1835, Vjazemskij as regular visitors.

Not surprisingly, perhaps, Kozlov's translations of the work of English, French, Italian and German poets provoked interest and curiosity among the *literati* of the four countries concerned. It was in France that his fame first found a foothold in the West. Connections between Russian and French *littérateurs* having been strengthened year by year, since the arrival in Paris of the triumphant Russian armies (1814) with their many French-speaking officers, some of whom chose to stay, it was natural that versions of Lamartine, Chénier and Chateaubriand should find a welcome on the shelves of Russophile and Russian-speaking Frenchmen, as well as of Russian expatriates. As a boy of twelve, Prosper Mérimée witnessed the victorious Russian troops camping on the Champs Elysées. Later he recorded how he had felt drawn to "ces hommes à grande barbe noire, vêtus á l'orientale, montant de petits chevaux et armés de longues lances. . . . "[47] From that early curiosity grew an interest in Russia and Russian literature to which the tale *Guzla* and numerous translations from Puškin and Lermontov, as well as lengthy studies of Gogol' and Turgenev, bear eloquent witness.[48]

46. D. Mirskij, *op.cit.*, p. 72.

47. Prosper Mérimée, *Mélanges historiques et littéraires* (Paris, 1855), p. 63.

48. See my paper, "Prosper Mérimée and E. A. Baratynsky," *Romance Notes*, vol. XI (1969), no. 2, pp. 45-52.

Mérimée and other interested Frenchmen had ample occasion to study Russians at first hand. French-speaking Russian officers continued to be present in large numbers after the Restoration. Alexander himself, playing a rôle close to his heart, "avec des airs de grande modestie . . . se metta diligemment en montre et en valeur."[49] And of those who frequented the *salons* of Mesdames Récamier, Cuvier and Ancelot, four at least – A. I. Turgenev, Puškin's friend Sergej Ivanovič Sobolevskij, Nikolaj Mel'gunov and Žukovskij – knew Kozlov, as well as his work.

Interest in Jean de Kosloff (as he signed himself, when writing to Chateaubriand) quickened in Paris in 1828. In that year, the royalist and dilettante Prince Evgenij Meščerskij, Second Secretary in the Embassy, published a number of Kozlov's poems – in French translation. Meščerskij had a model in J. P. Emile Dupré de Saint-Maure's *Anthologie russe, suivie de poésies originales* (Paris, 1823), and, almost inevitably, improved on it greatly. Dupré de Saint-Maure's effort is a treasure-trove of errors, semantic and otherwise. Since it was dedicated to the Tsar, however, to criticize it other than obliquely was difficult.[50]

Meščerskij's versions of Kozlov's elegies, at least two of which verge on paraphrase, also appeared in a progressive literary journal, the *Revue encyclopédique* which, under the fine management of Marc-Antoine Jullien de Paris (1819 – 33), gave a consistently full account of happenings in Russian literature. Unwittingly, Kozlov found an excellent agent. Not only were articles reprinted in *Revue encyclopédique* from *Messenger of Europe, Son of the Fatherland, The Well-Meaner, Moscow Telegraph* and four other periodicals – they were reprinted legally; Jullien secured mutual reprinting rights. More than this, Russian collaborators were sought and found: S. D. Poltoratskij, Ja. N. Tolstoj, even Vjazemskij.

Jullien attracted numerous talented helpers, two of whom, E. -J. Hérau and J. -M. Chopin, were familiar with Russian. For ten years (1809 – 19), Hérau had served as Professor of French

49. K. Waliszewski, *Le règne d'Alexandre Premier* (Paris, 1924), p. 246.

50. Further on this, see P. Berkov, "Izučenie russkoj literatury vo Frantsii," *Literaturnoe nasledstvo*, vols. 33-4, pp. 732-4.

Literature at Kazan' University.[51] Using A. I. Turgenev as a willing intermediary, the exhausted and homesick professor established firm contacts between Jullien's journal and Polevoj's pro-French *Moscow Telegraph*, even praising the Russian journal at Jullien's expense. Hérau's translations of Kozlov appeared in the *Revue encyclopédique* in July, 1829 and June, 1830.

J. M. Chopin was born and educated in Russia, a lucid and prolific writer and (though the calling did not then exist) cultural historian. His essay *De l'Etat Actual de la Russie, ou observations sur ses moeurs, son influence et sa littérature* appeared in Paris in 1822; Žukovskij bought a copy.[52] Within a year of its publication in St. Petersburg, Chopin had published – in Jullien's revue – a detailed review of *The Monk* (1826, no. 6).

Other translations of Kozlov's work appeared in France during the 1830s. Some were by French-speaking Russians, as in the awkward case of *Le moine: poème de Kozlof intitulé Černets; traduit en prose par la Princesse A. Abamelek* (Moscow, 1831). The Princess, who also put Lermontov to the test, was Baratynskij's sister-in-law; Kozlov did not gain by that fact. Others were by Russians permanently settled in Paris. Such was the case with *Le pénitent noir; histoire kiovienne* (St. Petersburg and Paris, 1836; Odessa, 1837; Moscow, 1839), a "free verse translation" by Prince N. Golitsyn. Finally, there were the versions of native-born Frenchmen, for example, *Tchernetz, ou le novice, de Koslow; poème en vers imité du russe par T. Villars* (Odessa, 1850).

1828 was also the year of Kozlov's German début. Not to be outdone by Meščerskij, Sigismund Schreiber translated both *The Monk* and *Princess Natal'ja Dolgorukaja* into weighty German iambics. Both "Der Mönch" and "Die Fürstin N. Dolgorukij" appeared in Schreiber's *Metrische Ubersetzungen aus dem Russischen*. The work, it must be admitted, was published in St. Petersburg, but quickly found its way, via Riga, to German libraries.

51. On Jullien and Hérau, see S. N. Durylin, "P. A. Vjazemskij i Revue encyclopédique," *Literaturnoe nasledstvo*, vol. 31 (1937) pp. 89-108.

52. Chopin's career was long. His *Révolution des peuples du nord; choix de nouvelles russes de Lermontoff, Pouchkine, von Wisine* appeared in 1853 (Paris).

A second propagandist for Kozlov in Germany was Friedrich Martin von Bodenstedt (1819 – 88). Bodenstedt, like Hérau (and also Thomas Shaw, author of the first detailed appraisal of Puškin to appear in a British periodical, *Blackwoods' Edinburgh Magazine*, 1845), spent some years teaching in Russia, in the household of Prince M. Golitsyn (1840 – 43) and in Tiflis. (It is interesting to observe how large a part such teachers played in the early phases of the introduction of Russian literature to Western audiences. Even such missionaries as George Borrow[53] and merchants as William David Lewis and Benjamin Beeson[54] could not resist the temptation to lecture on their return.) Despite an intensive study of Russian, however, Bodenstedt's versions of Kozlov were flawed by numerous textual errors. Kozlov was presented, in 1843, as "the apostle of Lermontov"(!); nor were the poems selected typical. All in all, the work was hardly an advance on Schreiber's. Bodenstedt's experience with Kozlov, however, was later put to good account in a three-volume edition of Puškin in translation (1854 – 5).[55] And his translations of Lermontov enjoyed a great vogue in Germany during the 1850s.[56]

Paradoxically, Kozlov was less well known in England, birthplace of Byron, source of Kozlov's inspiration, than in either Germany or France during the 1830s. The reason is simple; he was excluded from Sir John Bowring's pioneering anthology, *Specimens of the Russian Poets* (London, 1821 – 3). Bowring, a fine linguist, was the first to introduce Russian poetry to a wide English-speaking audience. His translations are both graceful and, in the main, faithful to the originals; unfortunately, however,

53. Borrow was in St. Petersburg, 1833-35, for the British and Foreign Bible Society, and in 1835 had published, at his own expense, *Targum, or Metrical Translations from Thirty Languages* (St. Petersburg). It contained Puškin's "The Black Shawl" and Zemphira's song, from *The Gypsies*.

54. My paternal great-grandfather, collaborator with George Cox on the first English *History of Russian Literature . . .* (London, D. A. Talboys, 1839).

55. Bodenstedt's *Koslow, Puschkin und Lermontow* (Leipzig, 1843), is considered in H. Rappich's study, "Friedrich Bodenstedts literarische Beziehungen zu Russland," *Zeitschrift für Slawistik*, 1963, Bd. 8, Heft 4, pp. 582-94.

56. On *Michael Lermontoffs Nachlass* (Berlin, 1852; 2 vols.), see N. A. Sigal, "Bodenstedt – perevodčik Lermontova," *Učonnyje zapiski Leningradskogo Gosudarstvennogo Universiteta*, 1941, no. 64, sec. 8, pp. 328-49. Bodenstedt, like J.-M. Chopin, lived long (and made a lecture tour of North America in 1881).

Bowring chose to concentrate on eighteenth-century poets, ignoring even Puškin.[57]

Not until 1830 did a piece by Kozlov appear in England. It was a translation of lines 135 – 54 of Puškin's "southern tale," *The Baxčisarian Fountain,* and appeared in the *New Monthly Magazine and Literary Journal* (London, July, 1830). The "Anecdotes of Russia," in which the piece was published, tell a curious story. (See p. 180.) A slight mystery attaches to the story. Kozlov, so the author of "Anecdotes of Russia" claims, had translated the whole of Puškin's tale into English ("The whole poem is translated in much the same style").[58] He greatly regretted, when it was too late, not having taken with him the whole poem, which Kozlov had offered to him. But no trace of the remainder of Kozlov's version of the tale exists; and, while its existence can never convincingly be disproved, there are grounds for suspecting that Kozlov never, in fact, translated the entire tale. *The Baxčisarian Fountain* was published on March 10, 1824. It is possible, though improbable, that Kozlov could have heard extracts from a manuscript copy before that date. But news of Byron's death, which occurred on April 19, reached St. Petersburg only a week later. Consequently Kozlov would have had to complete his translation in ten or twelve weeks at most, in order to send it to England before news of Byron's death was yet known in Russia. Even for one whose knowledge of English was perfect, the translation would have been a feat. Kozlov's command of it, as the charming but slightly stilted epistle to Countess Fiquelmont shows clearly, was not perfect; and Puškin's tale is of 578 lines.

Kozlov's epistle "To Countess Fiquelmont" also appeared in *New Monthly Magazine* for July, 1830. It was a handsome compliment both to Kutuzov's grand-daughter and to his own linguistic skills:

In desert blush'd a rose; its bloom
So sweetly bright, to desert smiled;
Thus are by thee my heavy gloom

57. On Bowring, see V. I. Kulešov, *Literaturnyje svjazi Rossii i zapadnoj Evropy v XIX veke* (Moscow, 1965), pp. 263-5.

58. *New Monthly Magazine . . .* (London) 1830, July, p. 80.

And broken heart from pain e'er wiled.
Let, O let heaven smile on thee
Still more beloved, and still more smiling.
Be ever bless'd – but ever be
The angel all my work beguiling.

As a serious student of contemporary Russian literature, Thomas B. Shaw (1813 – 62) could hardly ignore Kozlov; nor did he do so. While still teaching English Literature at the Aleksandrijskij lycée in St. Petersburg,[59] he sent a translation of Kozlov's poem "Kiev" to *Blackwoods' Edinburgh Magazine*. It was published in January, 1844 (vol. 55), p. 80. Shaw's study of Puškin appeared in the following year (vol. 57, 656 – 78; 58, 28 – 43, 140 – 57). It is a valiant effort, capturing much of the emotional elevation, and something of the plasticity of the apostrophe to Kiev.

Italians, finally, took a substantial interest in the author of *A Venetian Night*. How could they not do so, with such Italian émigrés as Count Mignato Ricci and Cristoforo Boccella in contact with Kozlov and Del'vig, in whose *Northern Flowers* the former's version of the dream scene from Tasso's *Gerusalemme Liberata* appeared in 1826? As for Kozlov's interest in Italy it was more than that of a connoisseur of foreign odes and ballads; his knowledge of Italian history and literature, like that of Baratynskij, who died by the Bay of Naples, perhaps excelled Žukovskij's. For him, as for his generation, Italy was an ideal land – a place of unending warmth, where the ancient gods lived on in frescoes and oils.[60] Small wonder what Princess Zinaida Volkonskaja corresponded with him from Rome as though anxious that he should see St. Peter's through her eyes.[61] Žukovskij, too, when he visited Venice and met Alessandro Manzoni in 1838, was at

59. The author of *Outlines of the English Literature, for the Use of the Imperial Lyceum* (St. Petersburg, 1847), Shaw in 1852 became Professor of English Literature at St. Petersburg University; for a crude sketch, see D. Brewster, *East-West Passage* (London, 1953), pp. 63-7.

60. See my article, "Borghese, Baratynsky and the Ideal Italy," *Forum Italicum*, (1970).

61. See "Princess Zinaida Volkonskaya," a paper by N. Gorodetsky in *Oxford Slavonic Papers* vol. 5 (1954), pp. 93-106.

pains to write detailed letters to the blind poet. "I did not let the opportunity go by," wrote the diligent Žukovskij, "but spoke to Manzoni about you; and he told me that he knows of you, and gave me a copy of your verses with your signature on it, telling me to convey his greetings when we meet." The letter is a monument to the lasting friendship between Kozlov and Žukovskij; it is as though Žukovskij knew, unprompted, what Kozlov would have cared to see had he been in Venice himself, his sight unimpaired. "Imagine from where I am writing to you – from Venice! On hearing the word, Tasso, Byron and thousands of gigantic and poetic shades of the past will rise before your closed eyes. I am living on the bank of the Grand Canal. I have a corner room; the windows, as everywhere in Italy, reach down to the floor and have balconies. . . . Immediately before my window rises up, and overshadows it, the huge granite column with St. Theodore on its capital, and beside it another, with the winged lion of St. Mark . . . In front of these is the so-called piazzetta, or little square, of St. Mark's, bounded at one end by the church, and at the other by the wonderful palace of the Doges, before which extends a wide embankment. . . ."[62]

Boccella did not forget Kozlov, on his return to Pisa. It was in that city, in 1835, that he published *Il monaco, di Kozlov; tradotta da C. Boccella*. Ricci, living in St. Petersburg, could more easily maintain contact with Kozlov, whom he mentions twice in letters to Puškin of 1828 – 9. It is clear, from one of these letters in which friendship struggles with unadulterated admiration, that Kozlov was on close terms with Zinaida Volkonskaja, so soon to leave again for Rome.[63] "Madame la Psse. Zénéide," wrote Ricci in

62. Letter of 4.10.38; see my article "V. A. Žukovskij and Alessandro Manzoni," *Forum Italicum*, 1971.

63. See Baratynskij's "Knjagine Z. A. Volkonskoj" (1829), and Puškin's and Kozlov's epistles, also so titled, of 1827 and 1825. Kozlov was on close terms with numerous foreigners in St. Petersburg, many of these being diplomats. The case of K. -L. Fiquelmont has been met. Among Latin envoys, two are noteworthy – J. M. Paez de la Cadena, Spanish Ambassador in 1825-35, and I. Guereiro, First Secretary in the Embassy of Portugal. The latter was a brilliant linguist, fluent in five languages, and sent Kozlov a technically competent eight-line epistle – in English:

To John Kosloff

By ruthless hands deprived of light

March, 1828, "a envoyé a M. Kosloff une ode de Dérjavin traduite par moi. . . . " Ricci seemingly regarded Kozlov's opinion highly where translations were concerned.

Kozlov's reputation was not limited to Europe during the nineteenth century. William David Lewis, whose honour it is first to have translated Russian verse into English (his tolerably competent versions of Neledinskij-Meletskij appeared in *The National Gazette and Literary Register*, of Philadelphia, on January 31, 1821), published, in 1841, a slim volume entitled *The Bakchesarian Fountain; by Alexander Pooshkine.*[64] In it also appeared a poem by Kozlov, "Silence." Later, C. T. Wilson included Kozlov's "The Village Orphan," "The Wreck," "The Dream of the Betrothed" and, for good measure, a passage from *The Monk*, in his *Russian Lyrics* (New York, 1880).

Kozlov's first verse collection, that of 1828, contained forty-eight pieces, more than thirty of which had already appeared in journals and almanacs. It was in the hope of publishing his work *in toto* that he prepared a second collection, that of 1833. The edition included all his published poems, re-written in the spring of 1832, and was well received; a second edition appeared nine months later, in which he made no additions and no alterations.

The prisoned bird more sweetly sings,
The dreaded veil of endless night
To him at length no terror brings.
Within himself the songster finds
A little world of heavenly sound
That earth's corporeal ties unbinds
And holier renders all around.

Like Puškin, (see N. O. Lerner, *Rukoju Puškina* (Leningrad, 1922), p. 23, Kozlov was personally acquainted with Paez de la Cadena, who discussed Catalan poetry with him. "M. Paez," wrote Aleksandra, Countess Laval' on July 20, 1831 ("Dva pis'ma grafini Lavalja," *Russkij arxiv*, 1886, bk. 3, pp. 316-8), "m'a chargé de vous dire qu'il sera charmé de vous faire passer quelques heures en vous faisant connaitre les poésies de son pays."

64. Lewis, a successful commission merchant, fought a duel with Harrison, the American Consul in St. Petersburg – and was committed to Peter and Paul Fortress. See *The Dictionary of American Biography*, 22 vols. (New York, 1933), vol. 11, pp. 226-7. His version of Puškin's "Eastern tale" was rapturously received by his friend N. I. Greč, in *Severnaja pčela* (July 18, 1851).

Kozlov appointed Žukovskij as his literary executor, and it was within nine months of the poet's death that the latter informed his readers that, "acting to fulfil the wishes" of the poet "with the strong hope of helping his fellow-countrymen," he "had gathered into one volume" all Kozlov's poems.[65] The claim was over-bold. Not only did a number of occasional and album pieces escape Žukovskij's notice; he saw fit to make various "stylistic" changes to Kozlov's texts, so diminishing the value of his work and of the (third) edition. "The Bride," "The Swimmer," "The Warrior," "The First Meeting" and "Erminija on Jordan's Banks," among others, underwent the "improving" process. But this was not the full extent of his temerity. He omitted whole phrases or passages from four poems. In "Brenda," the fifth strophe was removed; in "Byron in the Coliseum" the title was altered and stanza 2 omitted; from "The Oak" no less than four strophes were missing, presumed unsuitable, while in "To the Friend of my Spring, After a Long, Long Separation," two lines were simply re-written.

Not until 1892, under the general editorship of Arsenij I. Vvedenskij, was a *Complete Collection of the Works of I. I. Kozlov* published in Russia (St. Petersburg, A. F. Marx). The edition, in Vvedenskij's words, "rested on that of 1840, compiled, with love and knowledge of the matter, under the direction of V. Žukovskij." Vvedenskij, that is to say, ignored Žukovskij's emendations to the texts, choosing rather to preserve than to remove them. To its credit, however, the edition included twenty-six poems not found in the 1840 collection, as well as a brief biographical sketch and bibliographical notes. In this lies its principal value, Soviet editions having carefully restored the original readings of Kozlov's *MS*.

Kozlov, it will be obvious from the above, did not fare well in his own country. He was remembered in anthologies, especially by the elegy "On the Burial of the English General Sir John Moore" and his rendering of Thomas Moore's "Evening Bells," which, few would deny, is strikingly faithful to the swinging rhythm of the original. He was remembered, too, for the romances based on his

65. *Sobranie sočinenij I. I. Kozlova*, Pts. 1 and 2 (St. Petersburg, A. F. Smirdin, 1833), p. 3.

verse and sung in drawing-rooms throughout the century; Glinka set "A Venetian Night" to music, others "An Irish Song" (from Moore's "As a Beam O'er the Face of the Waters"), "Hebrew Melody" and "Desdemona's Song." The poems demand to be sung, and many Russians, like the future Academician F. I. Buslaev, simply sung them to tunes of their making. ("I saw a splendid example of onomatopoeic poetry in 'Evening Bells' . . . reading it aloud, I did not simply speak the words but, as it were, rang with them, imagining myself sitting in a belfry.")[66] Broadly speaking, however, it must be said that Kozlov's reputation, kept from oblivion by only a few, beloved pieces (those same pieces which still appear in verse anthologies),[67] suffered a sad decline in the last part of the nineteenth century. Could the Symbolists see a precursor in him, as in Baratynskij? They could not. Had his work the least appeal to Acmeists or Futurists? It had not. Yet Kozlov's reputation, so tarnished in spite of Vvedenskij's efforts, was to rise to great heights under the third Bolshevik tsar, Khrushchev; nor does it show signs of declining in this decade.

The fate of Kozlov's work in Soviet Russia is of interest both as a subject in the study of Soviet publishing policy and in a general historico-literary sense. For of all pre-Revolutionary Russian poets of some standing, he is perhaps the least known among the Soviet reading public.

If his name was spoken at all during the meetings at the end of which, in January 1918, it was resolved to "nationalize" Russian literature, there is no record of the mention. Credit for the proposal to nationalize the classics goes traditionally to Valerian Poljanskij, who claims it in his article "Načalo sovetskix izdatel' stv" of 1927.[68] Lenin agreed, largely, it seems, with a view to the future employment of large numbers of printing hands.[69] A number of liberal, emphatically non-Bolshevik *intelligenty* sat on the general committee formed to discuss the way in which nationalization would be brought into effect, and schism was thus

66. F. I. Buslaev, *Moi vospominanija* (Moscow, 1897), p. 77.

67. For example, *Russkie poety*, 4 vols. (Moscow, 1966), vol. 2, pp. 257-72.

68. V. Poljanskij, "Načalo Sovetskix izdatel'stv," *Pečat' i revoljutsija*, 1927, no. 7, pp. 233-40.

69. Poljanskij is the source.

inherent in the committee's very composition. It was agreed, at length, that the state should "monopolize" the publication and sale of the Russian classics for a period of five years only, 1918 – 23. The measure, it was understood, was provisional. A list of 57 authors and poets, the works of whom were declared the property of the state, appears in Poljanskij's article. The list, as a glance confirms, was quite arbitrary, some major authors having been excluded, presumably on the grounds of politicial unsuitability, others, parts of whose work one would have thought distinctly undesirable to the new régime, nevertheless finding a place. Thus Fet, despite his stated reactionary views, was included by the committee, while Deržavin, Kjuxel'beker, Baratynskij and Kozlov, to name only poets, were ignored.

Doubtless, financial gain was a major consideration in the passing of the decree. A profit of nine million roubles in the first year (1918) represented one half of the original investment. Doubtless, too, Kozlov was of little value in hard currency terms.

The move to nationalize the classics, it would seem, was prompted by the understandable desire to control all publication within Russia, not only to prevent the sale of works that might be harmful to the Bolsheviks, but also to promote dissemination, by increased and frequent printings, of those works in verse and prose judged to be helpful to the cause. Clearly, the Bolsheviks themselves would decide what was and was not useful. It can hardly be pretended that Kozlov's verse advances the aims of Communism.

Despite the nationalization of works by 57 authors or poets, however, private printing houses were allowed to continue to function. Concessions were forthcoming in the years of NEP. So, until 1929, Soviet readers might, theoretically, influence publishers, encouraging them to bring out certain authors and to neglect others. (In fact the autonomy of private presses was carefully weakened over the decade.) In the words of A. I. Nazarov, the first years of Soviet publishing were "a period of coexistence with two publishing systems – the old, bourgeois system, on the verge of death but fighting still, and the young, newly-born Soviet system."[70]

70. A. I. Nazarov, *Očerki istorii sovetskogo knigoizdatel'stva* (Moscow, 1952), p. 84.

What editions or selections of Kozlov's verse were published by "the old, bourgeois system, on the verge of death"? The answer is straightforward. Neither by state-owned nor by private printing houses was a single edition of poems by Kozlov produced during the period of coexistence. If any small privately-owned firm brought out editions of his verse, as G. F. Mirimanov published classics for children, I. Glazunov the works of Turgenev or Teatral the plays of Ostrovskij,[71] there is no record of them in the public catalogues of the Lenin Library in Moscow or the Saltykov -Ščedrin Public Library, Leningrad. No such group as Posrednik, the Tolstoyans' venture, existed to foster interest in Kozlov's work.

On the other hand, no official ban was placed on publication of his verse either before or after 1929. Indeed, works by pre-Revolutionary Russian writers cannot be said to have been proscribed, in an official manner, at any time since the October Revolution. If they are banished from public view, it is unofficially; new editions are not printed, references to earlier editions of undesirable works (such as certain monarchist poems by Kol'tsov, or passages by P. I. Mel'nikov-Pečerskij describing the life of religious sectarians) are unobtrusively removed from public catalogues in libraries.[72] It would seem that it was Soviet policy (although most certainly not stated or announced) to permit Kozlov's work, which was of no assistance to the Party, to lapse into obscurity.

Official Soviet sources do not admit the existence ot political motivation in the selection of pre-Revolutionary classics for republication.[73] Of course, the popularity of individual works and writers changes. The state itself can effect a sharp, artificial increase in "demand" for works simply by printing more. There

71. Teatral also published plays by Puškin and Čexov to which the Party found no objection.

72. For a charming admission in this respect, see K. N. Batjuškov, *Sočinenija* (Moscow, 1955), p. 409. The early poem "Bog," so it is stated, was excluded from the present edition together with "poems written during the poet's mental illness." "Mental illness" may be extended to cover a wide variety of "unfortunate pieces," including the rabidly religious.

73. The State printing house that deals with Russian classics, Xudožestvennaja Literatura, remains unwilling to grant interviews to interested parties.

are no best-sellers in the Soviet Union, only most-printeds.

There is no question, however, but that political utility was a factor in the choice of works for publication by the decree of January, 1918, and that it was intended to be one. Gosizdat was formed, not to compete commercially with rival bourgeois houses, but to assist the Party in the task of educating, or re-educating, the masses in the spirit of the new ideology. The idea may be found, already in a developed state, in Lenin's writings of 1905: "Not only may literature be an instrument of gain for no individual or group . . . it may not be an individual matter at all. It cannot be independent of general proletarian activities."[74]

Between 1918 and 1929 there was no change in official Soviet publishing policy, and a brief reading of the text of Lunačarskij's and Xalatov's *Questions of Cultural Development in the RSFSR* makes plain why no copies of Kozlov's verse were printed by the Soviets: "The Soviet State and the Communist Party have placed books at the service of socialist construction and demand that books wage an active struggle for the progress and reconstruction of the national economy, for proletarian ideology."[75]

Political factors, then, are of importance in the state's choice of pre-Revolutionary reading matter for its modern readers. Nekrasov has ranked high among most-printeds since 1924.[76] Saltykov-Ščedrin has also remained high, as has Uspenskij. Kozlov has remained consistently low since first being published at all.

The imminence of World War II did little or nothing to improve Kozlov's standing as it did for others. A new emphasis, in the 1930s, on nationalist themes, barely increased his popularity in the USSR, nor did a fresh and heavy emphasis on military and romantic themes, felt in the years immediately preceding the war. Puškin's *Poltava* was published twice in 1937 – 39; it is about a victory over foreigners.

An edition of Kozlov's verse did appear, however, in 1936. Printed in one volume by Zovetskij Pisatel', a series inaugurated by

74. V. I. Lenin, *Sočinenija* (3rd ed., 30 vols: Moscow, 1935), vol. 8, p. 387.

75. A. Lunačarskij, A. Xalatov, *Voprosy kul'turnogo stroitel'stva RSFSR: doklady na XVI-om vserossijskom s'ezde sovetov* (Moscow, 1929), p. 63.

76. See M. Friedberg, *Russian Classics in Soviet Jackets* (New York, 1962), pp. 188-9.

Gorkij in the last months of his life, it ran to 5000 copies and sold at ten roubles. It was, for the time and circumstances, extremely expensive. Nonetheless, it was fully annotated by E. Kuprejanova and, although printed on paper of poor quality, as were all prewar editions in the Sovetskij Pisatel' series, was most satisfactory from the general reader's viewpoint.

Although 5000 copies seems a small number, compared with recent Soviet editions – 275,000 copies of Puškin's *Stixotvorenija* in 1965, or 200,000 copies of Lermontov's *Stixotvorenija i poemy* in the preceding year[77] – that printing was no larger and no smaller than those of works by other poets of the Puškin era. In 1939, Sovetskij Pisatel' produced editions of the works of Benediktov and Žukovskij in 5000 copies only. In the relatively small number of poems by Žukovskij printed even in that edition is reflected both the poet's uselessness, from the national and military standpoint of 1939, and the shortage of paper for use in such a way.

Sovetskij Pisatel', in the pocket-size hard-cover series Biblioteka poeta, is the most important publisher of pre-Revolutionary Russian verse. The series is designed to please discriminating readers of poetry and to provide Russian verse that is no longer available elsewhere. In 1948, the house produced a second edition of Kozlov's verse, again in 5000 copies. Notes were by Medvedeva. Finally, in 1956, a third appeared – again in the so-called "small series" (*malaja serija*) of Biblioteka poeta. Like its two predecessors, it had fine prefaces, footnotes and explanatory notes. The introductions of Medvedeva and Kuprejanova are those of competent scholars.

The number of copies in which poets of Puškin's age are published, under the aegis of Sovetskij Pisatel', provides an interesting clue as to the esteem in which, in any given year, that part of the Soviet régime concerned with the publication of poetry holds them or wishes to appear to hold them. Esteem, of course, is by no means directly related to aesthetic merit. (More than other state printing houses, however, Sovetskij Pisatel' and Xudožest-

77. Regrettably, it is not possible to compare these figures with that of Vvedenskij's 1892 edition; A. F. Marks and Co., the publishers, did not print details of *tirage*, paper, format and so forth.

vennaja Literatura seem to cater to actual demand in a realistic way.) For example, Venevitnov's verse appeared in 1960 in 7500 copies only, while A. I. Odoevskij and Karolina Pavlova merited 20,000 and 25,000 respectively.[78] Batjuškov, Davydov and Del'vig – this last a little surprisingly, perhaps – appeared in no less than 50,000 copies each.[79] Thus Kozlov received no worse treatment at the hands of Sovetskij Pisatel' than any other poet of his time – and better treatment than several.

Printings of Kozlov's verse since 1936 have thus reversed the earlier trend. After the most recent Soviet edition, that edited most competently by I. Glikman (1960), came an increased awareness, both among Soviet critics and literary commentators and in the West, of the significance of Kozlov's place in Russian literary history and of his merit as a poet. That increased awareness has been marked by a number of critical studies of his work, most by Soviet students of the period, and there is now a body of post-war criticism that those interested may consult.[80]

It must be added, however, that between the publication of K. Ja. Grot's work in 1903 – 06, an invaluable source of information for all students of Kozlov's life, poetry and translations, and the 1960 Sovetskij Pisatel' edition, two scholars only have made real contributions to the general knowledge and appreciation of the poet's work. These are I. Medvedeva and E. Kuprejanova. They alone have made extensive use of the materials preserved in the archives of Puškinskij Dom and of TsGALI, and were the first to be but little indebted to pre-Revolutionary critics. The substance of their work, unfortunately, cannot be discussed here.

A general comment is apposite, however, on all Soviet criticism of Kozlov's work. Literary criticism in the Soviet Union, one need hardly emphasize, serves as a vehicle for the expression of political positions, no less in the 1970s than fifty years ago. On studying it carefully, one can discern nuances of political

78. I. Odoevskij, *Poln sob. stixotvorenij*, ed. M. A. Brikman (Leningrad, 1958); Karolina Pavlova, *Poln. sob. stix.*, ed. S. P. Gromov (Leningrad, 1964).

79. The three being edited by, respectively, G. P. Makogonenko, V. Orlov and I. V. Isakovič.

80. To consult it, however, one must visit a major Soviet library, in which copies of unpublished dissertations are held by Soviet law; but see also Bibliography, p. 244.

opinion that are unlikely to be found in the daily or weekly Soviet press. Soviet literary criticism, while generally dull and repetitious, provides politically more stimulating reading than *Izvestija* or *Pravda*.

It is no exaggeration to claim that Soviet studies of Kozlov (there have been no Western monographs), have been unimaginative in attitude and execution. Only too well does one sense a lack of real controversy among professional critics. There are differences of opinion, of course; but differences have been confined to a number of problems of aesthetic judgement and, especially, of methodology. Kozlov was, in the accepted Soviet view, (as judged by articles over the past two decades), a poet unprepared for action on behalf of the people, but a man with strong radical sympathies. His friendship with Puškin and respect for Byron are invariably mentioned in each new study or sketch, and his pieces dealing with Ypsylanty ("Plennyj grek v temnitse") and young men in revolt in a generalized way ("Molodoj pevets," "Prosti!"), noted with warm approval. He was not, and could not be, a Decembrist, but he was at least a sympathizer – such is the Soviet image. Ideologically neutral, his work neither assists nor harms the Party, and gives pleasure to a minority. For over three decades that minority has been allowed a harmless cultural pleasure.

In one final way, criticism of Kozlov's verse has faithfully reflected the general trend of Soviet literary criticism. Patristic tendencies are plain in each of the four Soviet editions – those of 1936, 1948, 1956 and 1960. Such tendencies have been in evidence in all branches of Soviet scholarly work since the time of Stalin's rise to power, and patently reflect a general enforcement of orthodoxy in the country, as in the ranks of the Party. Most frequently cited among the Radical Fathers have been the most venerable among them: Belinskij, Dobroljubov, Cernyševskij and, whenever possible, Lenin. It is most noteworthy, in this connection, that I. Glikman, writing in the 1960 (*bol'saja serija*) edition, has succeeded in paring such pious references to a bare minimum. That the trend is a sensible one, there can be no doubt, for to my knowledge there is no evidence of Lenin's ever having read Kozlov. ("In his few moments of leisure," according to the veteran Bolshevik P. N. Lepešinskij, Lenin "would glance through some little volume of Shakespeare, Schiller, Byron, Puškin . . . or even of such lesser poets as Baratynskij or Tjutčev."[81]

The availability of Kozlov's work to Soviet readers, it now seems reasonable to assume, will continue to depend on the unbroken publication of the series Biblioteka poeta. There is no sign that the series will be discontinued; on the contrary, it would seem that public demand has even influenced the volume and frequency of printings of a poet whose work can in no way help the Party. Perhaps, conversely, to keep his work from the bookshelves would be to harm the Party's image among the general public, both at home and abroad. As matters stand, Kozlov is not considered counter-revolutionary, and his future appears to be assured.

81. P. N. Lepešinskij, *Na povorote* (Moscow, 1955), p. 112.

A SHORT BIBLIOGRAPHY

Works by I. I. Kozlov

"Dnevnik I. I. Kozlova," introduced by K. Ja. Grot. *Starina i novizna* (St. Petersburg, 1906), no. 11, pp. 34-66.

"Pis'ma (6) I. I. Kozlova," introduced by A. Sivers. *Zven'ja*, vol. 9 (1951), pp. 469-486; letters to P. A. Barteneva, A. I. and S. I. Turgenev and P. S. Šiškin.

Sobranie stixotvorenij, 2 Pts. (St. Petersburg, 1833); 2nd ed. (A. F. Smirdin: St. Petersburg, 1834); 3rd ed. (St. Petersburg, 1840).

Stixotvorenija, ed. and with introduction by A. I. Vvedenskij. (St. Petersburg, 1892), 344 pp.

"Stixotvorenija," ed. and with notes by Ts. Vol'pe. *Kozlov I, Podolinskij A.; stixotvorenija.* (Leningrad, 1936), pp. 7-122.

Stixotvorenija, with introductory article by I. D. Glikman. (Leningrad, 1956), 349 pp.

Criticism of Works

Ajxen'val'd, Ju., "I. I. Kozlov." *Istorija russkoj literatury XIX-ogo veka*, vol. 1, D. N. Ovsjaniko-Kulikovskij ed. (Moscow, 1908), pp. 156-163.

Bulgarin, F. V., "*Černets*; kievskaja povest'; sočinenie I. Kozlova." *Severnaja pčela* (1825), nos. 47-49.

Glikman, I. D., "I. I. Kozlov." *I. I. Kozlov; stixotvorenija* (Leningrad, 1960), pp. 5-51.

Gogol', N. V., "O poezii Kozlova" (1831). *Poln. sob. soč.*, vol. 8 (Moscow-Leningrad, 1952), pp. 153-155; also in any complete ed. of Gogol'.

Grigor'ev, A., "Stixotvorenija I. Kozlova" (1855). *Sertum Bibliologicum v čest'*, A. I. Maleina ed. (St. Petersburg, 1922), pp. 242-248.

Polevoj, N. A., "Knjaginja N. B. Dolgorukaja." *Moskovskij telegraf* (1828), Pt. 19, pp. 336-357.

Truš, K., *Očerk literaturnoj dejatel'nosti I. I. Kozlova* (Moscow, 1899), 32 pp.

Vjazemskij, P. A., "*Černets*; sočinenie I. Kozlova." *Moskovskij telegraf* (1825), no. 2, pp. 312-320.

Žukovskij, V. A., "O stixotvorenijax I. I. Kozlova." *Sovremennik*, vol. 18 (1840), no. 2, pp. 83-88; also in any complete ed. of Žukovskij.

On Byron in Russia

Ejges, I. P., "K perevodam I. Kozlova iz Bajrona." *Zven'ja*, vol. 5 (1935), pp. 744-748.

Maslov, V. I., *Načal'nyj period bajronizma v Rossii.* (Kiev, 1915), esp. pp. 26-29.

Zdziechowski, M., *Byron i yego wiek; studya porownawczo-literackie.* (Krakow, 1894-1897).

Žirmunskij, V., *Puškin i Bajron* (Leningrad, 1924).

Biography: Kozlov

Danilov, N. M., "I. I. Kozlov; opyt peresmotra materialov dlja jego biografii." *Izvestija Otdela Russkogo Jazyka i Slovesnosti*, vol. 19 (1914), no. 2, pp. 150-210.

Grot, K. Ja., "K biografii I. I. Kozlova." *Ibid.*, vol. 9 (1904), pp. 74-95; also published separately in that year (St. Petersburg), 22 pp.

Selivanov, I. V., "Mojo znakomstvo s I. I. Kozlovym." *Russkij arxiv* (1903), no. 12, pp. 665-668.

Voejkova, A. A., "Pis'ma (39) I. I. Kozlovu." Solov'jov, N. V., *Istorija odnoj žizni: A. A. Voejkova*, vol. 2 (Petrograd, 1916), pp. 24-55.

Xomutov, A. S., intro., "32 pis'ma k I. I. Kozlovu." *Russkij arxiv* (1886), no. 2, pp. 177-195; no. 3, pp. 308-319; including letters from Baratynskij, Vjazemskij, Žukovskij (15), Zagoskin, A. I. Turgenev and Chateaubriand.

On Russian Verse Translation

Alekseev, M. P., ed., *Iz istorii russko-slavjanskix literaturnyx svjazej XIX-ogo veka.* (Moscow-Leningrad, 1963).

– "Problema xudožestvennogo perevoda." *Sbornik trudov Irkutskogo Universiteta*, vol. 18 (1931), no. 1, pp. 189-196.

Fjodorov, A. V., *Vvedenie v teoriju perevoda.* (Moscow, 1958), esp. Pt. II.

Levin, Ju. D., "Ob istoričeskoj evoljutsii printsipov perevoda." *Meždunarodnyje svjazi russkoj literatury* (Moscow, 1963), pp. 5-63.

Further Bibliographical Sources

Longinov, M. N., "Materialy dlja polnogo sobranija sočinenij I. I. Kozlova." *Russkij arxiv* (1864), no. 2, pp. 230-232.

Muratova, K., ed., *Istorija russkoj literatury XIX-ogo veka: bibliografičeskij ukazatel'.* (Moscow, 1962), pp. 370-371.

Truš, K., *op. cit.*, pp. 22-32; 85 items are given with references.

INDICES
I. WORKS OF IVAN KOZLOV

II. INDEX OF GENERAL WORDS